Required

Huck Finn

a Kipling or The Yearling

a Stevenson

Mutiny on The Bounty

Biography

Non - Fiction or 2 plays
or 3 poems or Travel
book or other biography

Tristram
By
Robinson

THE TRAGEDY OF
ROMEO AND JULIET
BY WILLIAM SHAKESPEARE

Edited by

GEORGE LYMAN KITTREDGE

GINN AND COMPANY

BOSTON · NEW YORK · CHICAGO

LONDON · ATLANTA · DALLAS · COLUMBUS · SAN FRANCISCO

The Athenæum Press

GINN AND COMPANY · PRO-
PRIETORS · BOSTON · U.S.A.

PREFACE

THE text is complete and agrees with that in Kittredge's edition of Shakespeare's *Works*. The numbering of the lines accords with that commonly used in citing the plays. This method is preferred to a new counting in order to facilitate reference to such standard works as Bartlett's *Concordance* and Schmidt's *Shakespeare-Lexicon*. In prose passages there results some slight irregularity in computation, but this does not indicate any omission in the text.

G. L. K.

CONTENTS

CONTENTS

INTRODUCTION

THE First Quarto[1] of ROMEO AND JULIET (1597) prints the play in a curtailed and corrupt form. The Second Quarto[2] (1599) is our authority for the text; but it is carelessly printed, and the First Quarto very often provides the correct reading where the Second has gone astray. The Third Quarto appeared in 1609; the Fourth is undated. These are of no textual authority, though they sometimes supply a good reading. The First Folio (1623) used the Third Quarto as printer's copy.

The date of composition is uncertain. On April 6, 1580, there was an earthquake[3] which terrified the audiences in the London theatres. Anthony Munday reports that 'at the play-houses the people came running foorth, supprised with great astonishment.'[4] Two days later a ballad was registered 'intituled comme from the plaie, comme from the playe: the house will fall so people saye: the earth quakes lett vs hast awaye.'[5] The Nurse, recalling an incident of Juliet's childhood, dates it by remarking "Tis since the earthquake now eleven years' and 'Since that time it is eleven years' (i, 3, 23, 35). Thus, some think, she fixes the date of the play as 1591. Doubtless Shakespeare remembered the London earthquake when he wrote the Nurse's speech, but his concern, like hers, was to determine Juliet's birthday ('Come Lammas Eve at night shall she be fourteen'), not to hand down to posterity the date of his drama.

[1] An | Excellent | conceited Tragedie | of | Romeo and Iuliet, | As it hath been often (with great applause) | plaid publiquely, by the right Ho- | nourable the L. of *Hunsdon* | his Seruants. | London, | Printed by Iohn Danter. | 1597.

[2] The | Most | Ex- | cellent and lamentable | Tragedie, of Romeo | and Iuliet. | *Newly corrected, augmented, and | amended:* As it hath bene sundry times publiquely acted, by the | right Honourable the Lord Chamberlaine | his Seruants. | London | Printed by Thomas Creede, for Cuthbert Burby, and are to | be sold at his shop neare the Exchange. | 1599.

[3] Stow, *Annales,* 1592, p. 1176; Gabriel Harvey, letter to Spenser, ed. Grosart, I, 40–66.

[4] *A View of Sundry Examples,* 1580.

[5] Arber, II, 368; Rollins, *Analytical Index to the Ballad-Entries,* 1924, No. 327, p. 36. For records of other ballads on the earthquake see Rollins, Nos. 663, 1838, 2224, 2714. Cf. Chambers, *Elizabethan Stage,* IV, 208.

For the play in its present form, 1591 is manifestly too early a date; and there is no good reason for thinking that this form is Shakespeare's revision of an earlier drama, whether his own or another's.[1] Differences in style and metre of course appear, but these accord with mood and circumstances in every case. The so-called 'lyrical period' (about 1595) fits all the conditions.[2] This brings ROMEO AND JULIET into close relation with *A Midsummer Night's Dream.* Which of the two is earlier is an open question—probably *A Midsummer Night's Dream,* though some scholars (oddly enough) maintain that *Pyramus and Thisbe,* as acted by Bottom and his friends, is a parody of the theme of ROMEO AND JULIET and, in particular, that Romeo's leaping the orchard wall in Act II is burlesqued by the business of Wall in that comic interlude.[3]

For his plot Shakespeare used a poem by Arthur Broke (or Brooke), printed in 1562, 'The Tragicall Historye of Romeus and Iuliet, written first in Italian by Bandell, and nowe in Englishe by Ar. Br.'[4] Broke's source was the ninth story in Part II of Matteo Bandello's *Novelle* (1554). This he knew in the French version in Boaistuau's *Histoires Tragiques* (1559), which adds some details and modifies others. Broke's *Romeus and Juliet,* though he follows the narrative faithfully, is by no means a mere versification of Boaistuau. He touches up many

[1] See Van Dam, *Anglia,* LI (1927), 39–62; E. K. Chambers, *William Shakespeare,* 1930, I, 343–345. The phrase 'Newly corrected, augmented, and amended' in the title page of the Second Quarto signifies merely the publisher's claim that his edition is more correct and complete than the pirated Quarto of 1597.

[2] For resemblance in phraseology between the Sonnets and the play see McClumpha, *Shakespeare-Jahrbuch,* XL (1904), 187–203.

[3] E. K. Chambers, *The Elizabethan Stage,* 1923, III, 98; *William Shakespeare,* 1930, I, 345.

[4] Edited by P. A. Daniel for the New Shakspere Society, 1875; and by J. J. Munro, 1908, in modern spelling and punctuation, with an elaborate discussion of versions of the tale, a 'table of correspondence' between the poem and the play, and much other material of value. Several details in *The Two Gentlemen of Verona* suggest that Shakespeare had read Broke's poem before he wrote that play, which must antedate *Romeo and Juliet.* See Munro, pp. lv–lvii.

details and adds many reflections. He develops the character of the Nurse with genuine humour; he inserts a long conversation between Romeo and the Friar, in which Romeo rages in despair and the Friar sternly counsels self-control; he describes Romeo's sorrows during his sojourn at Mantua. There is a prose translation of Boaistuau's text in Painter's *Palace of Pleasure*, Vol. II, No. 25 (1567), but Shakespeare does not seem to have taken anything from it.

Shakespeare's use of Broke's poem resembles his use of Holinshed in his English plays and of North's Plutarch in his Roman tragedies. It gave him the whole plot, and he does not hesitate to borrow such turns of phrase as take his fancy.[1] The character of the Nurse owes much to Broke, and now and then he makes a suggestion which Shakespeare has developed in the case of the other *dramatis personæ*; but Mercutio is barely foreshadowed in Broke's poem. All he says of him is contained in the following passage (foll. 7 v°–9 r°):

> The daunce once beyng donne,
> Fayre Iuliet turned to, her chayre with pleasant cheere:
> And glad she was her Romeus approched was so neere.
> At thone side of her chayre, her louer Romeo:
> And on the other side there sat one cald Mercutio.
> A courtier that eche where was highly had in pryce:
> For he was coorteous of his speche, and pleasant of deuice.
> Euen as a Lyon would emong the lambes be bolde:
> Such was emong the bashfull maydes, Mercutio to beholde.
> With frendly gripe he ceasd fayre Iuliets snowish hand
> A gyft he had that nature gaue him in his swathing band,
> That frosen mountayne yse was neuer halfe so cold
> As were his handes, though nere so neere the fire he dyd them holde.
> As soone as had the knight the vyrgins right hand raught:
> Within his trembling hand her left hath louing Romeus caught.
>
> .   .   .   .
>
> Meruayle no whit my heartes delight, my onely knight and fere,
> Mercutious ysy hande had all to frosen myne
> And of thy goodnes thou agayne hast warmed it with thine.

[1] For details as to characters and phraseology see R. A. Law, *Studies in English* (University of Texas), 1929, pp. 86 ff.

Here Broke is following Boaistuau closely and Boaistuau is
following Bandello. To their grotesquely eccentric incident
we owe the existence of Mercutio in the drama—merely the
existence, however, for Shakespeare's Mercutio is Shakespeare's
own creation.

In Broke's poem the action covers about nine months. Shakespeare condenses it to less than a week. The play begins on a
Sunday; Juliet drinks the sleeping potion at some time during
the night of Tuesday–Wednesday. Soon after three o'clock on
Wednesday morning the Nurse finds her in a trance that seems
to be death (iv, 4, 4, 25; iv, 5, 14), and the funeral follows in
the forenoon of this same Wednesday. Friar Laurence has told
Juliet that she will lie unconscious for two-and-forty hours
(iv, 1, 104–106). The exactness of this figure (instead of eight-
and-forty) is obviously meant to give us confidence in the
Friar's prescription (cf. v, 2, 24). In using two-and-forty,
however, as a basis for computation, one finds some difficulty
in determining the time at which Juliet awakes in the tomb
(v, 3, 147, 176). Hence the uncertainty whether the play ends
on Thursday or on Friday. Thursday seems preferable; but the
problem would never occur to an audience.[1]

The romantic history of Romeo and Juliet was more or less
familiar to Elizabethans before Shakespeare wrote. Broke, in
his preface, speaks of a drama on the subject which he had seen
acted: 'Though I saw the same argument lately set foorth on
stage with more commendation, then I can looke for: (being
there much better set forth then I haue or can dooe) yet the
same matter penned as it is, may serue to lyke good effect.'
The performance which Broke commends may have been a
Christmas show at the Inner Temple.[2] It is just possible that
Jacob Struijs's Dutch play *Romeo en Juliette* (1630) was
founded on it.[3] Perhaps some of Broke's changes in Boaistuau's

[1]See Daniel, *New Shakspere Society Transactions*, 1877–79, p. 194;
Rolfe's edition, pp. 202–203, 219; Dowden's edition, pp. xxix–xxxi; Munro,
p. 132.
[2]See Cunliffe, *Modern Language Review*, VII (1912), 517, 518.
[3]See H. de W. Fuller, *Modern Philology*, IV (1906), 75 ff.

tale were suggested by the play he mentions; but there is no reason to suppose that Shakespeare was influenced by it. Broke's poem is the only source from which he appears to have drawn.

The plot of ROMEO AND JULIET has a long and complicated history. In a Greek romance of the third or fourth century, the *Ephesiaca* of one Xenophon of Ephesus (perhaps a pseudonym), the heroine, Anthia—separated by miscellaneous adventures from her husband Habrocomes, and anxious to avoid an adulterous second marriage—begs a physician to provide her with a deadly poison. He substitutes a sleeping draught, and she awakes in the tomb. She resolves to die of starvation, but robbers find her and carry her off. After many perils, Anthia and her husband are reunited (Books iii–iv). There is a rather similar episode in another Greek romance, the *Babyloniaca* of Iamblichus Syrus, which dates from the middle of the second century.[1] Some form of this ancient tale, combined with a tragic story of star-crossed lovers, forms the substance of Shakespeare's plot. Such a combination is found in the 33d story in *Il Novellino* of Masuccio Salernitano (1476) and in Luigi da Porto's *Hystoria di due nobili Amanti* (printed *ca.* 1525). Da Porto may have drawn from Masuccio, but he says he heard the story from a Veronese comrade. In Masuccio the scene is Siena; in Da Porto it is Verona. Da Porto was the first to call the hero and heroine Romeo and Giulietta and to associate them with the Montecchi and the Cappelletti. Bandello's novel is derived from Da Porto, but may owe something to a previous derivative—'L'infelice amore de i due fedelissimi amanti Giulia e Romeo' (1553), usually ascribed to Gherardo Bolderi, *alias* Boldiero.

A few points of resemblance between ROMEO AND JULIET and Luigi Groto's tragedy *La Hadriana* (1578), if not fortuitous, require an elaborate theory to account for them: namely, that both the *Hadriana* and the lost play which Broke had seen, drew from some Italian version that has not survived, and that Shakespeare made use of the lost play. Coincidence seems more probable; but thought is free.

[1] Epitome in Photius, *Bibliotheca*, 94 (ed. Bekker, pp. 73 ff.).

Otway, in his tragedy entitled *The History and Fall of Caius Marius* (acted in 1679 or 1680, published in 1680),[1] borrows a large part of Shakespeare's ROMEO AND JULIET, almost word for word. The Prologue frankly acknowledges the debt and pays a splendid tribute to Shakespeare's supremacy:

> Our *Shakespear* wrote too in an Age as blest,
> The happiest Poet of his time and best.
> A gracious Prince's Favour chear'd his Muse,
> A constant Favour he ne'er fear'd to lose.
> Therefore he wrote with Fancy unconfin'd,
> And Thoughts that were Immortal as his Mind.
> And from the Crop of his luxuriant Pen
> E're since succeeding Poets humbly glean,
> Though much the most unworthy of the Throng,
> Our this-day's Poet fears h' has done him wrong.
> Like greedy Beggars that steal Sheaves away,
> You'll find h' has rifled him of half a Play.
> Amidst this baser Dross you'll see it shine
> Most beautifull, amazing, and Divine.

ROMEO AND JULIET (like *Macbeth*) is a fatalistic drama. The Prologue announces the tragedy of 'a pair of star-cross'd lovers.' Romeo, on his way to Capulet's festivity, brings fate and providence into that contradictory union which is characteristic of bewildered mortals (i, 4, 106–113):

> My mind misgives
> Some consequence, yet hanging in the stars,
> Shall bitterly begin his fearful date
> With this night's revels and expire the term
> Of a despised life, clos'd in my breast
> By some vile forfeit of untimely death.
> But he that hath the steerage of my course
> Direct my sail!

Only by suicide can he defy the stars (v, 1, 24) and 'shake the yoke of inauspicious stars from this world-wearied flesh' (v, 3, 11i, 112). In almost every act of the play there are what we call presentiments, and, at the end,

> A glooming peace this morning with it brings.
> The sun for sorrow will not show his head.

[1]See Hazelton Spencer, *Shakespeare Improved*, 1927, pp. 100, 292–298.

THE TRAGEDY OF
ROMEO AND JULIET

Chorus.

Escalus, Prince of Verona.
Paris, a young Count, kinsman to the *Prince*.
Montague,
Capulet, } heads of two houses at variance with each other.
An old Man, of the Capulet family.
Romeo, son to *Montague*.
Mercutio, kinsman to the *Prince*, and friend to *Romeo*.
Benvolio, nephew to *Montague*, and friend to *Romeo*.
Tybalt, nephew to *Lady Capulet*.
Friar Laurence,
Friar John, } Franciscans.
Balthasar, servant to *Romeo*.
Abram, servant to *Montague*.
Sampson,
Gregory, } servants to *Capulet*.
Peter, servant to *Juliet's* nurse.
An Apothecary.
Three Musicians.
An Officer.

Lady Montague, wife to *Montague*.
Lady Capulet, wife to *Capulet*.
Juliet, daughter to *Capulet*.
Nurse to *Juliet*.

Citizens of Verona; Gentlemen and Gentlewomen of both houses; Maskers, Torchbearers, Pages, Guards, Watchmen, Servants, and Attendants.

SCENE.—*Verona; Mantua.*]

THE TRAGEDY OF
ROMEO AND JULIET

THE PROLOGUE.

[Enter *Chorus*.]

Chor. Two households, both alike in dignity,
In fair Verona, where we lay our scene,
From ancient grudge break to new mutiny,
Where civil blood makes civil hands unclean.
From forth the fatal loins of these two foes   5
A pair of star-cross'd lovers take their life;
Whose misadventur'd piteous overthrows
Doth with their death bury their parents' strife.
The fearful passage of their death-mark'd love,
And the continuance of their parents' rage,   10
Which, but their children's end, naught could remove,
Is now the two hours' traffic of our stage;
The which if you with patient ears attend,
What here shall miss, our toil shall strive to mend.   [*Exit.*]

Act I. Scene I. [*Verona. A public place.*]

Enter *Sampson* and *Gregory* (with swords and bucklers) of
the house of *Capulet*.

Samp. Gregory, on my word, we'll not carry coals.
Greg. No, for then we should be colliers.
Samp. I mean, an we be in choler, we'll draw.
Greg. Ay, while you live, draw your neck out of collar.   6
Samp. I strike quickly, being moved.
Greg. But thou art not quickly moved to strike.
Samp. A dog of the house of Montague moves me.   10

Greg. To move is to stir, and to be valiant is to stand. Therefore, if thou art moved, thou runn'st away.

Samp. A dog of that house shall move me to stand. I will take the wall of any man or maid of Montague's.   16

Greg. That shows thee a weak slave; for the weakest goes to the wall.

Samp. 'Tis true; and therefore women, being the weaker vessels, are ever thrust to the wall. Therefore I will push Montague's men from the wall and thrust his maids to the wall.

Greg. The quarrel is between our masters and us their men.

Samp. 'Tis all one. I will show myself a tyrant. When I have fought with the men, I will be cruel with the maids— I will cut off their heads.

Greg. The heads of the maids?   29

Samp. Ay, the heads of the maids, or their maidenheads. Take it in what sense thou wilt.

Greg. They must take it in sense that feel it.

Samp. Me they shall feel while I am able to stand; and 'tis known I am a pretty piece of flesh.   35

Greg. 'Tis well thou art not fish; if thou hadst, thou hadst been poor-John. Draw thy tool! Here comes two of the house of Montagues.

Enter two other *Servingmen* [*Abram* and *Balthasar*].

Samp. My naked weapon is out. Quarrel! I will back thee.

Greg. How? turn thy back and run?   41

Samp. Fear me not.

Greg. No, marry. I fear thee!

Samp. Let us take the law of our sides; let them begin.   45

Greg. I will frown as I pass by, and let them take it as they list.

Samp. Nay, as they dare. I will bite my thumb at them; which is disgrace to them, if they bear it.   50

Abr. Do you bite your thumb at us, sir?

Samp. I do bite my thumb, sir.

Abr. Do you bite your thumb at us, sir?

Samp. [*aside to Gregory*] Is the law of our side if I say ay?

Greg. [*aside to Sampson*] No.   56

Samp. No, sir, I do not bite my thumb at you, sir; but I
bite my thumb, sir.

Greg. Do you quarrel, sir?

Abr. Quarrel, sir? No, sir.   60

Samp. But if you do, sir, I am for you. I serve as good a
man as you.

Abr. No better.

Samp. Well, sir.

Enter *Benvolio.*

Greg. [*aside to Sampson*] Say 'better.' Here comes one of
my master's kinsmen.   66

Samp. Yes, better, sir.

Abr. You lie.

Samp. Draw, if you be men. Gregory, remember thy swashing blow.   *They fight.*

Ben. Part, fools! [*Beats down their swords.*]
Put up your swords. You know not what you do.   72

Enter *Tybalt.*

Tyb. What, art thou drawn among these heartless hinds?
Turn thee, Benvolio! look upon thy death.

Ben. I do but keep the peace. Put up thy sword,   75
Or manage it to part these men with me.

Tyb. What, drawn, and talk of peace? I hate the word
As I hate hell, all Montagues, and thee.
Have at thee, coward!   [*They*] *fight.*

Enter [an *Officer*, and] three or four *Citizens* with clubs or
partisans.

Officer. Clubs, bills, and partisans! Strike! beat them down!
Citizens. Down with the Capulets! Down with the Montagues!   81

Enter *Old Capulet* in his gown, and his *Wife*.

Cap. What noise is this? Give me my long sword, ho!
Wife. A crutch, a crutch! Why call you for a sword?
Cap. My sword, I say! Old Montague is come
And flourishes his blade in spite of me.   85

Enter *Old Montague* and his *Wife*.

Mon. Thou villain Capulet!—Hold me not, let me go.
M. Wife. Thou shalt not stir one foot to seek a foe.

Enter *Prince Escalus*, with his *Train*.

Prince. Rebellious subjects, enemies to peace,
Profaners of this neighbour-stained steel—
Will they not hear? What, ho! you men, you beasts,   9c
That quench the fire of your pernicious rage
With purple fountains issuing from your veins!
On pain of torture, from those bloody hands
Throw your mistempered weapons to the ground
And hear the sentence of your moved prince.   95
Three civil brawls, bred of an airy word
By thee, old Capulet, and Montague,
Have thrice disturb'd the quiet of our streets
And made Verona's ancient citizens
Cast by their grave beseeming ornaments   100
To wield old partisans, in hands as old,
Cank'red with peace, to part your cank'red hate.

If ever you disturb our streets again,
Your lives shall pay the forfeit of the peace.
For this time all the rest depart away.   105
You, Capulet, shall go along with me;
And, Montague, come you this afternoon,
To know our farther pleasure in this case,
To old Freetown, our common judgment place.
Once more, on pain of death, all men depart.   110
          Exeunt [all but Montague, his Wife, and Benvolio].
   Mon. Who set this ancient quarrel new abroach?
Speak, nephew, were you by when it began?
   Ben. Here were the servants of your adversary
And yours, close fighting ere I did approach.
I drew to part them. In the instant came   115
The fiery Tybalt, with his sword prepar'd;
Which, as he breath'd defiance to my ears,
He swung about his head and cut the winds,
Who, nothing hurt withal, hiss'd him in scorn.
While we were interchanging thrusts and blows,   120
Came more and more, and fought on part and part,
Till the Prince came, who parted either part.
   M. Wife. O, where is Romeo? Saw you him to-day?
Right glad I am he was not at this fray.
   Ben. Madam, an hour before the worshipp'd sun   125
Peer'd forth the golden window of the East,
A troubled mind drave me to walk abroad;
Where, underneath the grove of sycamore
That westward rooteth from the city's side,
So early walking did I see your son.   130
Towards him I made; but he was ware of me
And stole into the covert of the wood.
I—measuring his affections by my own,
Which then most sought where most might not be found,

Being one too many by my weary self—   135
Pursu'd my humour, not pursuing his,
And gladly shunn'd who gladly fled from me.

   Mon. Many a morning hath he there been seen,
With tears augmenting the fresh morning's dew,
Adding to clouds more clouds with his deep sighs;   140
But all so soon as the all-cheering sun
Should in the farthest East begin to draw
The shady curtains from Aurora's bed,
Away from light steals home my heavy son
And private in his chamber pens himself,   145
Shuts up his windows, locks fair daylight out,
And makes himself an artificial night.
Black and portentous must this humour prove
Unless good counsel may the cause remove.

   Ben. My noble uncle, do you know the cause?   150
   Mon. I neither know it nor can learn of him.
   Ben. Have you importun'd him by any means?
   Mon. Both by myself and many other friends;
But he, his own affections' counsellor,
Is to himself—I will not say how true—   155
But to himself so secret and so close,
So far from sounding and discovery,
As is the bud bit with an envious worm
Ere he can spread his sweet leaves to the air
Or dedicate his beauty to the sun.   160
Could we but learn from whence his sorrows grow,
We would as willingly give cure as know.

Enter Romeo.

   Ben. See, where he comes. So please you step aside,
I'll know his grievance, or be much denied.

   Mon. I would thou wert so happy by thy stay   165
To hear true shrift. Come, madam, let's away.
                      Exeunt [Montague and Wife].
   Ben. Good morrow, cousin.
   Rom.   Is the day so young?
   Ben. But new struck nine.
   Rom.   Ay me! sad hours seem long.
Was that my father that went hence so fast?
   Ben. It was. What sadness lengthens Romeo's hours?   170
   Rom. Not having that which having makes them short.
   Ben. In love?
   Rom. Out—
   Ben. Of love?
   Rom. Out of her favour where I am in love.   175
   Ben. Alas that love, so gentle in his view,
Should be so tyrannous and rough in proof!
   Rom. Alas that love, whose view is muffled still,
Should without eyes see pathways to his will!
Where shall we dine? O me! What fray was here?   180
Yet tell me not, for I have heard it all.
Here's much to do with hate, but more with love.
Why then, O brawling love! O loving hate!
O anything, of nothing first create!
O heavy lightness! serious vanity!   185
Misshapen chaos of well-seeming forms!
Feather of lead, bright smoke, cold fire, sick health!
Still-waking sleep, that is not what it is!
This love feel I, that feel no love in this.
Dost thou not laugh?
   Ben.   No, coz, I rather weep.   190
   Rom. Good heart, at what?
   Ben.   At thy good heart's oppression.
   Rom. Why, such is love's transgression.

Griefs of mine own lie heavy in my breast,
Which thou wilt propagate, to have it prest
With more of thine. This love that thou hast shown   195
Doth add more grief to too much of mine own.
Love is a smoke rais'd with the fume of sighs;
Being purg'd, a fire sparkling in lovers' eyes;
Being vex'd, a sea nourish'd with lovers' tears.
What is it else? A madness most discreet,   200
A choking gall, and a preserving sweet.
Farewell, my coz.

   Ben.   Soft! I will go along.
An if you leave me so, you do me wrong.
   Rom. Tut! I have lost myself; I am not here:
This is not Romeo, he's some other where.   205
   Ben. Tell me in sadness, who is that you love?
   Rom. What, shall I groan and tell thee?
   Ben.   Groan? Why, no;
But sadly tell me who.
   Rom. Bid a sick man in sadness make his will.
Ah, word ill urg'd to one that is so ill!   210
In sadness, cousin, I do love a woman.
   Ben. I aim'd so near when I suppos'd you lov'd.
   Rom. A right good markman! And she's fair I love.
   Ben. A right fair mark, fair coz, is soonest hit.
   Rom. Well, in that hit you miss. She'll not be hit   215
With Cupid's arrow. She hath Dian's wit,
And, in strong proof of chastity well arm'd,
From Love's weak childish bow she lives unharm'd.
She will not stay the siege of loving terms,
Nor bide th' encounter of assailing eyes,   220
Nor ope her lap to saint-seducing gold.
O, she is rich in beauty; only poor
That, when she dies, with beauty dies her store.

Ben. Then she hath sworn that she will still live chaste?
Rom. She hath, and in that sparing makes huge waste;   225
For beauty, starv'd with her severity,
Cuts beauty off from all posterity.
She is too fair, too wise, wisely too fair,
To merit bliss by making me despair.
She hath forsworn to love, and in that vow   230
Do I live dead that live to tell it now.
  Ben. Be rul'd by me: forget to think of her.
  Rom. O, teach me how I should forget to think!
  Ben. By giving liberty unto thine eyes.
Examine other beauties.
  Rom.   'Tis the way   235
To call hers (exquisite) in question more.
These happy masks that kiss fair ladies' brows,
Being black puts us in mind they hide the fair.
He that is strucken blind cannot forget
The precious treasure of his eyesight lost.   240
Show me a mistress that is passing fair,
What doth her beauty serve but as a note
Where I may read who pass'd that passing fair?
Farewell. Thou canst not teach me to forget.
  Ben. I'll pay that doctrine, or else die in debt.   245
                                              Exeunt.

[Scene II. *A Street.*]

Enter *Capulet, County Paris,* and [*Servant*]—the *Clown.*

  Cap. But Montague is bound as well as I,
In penalty alike; and 'tis not hard, I think,
For men so old as we to keep the peace.
  Par. Of honourable reckoning are you both,

And pity 'tis you liv'd at odds so long. 5
But now, my lord, what say you to my suit?
  Cap. But saying o'er what I have said before:
My child is yet a stranger in the world,
She hath not seen the change of fourteen years;
Let two more summers wither in their pride 10
Ere we may think her ripe to be a bride.
  Par. Younger than she are happy mothers made.
  Cap. And too soon marr'd are those so early made.
The earth hath swallowed all my hopes but she;
She is the hopeful lady of my earth. 15
But woo her, gentle Paris, get her heart;
My will to her consent is but a part.
An she agree, within her scope of choice
Lies my consent and fair according voice.
This night I hold an old accustom'd feast, 20
Whereto I have invited many a guest,
Such as I love; and you among the store,
One more, most welcome, makes my number more.
At my poor house look to behold this night
Earth-treading stars that make dark heaven light. 25
Such comfort as do lusty young men feel
When well-apparell'd April on the heel
Of limping Winter treads, even such delight
Among fresh female buds shall you this night
Inherit at my house. Hear all, all see, 30
And like her most whose merit most shall be;
Which, on more view of many, mine, being one,
May stand in number, though in reck'ning none.
Come, go with me. [*To Servant, giving him a paper*] Go,
    sirrah, trudge about
Through fair Verona; find those persons out 35

Whose names are written there, and to them say,
My house and welcome on their pleasure stay.

        Exeunt [*Capulet and Paris*].

 Serv. Find them out whose names are written here? It is
written that the shoemaker should meddle with his yard and
the tailor with his last, the fisher with his pencil and the painter
with his nets; but I am sent to find those persons whose names
are here writ, and can never find what names the writing person hath here writ. I must to the learned. In good time! 45

    Enter *Benvolio* and *Romeo*.

 Ben. Tut, man, one fire burns out another's burning;
 One pain is less'ned by another's anguish;
Turn giddy, and be holp by backward turning;
 One desperate grief cures with another's languish.
Take thou some new infection to thy eye,   50
And the rank poison of the old will die.

 Rom. Your plantain leaf is excellent for that.

 Ben. For what, I pray thee?

 Rom.   For your broken shin.

 Ben. Why, Romeo, art thou mad?

 Rom. Not mad, but bound more than a madman is; 55
Shut up in prison, kept without my food,
Whipp'd and tormented and—God-den, good fellow.

 Serv. God gi' go-den. I pray, sir, can you read?

 Rom. Ay, mine own fortune in my misery.   60

 Serv. Perhaps you have learned it without book. But I pray,
can you read anything you see?

 Rom. Ay, if I know the letters and the language.

 Serv. Ye say honestly. Rest you merry!   65

 Rom. Stay, fellow; I can read.   *He reads.*

'Signior Martino and his wife and daughters;
County Anselmo and his beauteous sisters;
The lady widow of Vitruvio;
Signior Placentio and his lovely nieces;
Mercutio and his brother Valentine;   **70**
Mine uncle Capulet, his wife, and daughters;
My fair niece Rosaline and Livia;
Signior Valentio and his cousin Tybalt;
Lucio and the lively Helena.'

[*Gives back the paper.*] A fair assembly. Whither should they
 come?   75
 Serv. Up.
 Rom. Whither?
 Serv. To supper, to our house.
 Rom. Whose house?
 Serv. My master's.   80
 Rom. Indeed I should have ask'd you that before.
 Serv. Now I'll tell you without asking. My master is the
great rich Capulet; and if you be not of the house of
Montagues, I pray come and crush a cup of wine. Rest you
merry!   *Exit.*
 Ben. At this same ancient feast of Capulet's   86
Sups the fair Rosaline whom thou so lov'st;
With all the admired beauties of Verona.
Go thither, and with unattainted eye
Compare her face with some that I shall show,   90
And I will make thee think thy swan a crow.
 Rom. When the devout religion of mine eye
 Maintains such falsehood, then turn tears to fires;
And these, who, often drown'd, could never die,
 Transparent heretics, be burnt for liars!   95
One fairer than my love? The all-seeing sun
Ne'er saw her match since first the world begun.

Ben. Tut! you saw her fair, none else being by,
Herself pois'd with herself in either eye;
But in that crystal scales let there be weigh'd   100
Your lady's love against some other maid
That I will show you shining at this feast,
And she shall scant show well that now seems best.
    Rom. I'll go along, no such sight to be shown,
But to rejoice in splendour of my own.   105
                                                  [*Exeunt.*]

[Scene III. Capulet's *house.*]

Enter *Capulet's Wife*, and *Nurse*.

Wife. Nurse, where's my daughter? Call her forth to me.
Nurse. Now, by my maidenhead at twelve year old,
I bade her come. What, lamb! what, ladybird!
God forbid! Where's this girl? What, Juliet!

Enter *Juliet*.

Jul. How now? Who calls?
Nurse.   Your mother.
Jul.   Madam, I am here.
What is your will?   6
    Wife. This is the matter—Nurse, give leave awhile,
We must talk in secret. Nurse, come back again;
I have rememb'red me, thou 's hear our counsel.
Thou knowest my daughter 's of a pretty age.   10
    Nurse. Faith, I can tell her age unto an hour.
    Wife. She's not fourteen.
    Nurse.   I'll lay fourteen of my teeth—
And yet, to my teen be it spoken, I have but four—

She is not fourteen. How long is it now
To Lammastide?

   Wife.   A fortnight and odd days.   15

   Nurse. Even or odd, of all days in the year,
Come Lammas Eve at night shall she be fourteen.
Susan and she (God rest all Christian souls!)
Were of an age. Well, Susan is with God;
She was too good for me. But, as I said,   20
On Lammas Eve at night shall she be fourteen;
That shall she, marry; I remember it well.
'Tis since the earthquake now eleven years;
And she was wean'd (I never shall forget it),
Of all the days of the year, upon that day;   25
For I had then laid wormwood to my dug,
Sitting in the sun under the dovehouse wall.
My lord and you were then at Mantua.
Nay, I do bear a brain. But, as I said,
When it did taste the wormwood on the nipple   30
Of my dug and felt it bitter, pretty fool,
To see it tetchy and fall out with the dug!
Shake, quoth the dovehouse! 'Twas no need, I trow,
To bid me trudge.
And since that time it is eleven years,   35
For then she could stand high-lone; nay, by th' rood,
She could have run and waddled all about;
For even the day before, she broke her brow;
And then my husband (God be with his soul!
'A was a merry man) took up the child.   40
'Yea,' quoth he, 'dost thou fall upon thy face?
Thou wilt fall backward when thou hast more wit;
Wilt thou not, Jule?' and, by my holidam,
The pretty wretch left crying, and said 'Ay.'
To see now how a jest shall come about!   45

I warrant, an I should live a thousand years,
I never should forget it. 'Wilt thou not, Jule?' quoth he,
And, pretty fool, it stinted, and said 'Ay.'
    Wife. Enough of this. I pray thee hold thy peace.
    Nurse. Yes, madam. Yet I cannot choose but laugh   50
To think it should leave crying and say 'Ay.'
And yet, I warrant, it had upon it brow
A bump as big as a young cock'rel's stone;
A perilous knock; and it cried bitterly.
'Yea,' quoth my husband, 'fall'st upon thy face?   55
Thou wilt fall backward when thou comest to age;
Wilt thou not, Jule?' It stinted, and said 'Ay.'
    Jul. And stint thou too, I pray thee, nurse, say I.
    Nurse. Peace, I have done. God mark thee to his grace!
Thou wast the prettiest babe that e'er I nurs'd.   60
An I might live to see thee married once,
I have my wish.
    Wife. Marry, that 'marry' is the very theme
I came to talk of. Tell me, daughter Juliet,
How stands your disposition to be married?   65
    Jul. It is an honour that I dream not of.
    Nurse. An honour? Were not I thine only nurse,
I would say thou hadst suck'd wisdom from thy teat.
    Wife. Well, think of marriage now. Younger than you,
Here in Verona, ladies of esteem,   70
Are made already mothers. By my count,
I was your mother much upon these years
That you are now a maid. Thus then in brief:
The valiant Paris seeks you for his love.
    Nurse. A man, young lady! lady, such a man   75
As all the world—why he's a man of wax.
    Wife. Verona's summer hath not such a flower.
    Nurse. Nay, he's a flower, in faith—a very flower.

Wife. What say you? Can you love the gentleman?
This night you shall behold him at our feast.   80
Read o'er the volume of young Paris' face,
And find delight writ there with beauty's pen;
Examine every married lineament,
And see how one another lends content;
And what obscur'd in this fair volume lies   85
Find written in the margent of his eyes.
This precious book of love, this unbound lover,
To beautify him only lacks a cover.
The fish lives in the sea, and 'tis much pride
For fair without the fair within to hide.   90
That book in many's eyes doth share the glory,
That in gold clasps locks in the golden story;
So shall you share all that he doth possess,
By having him making yourself no less.

   Nurse. No less? Nay, bigger! Women grow by men.   95
   Wife. Speak briefly, can you like of Paris' love?
   Jul. I'll look to like, if looking liking move;
But no more deep will I endart mine eye
Than your consent gives strength to make it fly.

Enter *Servingman.*

   Serv. Madam, the guests are come, supper serv'd up, you
call'd, my young lady ask'd for, the nurse curs'd in the pantry,
and everything in extremity. I must hence to wait. I beseech
you follow straight.

   Wife. We follow thee. *Exit* [*Servingman*]. Juliet, the
     County stays.   105
   Nurse. Go, girl, seek happy nights to happy days.

                         Exeunt.

[Scene IV. *A street.*]

Enter *Romeo, Mercutio, Benvolio*, with five or six other
Maskers; Torchbearers.

Rom. What, shall this speech be spoke for our excuse?
Or shall we on without apology?
Ben. The date is out of such prolixity.
We'll have no Cupid hoodwink'd with a scarf,
Bearing a Tartar's painted bow of lath,   5
Scaring the ladies like a crowkeeper;
Nor no without-book prologue, faintly spoke
After the prompter, for our entrance;
But, let them measure us by what they will,
We'll measure them a measure, and be gone.   10
Rom. Give me a torch. I am not for this ambling.
Being but heavy, I will bear the light.
Mer. Nay, gentle Romeo, we must have you dance.
Rom. Not I, believe me. You have dancing shoes
With nimble soles; I have a soul of lead   15
So stakes me to the ground I cannot move.
Mer. You are a lover. Borrow Cupid's wings
And soar with them above a common bound.
Rom. I am too sore enpierced with his shaft
To soar with his light feathers; and so bound   20
I cannot bound a pitch above dull woe.
Under love's heavy burthen do I sink.
Mer. And, to sink in it, should you burthen love—
Too great oppression for a tender thing.
Rom. Is love a tender thing? It is too rough,   25
Too rude, too boist'rous, and it pricks like thorn.
Mer. If love be rough with you, be rough with love.
Prick love for pricking, and you beat love down.

Give me a case to put my visage in.
A visor for a visor! What care I   30
What curious eye doth quote deformities?
Here are the beetle brows shall blush for me.

   Ben. Come, knock and enter; and no sooner in
But every man betake him to his legs.

   Rom. A torch for me! Let wantons light of heart   35
Tickle the senseless rushes with their heels;
For I am proverb'd with a grandsire phrase,
I'll be a candle-holder and look on;
The game was ne'er so fair, and I am done.

   Mer. Tut! dun's the mouse, the constable's own word! 40
If thou art Dun, we'll draw thee from the mire
Of this sir-reverence love, wherein thou stick'st
Up to the ears. Come, we burn daylight, ho!

   Rom. Nay, that's not so.

   Mer.   I mean, sir, in delay
We waste our lights in vain, like lamps by day.   45
Take our good meaning, for our judgment sits
Five times in that ere once in our five wits.

   Rom. And we mean well, in going to this masque;
But 'tis no wit to go.

   Mer.   Why, may one ask?

   Rom. I dreamt a dream to-night.

   Mer.   And so did I.   50

   Rom. Well, what was yours?

   Mer.   That dreamers often lie.

   Rom. In bed asleep, while they do dream things true.

   Mer. O, then I see Queen Mab hath been with you.
She is the fairies' midwife, and she comes
In shape no bigger than an agate stone   55
On the forefinger of an alderman,
Drawn with a team of little atomies

Athwart men's noses as they lie asleep;
Her wagon spokes made of long spinners' legs,
The cover, of the wings of grasshoppers;   60
Her traces, of the smallest spider's web;
Her collars, of the moonshine's wat'ry beams;
Her whip, of cricket's bone; the lash, of film;
Her wagoner, a small grey-coated gnat,
Not half so big as a round little worm   65
Prick'd from the lazy finger of a maid;
Her chariot is an empty hazelnut,
Made by the joiner squirrel or old grub,
Time out o' mind the fairies' coachmakers.
And in this state she gallops night by night   70
Through lovers' brains, and then they dream of love;
O'er courtiers' knees, that dream on cursies straight;
O'er lawyers' fingers, who straight dream on fees;
O'er ladies' lips, who straight on kisses dream,
Which oft the angry Mab with blisters plagues,   75
Because their breaths with sweetmeats tainted are.
Sometime she gallops o'er a courtier's nose,
And then dreams he of smelling out a suit;
And sometime comes she with a tithe-pig's tail
Tickling a parson's nose as 'a lies asleep,   80
Then dreams he of another benefice.
Sometimes she driveth o'er a soldier's neck,
And then dreams he of cutting foreign throats,
Of breaches, ambuscadoes, Spanish blades,
Of healths five fadom deep; and then anon   85
Drums in his ear, at which he starts and wakes,
And being thus frighted, swears a prayer or two
And sleeps again. This is that very Mab
That plats the manes of horses in the night
And bakes the elflocks in foul sluttish hairs,   90

Which once untangled much misfortune bodes.
This is the hag, when maids lie on their backs,
That presses them and learns them first to bear,
Making them women of good carriage.
This is she—
   Rom.   Peace, peace, Mercutio, peace!   95
Thou talk'st of nothing.
   Mer.   True, I talk of dreams;
Which are the children of an idle brain,
Begot of nothing but vain fantasy;
Which is as thin of substance as the air,
And more inconstant than the wind, who wooes   100
Even now the frozen bosom of the North
And, being anger'd, puffs away from thence,
Turning his face to the dew-dropping South.
   Ben. This wind you talk of blows us from ourselves.
Supper is done, and we shall come too late.   105
   Rom. I fear, too early; for my mind misgives
Some consequence, yet hanging in the stars,
Shall bitterly begin his fearful date
With this night's revels and expire the term
Of a despised life, clos'd in my breast,   110
By some vile forfeit of untimely death.
But he that hath the steerage of my course
Direct my sail! On, lusty gentlemen!
   Ben. Strike, drum.
             They march about the stage. [*Exeunt.*]

[Scene V. Capulet's *house*.]

Servingmen come forth with napkins.

1. Serv. Where's Potpan, that he helps not to take away?
He shift a trencher! he scrape a trencher!

2. Serv. When good manners shall lie all in one or two men's
hands, and they unwash'd too, 'tis a foul thing.   6

1. Serv. Away with the join-stools, remove the court-cubbert,
look to the plate. Good thou, save me a piece of marchpane
and, as thou loves me, let the porter let in Susan Grindstone
and Nell. Anthony, and Potpan!   11

2. Serv. Ay, boy, ready.

1. Serv. You are look'd for and call'd for, ask'd for and
sought for, in the great chamber.

3. Serv. We cannot be here and there too. Cheerly, boys!
Be brisk awhile, and the longer liver take all.   *Exeunt.*

[Enter the *Maskers*.] Enter, [with *Servants, Capulet,* his *Wife,
Juliet, Tybalt,* and] all the *Guests* and *Gentlewomen* to the
Maskers.

Cap. Welcome, gentlemen! Ladies that have their toes
Unplagu'd with corns will have a bout with you.
Ah ha, my mistresses! which of you all   20
Will now deny to dance? She that makes dainty,
She I'll swear hath corns. Am I come near ye now?
Welcome, gentlemen! I have seen the day
That I have worn a visor and could tell
A whispering tale in a fair lady's ear,   25
Such as would please. 'Tis gone, 'tis gone, 'tis gone!
You are welcome, gentlemen! Come, musicians, play.
A hall, a hall! give room! and foot it, girls.
                Music plays, and they dance.

More light, you knaves! and turn the tables up,
And quench the fire, the room is grown too hot.   30
Ah, sirrah, this unlook'd-for sport comes well.
Nay, sit, nay, sit, good cousin Capulet,
For you and I are past our dancing days.
How long is't now since last yourself and I
Were in a mask?

  2. Cap. By'r Lady, thirty years.   35
  Cap. What, man? 'Tis not so much, 'tis not so much!
'Tis since the nuptial of Lucentio,
Come Pentecost as quickly as it will,
Some five-and-twenty years, and then we mask'd.

  2. Cap. 'Tis more, 'tis more! His son is elder, sir;   40
His son is thirty.

  Cap. Will you tell me that?
His son was but a ward two years ago.

  Rom. [*to a Servingman*] What lady's that, which doth en-
   rich the hand
Of yonder knight?

  Serv. I know not, sir.   45

  Rom. O, she doth teach the torches to burn bright!
It seems she hangs upon the cheek of night
Like a rich jewel in an Ethiop's ear—
Beauty too rich for use, for earth too dear!
So shows a snowy dove trooping with crows   50
As yonder lady o'er her fellows shows.
The measure done, I'll watch her place of stand
And, touching hers, make blessed my rude hand.
Did my heart love till now? Forswear it, sight!
For I ne'er saw true beauty till this night.   55

  Tyb. This, by his voice, should be a Montague.
Fetch me my rapier, boy. What, dares the slave
Come hither, cover'd with an antic face,

To fleer and scorn at our solemnity?
Now, by the stock and honour of my kin,   60
To strike him dead I hold it not a sin.
   Cap. Why, how now, kinsman? Wherefore storm you so?
   Tyb. Uncle, this is a Montague, our foe;
A villain, that is hither come in spite
To scorn at our solemnity this night.   65
   Cap. Young Romeo is it?
   Tyb.   'Tis he, that villain Romeo.
   Cap. Content thee, gentle coz, let him alone.
'A bears him like a portly gentleman,
And, to say truth, Verona brags of him
To be a virtuous and well-govern'd youth.   70
I would not for the wealth of all this town
Here in my house do him disparagement.
Therefore be patient, take no note of him.
It is my will; the which if thou respect,
Show a fair presence and put off these frowns,   75
An ill-beseeming semblance for a feast.
   Tyb. It fits when such a villain is a guest.
I'll not endure him.
   Cap.   He shall be endur'd.
What, goodman boy? I say he shall. Go to!
Am I the master here, or you? Go to!   80
You'll not endure him? God shall mend my soul!
You'll make a mutiny among my guests!
You will set cock-a-hoop! you'll be the man!
   Tyb. Why, uncle, 'tis a shame.
   Cap.   Go to, go to!
You are a saucy boy. Is't so, indeed?   85
This trick may chance to scathe you. I know what.
You must contrary me! Marry, 'tis time.—
Well said, my hearts!—You are a princox—go!

Be quiet, or—More light, more light!—For shame!
I'll make you quiet; what!—Cheerly, my hearts!   90
   Tyb. Patience perforce with wilful choler meeting
Makes my flesh tremble in their different greeting.
I will withdraw; but this intrusion shall,
Now seeming sweet, convert to bitt'rest gall.   *Exit.*
   Rom. If I profane with my unworthiest hand   95
   This holy shrine, the gentle fine is this:
My lips, two blushing pilgrims, ready stand
   To smooth that rough touch with a tender kiss.
   Jul. Good pilgrim, you do wrong your hand too much,
   Which mannerly devotion shows in this;   100
For saints have hands that pilgrims' hands do touch,
   And palm to palm is holy palmers' kiss.
   Rom. Have not saints lips, and holy palmers too?
   Jul. Ay, pilgrim, lips that they must use in pray'r.
   Rom. O, then, dear saint, let lips do what hands do!   105
They pray; grant thou, lest faith turn to despair.
   Jul. Saints do not move, though grant for prayers' sake.
   Rom. Then move not while my prayer's effect I take.
Thus from my lips, by thine my sin is purg'd.   [*Kisses her.*]
   Jul. Then have my lips the sin that they have took.   110
   Rom. Sin from my lips? O trespass sweetly urg'd!
Give me my sin again.   [*Kisses her.*]
   Jul.   You kiss by th' book.
   Nurse. Madam, your mother craves a word with you.
   Rom. What is her mother?
   Nurse.   Marry, bachelor,
Her mother is the lady of the house.   115
And a good lady, and a wise and virtuous.
I nurs'd her daughter that you talk'd withal.
I tell you, he that can lay hold of her
Shall have the chinks.

Rom.   Is she a Capulet?

O dear account! my life is my foe's debt.   120

   Ben. Away, be gone; the sport is at the best.

   Rom. Ay, so I fear; the more is my unrest.

   Cap. Nay, gentlemen, prepare not to be gone;

We have a trifling foolish banquet towards.

Is it e'en so? Why then, I thank you all.   125

I thank you, honest gentlemen. Good night.

More torches here! [*Exeunt Maskers.*] Come on then, let's
    to bed.

Ah, sirrah, by my fay, it waxes late;

I'll to my rest.

                       Exeunt [all but Juliet and Nurse].

   Jul. Come hither, nurse. What is yond gentleman?   130

   Nurse. The son and heir of old Tiberio.

   Jul. What's he that now is going out of door?

   Nurse. Marry, that, I think, be young Petruchio.

   Jul. What's he that follows there, that would not **dance**?

   Nurse. I know not.   135

   Jul. Go ask his name.—If he be married,

My grave is like to be my wedding bed.

   Nurse. His name is Romeo, and a Montague,

The only son of your great enemy.

   Jul. My only love, sprung from my only hate!   140

Too early seen unknown, and known too late!

Prodigious birth of love it is to me

That I must love a loathed enemy.

   Nurse. What's this? what's this?

   Jul.   A rhyme I learnt even now

Of one I danc'd withal.

               One calls within, 'Juliet.'

   Nurse.   Anon, anon!   145

Come, let's away; the strangers all are gone.   *Exeunt.*

[PROLOGUE.]

[Enter *Chorus.*]

Chor. Now old desire doth in his deathbed lie,
   And young affection gapes to be his heir;
That fair for which love groan'd for and would die,
   With tender Juliet match'd, is now not fair.
Now Romeo is belov'd, and loves again,   5
   Alike bewitched by the charm of looks;
But to his foe suppos'd he must complain,
   And she steal love's sweet bait from fearful **hooks.**
Being held a foe, he may not have access
   To breathe such vows as lovers use to swear,   10
And she as much in love, her means much less
   To meet her new beloved anywhere;
But passion lends them power, time means, to meet,
Temp'ring extremities with extreme sweet.

                         [*Exit.*]

[Scene I. *A lane by the wall of* Capulet's *orchard.*]

Enter *Romeo* alone.

Rom. Can I go forward when my heart is here?
Turn back, dull earth, and find thy centre out.
       [*Climbs the wall and leaps down within it.*]

Enter *Benvolio* with *Mercutio.*

Ben. Romeo! my cousin Romeo! Romeo!
Mer.   He is wise,
And, on my life, hath stol'n him home to bed.

   Ben. He ran this way, and leapt this orchard wall.   5
Call, good Mercutio.
   Mer.   Nay, I'll conjure too.
Romeo! humours! madman! passion! lover!
Appear thou in the likeness of a sigh;
Speak but one rhyme, and I am satisfied!
Cry but 'Ay me!' pronounce but 'love' and 'dove';   10
Speak to my gossip Venus one fair word,
One nickname for her purblind son and heir,
Young Adam Cupid, he that shot so trim
When King Cophetua lov'd the beggar maid!
He heareth not, he stirreth not, he moveth not;   15
The ape is dead, and I must conjure him.
I conjure thee by Rosaline's bright eyes,
By her high forehead and her scarlet lip,
By her fine foot, straight leg, and quivering thigh,
And the demesnes that there adjacent lie,   20
That in thy likeness thou appear to us!
   Ben. An if he hear thee, thou wilt anger him.
   Mer. This cannot anger him. 'Twould anger him
To raise a spirit in his mistress' circle
Of some strange nature, letting it there stand   25
Till she had laid it and conjur'd it down.
That were some spite; my invocation
Is fair and honest: in his mistress' name,
I conjure only but to raise up him.
   Ben. Come, he hath hid himself among these trees   30
To be consorted with the humorous night.
Blind is his love and best befits the dark.
   Mer. If love be blind, love cannot hit the mark.
Now will he sit under a medlar tree
And wish his mistress were that kind of fruit   35
As maids call medlars when they laugh alone.

O, Romeo, that she were, O that she were
An open et cetera, thou a pop'rin pear!
Romeo, good night. I'll to my truckle-bed;
This field-bed is too cold for me to sleep.   **40**
Come, shall we go?

   Ben.   Go then, for 'tis in vain
To seek him here that means not to be found.

Exeunt.

[Scene II. Capulet's *orchard*.]

[Enter *Romeo*.]

Rom. He jests at scars that never felt a wound.

[Enter *Juliet* above at a window.]

But soft! What light through yonder window breaks?
It is the East, and Juliet is the sun!
Arise, fair sun, and kill the envious moon,
Who is already sick and pale with grief   5
That thou her maid art far more fair than she.
Be not her maid, since she is envious.
Her vestal livery is but sick and green,
And none but fools do wear it. Cast it off.
It is my lady; O, it is my love!   10
O that she knew she were!
She speaks, yet she says nothing. What of that?
Her eye discourses; I will answer it.
I am too bold; 'tis not to me she speaks.
Two of the fairest stars in all the heaven,   15
Having some business, do entreat her eyes
To twinkle in their spheres till they return.
What if her eyes were there, they in her head?

The brightness of her cheek would shame those stars
As daylight doth a lamp; her eyes in heaven   20
Would through the airy region stream so bright
That birds would sing and think it were not night.
See how she leans her cheek upon her hand!
O that I were a glove upon that hand,
That I might touch that cheek!
  Jul.   Ay me!
  Rom.   She speaks.   25
O, speak again, bright angel! for thou art
As glorious to this night, being o'er my head,
As is a winged messenger of heaven
Unto the white-upturned wond'ring eyes
Of mortals that fall back to gaze on him   30
When he bestrides the lazy-pacing clouds
And sails upon the bosom of the air.
  Jul. O Romeo, Romeo! wherefore art thou Romeo?
Deny thy father and refuse thy name!
Or, if thou wilt not, be but sworn my love,   35
And I'll no longer be a Capulet.
  Rom. [*aside*] Shall I hear more, or shall I speak at this?
  Jul. 'Tis but thy name that is my enemy.
Thou art thyself, though not a Montague.
What's Montague? It is nor hand, nor foot,   40
Nor arm, nor face, nor any other part
Belonging to a man. O, be some other name!
What's in a name? That which we call a rose
By any other name would smell as sweet.
So Romeo would, were he not Romeo call'd,   45
Retain that dear perfection which he owes
Without that title. Romeo, doff thy name;
And for that name, which is no part of thee,
Take all myself.

Rom.   I take thee at thy word.
Call me but love, and I'll be new baptiz'd;   50
Henceforth I never will be Romeo.

Jul. What man art thou that, thus bescreen'd in night,
So stumblest on my counsel?

Rom.   By a name
I know not how to tell thee who I am.
My name, dear saint, is hateful to myself,   55
Because it is an enemy to thee.
Had I it written, I would tear the word.

Jul. My ears have yet not drunk a hundred words
Of that tongue's utterance, yet I know the sound.
Art thou not Romeo, and a Montague?   60

Rom. Neither, fair saint, if either thee dislike.

Jul. How cam'st thou hither, tell me, and wherefore?
The orchard walls are high and hard to climb,
And the place death, considering who thou art,
If any of my kinsmen find thee here.   65

Rom. With love's light wings did I o'erperch these walls;
For stony limits cannot hold love out,
And what love can do, that dares love attempt.
Therefore thy kinsmen are no let to me.

Jul. If they do see thee, they will murther thee.   70

Rom. Alack, there lies more peril in thine eye
Than twenty of their swords! Look thou but sweet,
And I am proof against their enmity.

Jul. I would not for the world they saw thee here.

Rom. I have night's cloak to hide me from their sight;   75
And but thou love me, let them find me here.
My life were better ended by their hate
Than death prorogued, wanting of thy love.

Jul. By whose direction found'st thou out this place?

Rom. By love, that first did prompt me to enquire.   80

He lent me counsel, and I lent him eyes.
I am no pilot; yet, wert thou as far
As that vast shore wash'd with the farthest sea,
I would adventure for such merchandise.

 Jul. Thou knowest the mask of night is on my face; 85
Else would a maiden blush bepaint my cheek
For that which thou hast heard me speak to-night.
Fain would I dwell on form—fain, fain deny
What I have spoke; but farewell compliment!
Dost thou love me? I know thou wilt say 'Ay';   90
And I will take thy word. Yet, if thou swear'st,
Thou mayst prove false. At lovers' perjuries,
They say Jove laughs. O gentle Romeo,
If thou dost love, pronounce it faithfully.
Or if thou thinkest I am too quickly won,   95
I'll frown, and be perverse, and say thee nay,
So thou wilt woo; but else, not for the world.
In truth, fair Montague, I am too fond,
And therefore thou mayst think my haviour light;
But trust me, gentleman, I'll prove more true   100
Than those that have more cunning to be strange.
I should have been more strange, I must confess,
But that thou overheard'st, ere I was ware,
My true-love passion. Therefore pardon me,
And not impute this yielding to light love,   105
Which the dark night hath so discovered.

 Rom. Lady, by yonder blessed moon I swear,
That tips with silver all these fruit-tree tops—

 Jul. O, swear not by the moon, th' inconstant moon,
That monthly changes in her circled orb,   110
Lest that thy love prove likewise variable.

 Rom. What shall I swear by?

 Jul.   Do not swear at all;

Or if thou wilt, swear by thy gracious self,
Which is the god of my idolatry,
And I'll believe thee.

 Rom.   If my heart's dear love——   115
 Jul. Well, do not swear. Although I joy in thee,
I have no joy of this contract to-night.
It is too rash, too unadvis'd, too sudden;
Too like the lightning, which doth cease to be
Ere one can say 'It lightens.' Sweet, good night! 120
This bud of love, by summer's ripening breath,
May prove a beauteous flow'r when next we meet.
Good night, good night! As sweet repose and rest
Come to thy heart as that within my breast!

 Rom. O, wilt thou leave me so unsatisfied? 125
 Jul. What satisfaction canst thou have to-night?
 Rom. Th' exchange of thy love's faithful vow for mine.
 Jul. I gave thee mine before thou didst request it;
And yet I would it were to give again.

 Rom. Would'st thou withdraw it? For what purpose,
  love?
 Jul. But to be frank and give it thee again. 131
And yet I wish but for the thing I have.
My bounty is as boundless as the sea,
My love as deep; the more I give to thee,
The more I have, for both are infinite. 135
I hear some noise within. Dear love, adieu!

         [*Nurse*] *calls within.*

Anon, good nurse! Sweet Montague, be true.
Stay but a little, I will come again.   [*Exit.*]

 Rom. O blessed, blessed night! I am afeard,
Being in night, all this is but a dream, 140
Too flattering-sweet to be substantial.

[Enter *Juliet* above.]

Jul. Three words, dear Romeo, and good night indeed.
If that thy bent of love be honourable,
Thy purpose marriage, send me word to-morrow,
By one that I'll procure to come to thee,   145
Where and what time thou wilt perform the rite;
And all my fortunes at thy foot I'll lay
And follow thee my lord throughout the world.
    Nurse. (*within*) Madam!
    Jul. I come, anon.—But if thou meanest not well,   150
I do beseech thee—
    Nurse. (*within*) Madam!
    Jul.   By-and-by I come.—
To cease thy suit and leave me to my grief.
To-morrow will I send.
    Rom.   So thrive my soul—
    Jul. A thousand times good night!   *Exit.*
    Rom. A thousand times the worse, to want thy light! 156
Love goes toward love as schoolboys from their books;
But love from love, towards school with heavy looks.

Enter *Juliet* again, [above].

    Jul. Hist! Romeo, hist! O for a falc'ner's voice
To lure this tassel-gentle back again!   160
Bondage is hoarse and may not speak aloud;
Else would I tear the cave where Echo lies,
And make her airy tongue more hoarse than mine
With repetition of my Romeo's name.
Romeo!   165
    Rom. It is my soul that calls upon my name.
How silver-sweet sound lovers' tongues by night,
Like softest music to attending ears!

Jul. Romeo!

Rom.   My dear?

Jul.   At what o'clock to-morrow
Shall I send to thee?

   Rom.   By the hour of nine.   170

 Jul. I will not fail. 'Tis twenty years till then.
I have forgot why I did call thee back.

   Rom. Let me stand here till thou remember it.

   Jul. I shall forget, to have thee still stand there,
Rememb'ring how I love thy company.   175

   Rom. And I'll still stay, to have thee still forget,
Forgetting any other home but this.

   Jul. 'Tis almost morning. I would have thee gone—
And yet no farther than a wanton's bird,
That lets it hop a little from her hand,   180
Like a poor prisoner in his twisted gyves,
And with a silk thread plucks it back again,
So loving-jealous of his liberty.

   Rom. I would I were thy bird.

   Jul.   Sweet, so would I.
Yet I should kill thee with much cherishing.   185
Good night, good night! Parting is such sweet sorrow,
That I shall say good night till it be morrow.

                        [Exit.]

   Rom. Sleep dwell upon thine eyes, peace in thy breast!
Would I were sleep and peace, so sweet to rest!
Hence will I to my ghostly father's cell,   190
His help to crave and my dear hap to tell.

                           Exit.

[Scene III. Friar Laurence's *cell*.]

Enter *Friar* [*Laurence*] alone, with a basket.

Friar.   The grey-ey'd morn smiles on the frowning
   night,
Check'ring the Eastern clouds with streaks of light;
And flecked darkness like a drunkard reels
From forth day's path and Titan's fiery wheels.
Now, ere the sun advance his burning eye   5
The day to cheer and night's dank dew to dry,
I must up-fill this osier cage of ours
With baleful weeds and precious-juiced flowers.
The earth that's nature's mother is her tomb.
What is her burying grave, that is her womb;   10
And from her womb children of divers kind
We sucking on her natural bosom find;
Many for many virtues excellent,
None but for some, and yet all different.
O, mickle is the powerful grace that lies   15
In plants, herbs, stones, and their true qualities;
For naught so vile that on the earth doth live
But to the earth some special good doth give;
Nor aught so good but, strain'd from that fair use,
Revolts from true birth, stumbling on abuse.   20
Virtue itself turns vice, being misapplied,
And vice sometime 's by action dignified.
Within the infant rind of this small flower
Poison hath residence, and medicine power;
For this, being smelt, with that part cheers each part;   25
Being tasted, slays all senses with the heart.
Two such opposed kings encamp them still
In man as well as herbs—grace and rude will;

And where the worser is predominant,
Full soon the canker death eats up that plant.   30

Enter Romeo.

  Rom. Good morrow, father.
  Friar.   Benedicite!
What early tongue so sweet saluteth me?
Young son, it argues a distempered head
So soon to bid good morrow to thy bed.
Care keeps his watch in every old man's eye,   35
And where care lodges sleep will never lie;
But where unbruised youth with unstuff'd brain
Doth couch his limbs, there golden sleep doth reign.
Therefore thy earliness doth me assure
Thou art uprous'd with some distemp'rature;   40
Or if not so, then here I hit it right—
Our Romeo hath not been in bed to-night.
  Rom.   That last is true—the sweeter rest was mine.
  Friar. God pardon sin! Wast thou with Rosaline?
  Rom. With Rosaline, my ghostly father? No.   45
I have forgot that name, and that name's woe.
  Friar. That's my good son! But where hast thou been then?
  Rom. I'll tell thee ere thou ask it me again.
I have been feasting with mine enemy,
Where on a sudden one hath wounded me   50
That's by me wounded. Both our remedies
Within thy help and holy physic lies.
I bear no hatred, blessed man, for, lo,
My intercession likewise steads my foe.
  Friar. Be plain, good son, and homely in thy drift.   55
Riddling confession finds but riddling shrift.
  Rom. Then plainly know my heart's dear love is set
On the fair daughter of rich Capulet;

As mine on hers, so hers is set on mine,
And all combin'd, save what thou must combine   60
By holy marriage. When, and where, and how
We met, we woo'd, and made exchange of vow,
I'll tell thee as we pass; but this I pray,
That thou consent to marry us to-day.

   Friar. Holy Saint Francis! What a change is here!   65
Is Rosaline, that thou didst love so dear,
So soon forsaken? Young men's love then lies
Not truly in their hearts, but in their eyes.
Jesu Maria! What a deal of brine
Hath wash'd thy sallow cheeks for Rosaline!   70
How much salt water thrown away in waste,
To season love, that of it doth not taste!
The sun not yet thy sighs from heaven clears,
Thy old groans ring yet in mine ancient ears.
Lo, here upon thy cheek the stain doth sit   75
Of an old tear that is not wash'd off yet.
If e'er thou wast thyself, and these woes thine,
Thou and these woes were all for Rosaline.
And art thou chang'd? Pronounce this sentence then:
Women may fall when there's no strength in men.   80

   Rom. Thou chid'st me oft for loving Rosaline.
   Friar. For doting, not for loving, pupil mine.
   Rom. And bad'st me bury love.
   Friar.   Not in a grave
To lay one in, another out to have.
   Rom. I pray thee chide not. She whom I love now   85
Doth grace for grace and love for love allow.
The other did not so.
   Friar.   O, she knew well
Thy love did read by rote, that could not spell.
But come, young waverer, come go with me.

In one respect I'll thy assistant be;   90
For this alliance may so happy prove
To turn your households' rancour to pure love.

Rom. O, let us hence! I stand on sudden haste.

Friar. Wisely, and slow. They stumble that run fast.

Exeunt.

[Scene IV. *A street.*]

Enter *Benvolio* and *Mercutio.*

Mer. Where the devil should this Romeo be?
Came he not home to-night?

Ben. Not to his father's. I spoke with his man.

Mer. Why, that same pale hard-hearted wench, that Rosaline,
Torments him so that he will sure run mad.   5

Ben. Tybalt, the kinsman to old Capulet,
Hath sent a letter to his father's house.

Mer. A challenge, on my life.

Ben. Romeo will answer it.

Mer. Any man that can write may answer a letter.   10

Ben. Nay, he will answer the letter's master, how he dares,
being dared.

Mer. Alas, poor Romeo, he is already dead! stabb'd with
a white wench's black eye; shot through the ear with a love
song; the very pin of his heart cleft with the blind bow-boy's
butt-shaft; and is he a man to encounter Tybalt?

Ben. Why, what is Tybalt?   18

Mer. More than Prince of Cats, I can tell you. O, he's the
courageous captain of compliments. He fights as you sing
pricksong—keeps time, distance, and proportion; rests me
his minim rest, one, two, and the third in your bosom! the
very butcher of a silk button, a duellist, a duellist! a gentle-

man of the very first house, of the first and second cause. Ah,
the immortal passado! the punto reverso! the hay!

Ben. The what?   28

Mer. The pox of such antic, lisping, affecting fantasticoes—
these new tuners of accent! 'By Jesu, a very good blade! a very
tall man! a very good whore!' Why, is not this a lamentable
thing, grandsir, that we should be thus afflicted with these
strange flies, these fashion-mongers, these pardona-mi's, who
stand so much on the new form that they cannot sit at ease on
the old bench? O, their bones, their bones!   37

Enter *Romeo*.

Ben. Here comes Romeo! here comes Romeo!

Mer. Without his roe, like a dried herring. O flesh, flesh,
how art thou fishified! Now is he for the numbers that
Petrarch flowed in. Laura, to his lady, was but a kitchen
wench (marry, she had a better love to berhyme her), Dido a
dowdy, Cleopatra a gypsy, Helen and Hero hildings and
harlots, Thisbe a gray eye or so, but not to the purpose. Signior
Romeo, bon jour! There's a French salutation to your French
slop. You gave us the counterfeit fairly last night.

Rom. Good morrow to you both. What counterfeit did I
give you?   50

Mer. The slip, sir, the slip. Can you not conceive?

Rom. Pardon, good Mercutio. My business was great, and
in such a case as mine a man may strain courtesy.   55

Mer. That's as much as to say, such a case as yours constrains
a man to bow in the hams.

Rom. Meaning, to cursy.

Mer. Thou hast most kindly hit it.

Rom. A most courteous exposition.   60

Mer. Nay, I am the very pink of courtesy.

Rom. Pink for flower.

Mer. Right.

Rom. Why, then is my pump well-flower'd.

Mer. Well said! Follow me this jest now till thou hast worn out thy pump, that, when the single sole of it is worn, the jest may remain, after the wearing, solely singular.

Rom. O single-sol'd jest, solely singular for the singleness!

Mer. Come between us, good Benvolio! My wits faint.   71

Rom. Swits and spurs, swits and spurs! or I'll cry a match.

Mer. Nay, if our wits run the wild-goose chase, I am done; for thou hast more of the wild goose in one of thy wits than, I am sure, I have in my whole five. Was I with you there for the goose?

Rom. Thou wast never with me for anything when thou wast not there for the goose.   80

Mer. I will bite thee by the ear for that jest.

Rom. Nay, good goose, bite not!

Mer. Thy wit is a very bitter sweeting; it is a most sharp sauce.

Rom. And is it not, then, well serv'd in to a sweet goose?   86

Mer. O, here's a wit of cheveril, that stretches from an inch narrow to an ell broad!

Rom. I stretch it out for that word 'broad,' which, added to the goose, proves thee far and wide a broad goose.   91

Mer. Why, is not this better now than groaning for love? Now art thou sociable, now art thou Romeo; now art thou what thou art, by art as well as by nature. For this drivelling love is like a great natural that runs lolling up and down to hide his bauble in a hole.

Ben. Stop there, stop there!

Mer. Thou desirest me to stop in my tale against the hair.   100

Ben. Thou wouldst else have made thy tale large.

Mer. O, thou art deceiv'd! I would have made it short; for

I was come to the whole depth of my tale, and meant indeed
to occupy the argument no longer.   106

Rom. Here's goodly gear!

Enter *Nurse* and her *Man* [*Peter*].

Mer. A sail, a sail!

Ben. Two, two! a shirt and a smock.

Nurse. Peter!   110

Peter. Anon.

Nurse. My fan, Peter.

Mer. Good Peter, to hide her face; for her fan's the fairer
face of the two.

Nurse. God ye good morrow, gentlemen.   115

Mer. God ye good-den, fair gentlewoman.

Nurse. Is it good-den?

Mer. 'Tis no less, I tell ye; for the bawdy hand of the dial is
now upon the prick of noon.

Nurse. Out upon you! What a man are you!

Rom. One, gentlewoman, that God hath made for himself
to mar.   122

Nurse. By my troth, it is well said. 'For himself to mar,'
quoth 'a? Gentlemen, can any of you tell me where I may find
the young Romeo?

Rom. I can tell you; but young Romeo will be older when
you have found him than he was when you sought him. I am
the youngest of that name, for fault of a worse.

Nurse. You say well.   130

Mer. Yea, is the worst well? Very well took, i' faith! wisely,
wisely.

Nurse. If you be he, sir, I desire some confidence with you.

Ben. She will endite him to some supper.   135

Mer. A bawd, a bawd, a bawd! So ho!

Rom. What hast thou found?

Mer. No hare, sir; unless a hare, sir, in a lenten pie, that is
something stale and hoar ere it be spent.   140

> *He walks by them and sings.*
>
>> An old hare hoar,
>> And an old hare hoar,
>> Is very good meat in Lent;
>> But a hare that is hoar
>> Is too much for a score   145
>> When it hoars ere it be spent.

Romeo, will you come to your father's? We'll to dinner thither.
  Rom. I will follow you.
  Mer. Farewell, ancient lady. Farewell,   150
[*sings*] lady, lady, lady.

>   *Exeunt Mercutio, Benvolio.*

  Nurse. Marry, farewell! I pray you, sir, what saucy merchant
was this that was so full of his ropery?
  Rom. A gentleman, nurse, that loves to hear himself talk
and will speak more in a minute than he will stand to in a
month.   157
  Nurse. An 'a speak anything against me, I'll take him down,
an 'a were lustier than he is, and twenty such Jacks; and if I
cannot, I'll find those that shall. Scurvy knave! I am none of
his flirt-gills; I am none of his skains-mates. And thou must
stand by too, and suffer every knave to use me at his pleasure!
  Peter. I saw no man use you at his pleasure. If I had, my
weapon should quickly have been out, I warrant you. I dare
draw as soon as another man, if I see occasion in a good quarrel,
and the law on my side.   169
  Nurse. Now, afore God, I am so vex'd that every part about
me quivers. Scurvy knave! Pray you, sir, a word; and, as I
told you, my young lady bid me enquire you out. What she
bid me say, I will keep to myself; but first let me tell ye, if ye

should lead her into a fool's paradise, as they say, it were a very
gross kind of behaviour, as they say; for the gentlewoman is
young; and therefore, if you should deal double with her, truly
it were an ill thing to be off'red to any gentlewoman, and very
weak dealing.   181

Rom. Nurse, commend me to thy lady and mistress. I protest unto thee—

Nurse. Good heart, and i' faith I will tell her as much. Lord,
Lord! she will be a joyful woman.   186

Rom. What wilt thou tell her, nurse? Thou dost not mark
me.

Nurse. I will tell her, sir, that you do protest, which, as I take
it, is a gentlemanlike offer.   190

Rom. Bid her devise
Some means to come to shrift this afternoon;
And there she shall at Friar Laurence' cell
Be shriv'd and married. Here is for thy pains.

Nurse. No, truly, sir; not a penny.   195

Rom. Go to! I say you shall.

Nurse. This afternoon, sir? Well, she shall be there.

Rom. And stay, good nurse, behind the abbey wall.
Within this hour my man shall be with thee
And bring thee cords made like a tackled stair,   200
Which to the high topgallant of my joy
Must be my convoy in the secret night.
Farewell. Be trusty, and I'll quit thy pains.
Farewell. Commend me to thy mistress.

Nurse. Now God in heaven bless thee! Hark you, sir.   205

Rom. What say'st thou, my dear nurse?

Nurse. Is your man secret? Did you ne'er hear say,
Two may keep counsel, putting one away?

Rom. I warrant thee my man's as true as steel.   209

Nurse. Well, sir, my mistress is the sweetest lady. Lord,

Lord! when 'twas a little prating thing—O, there is a nobleman in town, one Paris, that would fain lay knife aboard; but
she, good soul, had as lieve see a toad, a very toad, as see him.
I anger her sometimes, and tell her that Paris is the properer
man; but I'll warrant you, when I say so, she looks as pale as
any clout in the versal world. Doth not rosemary and Romeo
begin both with a letter?   217

   Rom. Ay, nurse; what of that? Both with an R.

   Nurse. Ah, mocker! that's the dog's name. R is for the—
No; I know it begins with some other letter; and she hath
the prettiest sententious of it, of you and rosemary, that it
would do you good to hear it.   222

   Rom. Commend me to thy lady.

   Nurse. Ay, a thousand times. [*Exit Romeo.*] Peter!

   Peter. Anon.

   Nurse. Peter, take my fan, and go before, and apace.

                                                      Exeunt.

[Scene V. Capulet's *orchard*.]

Enter *Juliet*.

   Jul. The clock struck nine when I did send the nurse;
In half an hour she promis'd to return.
Perchance she cannot meet him. That's not so.
O, she is lame! Love's heralds should be thoughts,
Which ten times faster glide than the sun's beams   5
Driving back shadows over low'ring hills.
Therefore do nimble-pinion'd doves draw Love,
And therefore hath the wind-swift Cupid wings.
Now is the sun upon the highmost hill
Of this day's journey, and from nine till twelve   10
Is three long hours; yet she is not come.

Had she affections and warm youthful blood,
She would be as swift in motion as a ball;
My words would bandy her to my sweet love,
And his to me.   15
But old folks, many feign as they were dead—
Unwieldy, slow, heavy and pale as lead.

Enter *Nurse* [and *Peter*].

O God, she comes! O honey nurse, what news?
Hast thou met with him? Send thy man away.
    Nurse. Peter, stay at the gate.   20
                                        [*Exit Peter.*]
    Jul. Now, good sweet nurse—O Lord, why look'st thou
        sad?
Though news be sad, yet tell them merrily;
If good, thou shamest the music of sweet news
By playing it to me with so sour a face.
    Nurse. I am aweary, give me leave awhile.   25
Fie, how my bones ache! What a jaunce have I had!
    Jul. I would thou hadst my bones, and I thy news.
Nay, come, I pray thee speak. Good, good nurse, speak.
    Nurse. Jesu, what haste! Can you not stay awhile?
Do you not see that I am out of breath?   30
    Jul. How art thou out of breath when thou hast breath
To say to me that thou art out of breath?
The excuse that thou dost make in this delay
Is longer than the tale thou dost excuse.
Is thy news good or bad? Answer to that.   35
Say either, and I'll stay the circumstance.
Let me be satisfied, is't good or bad?
    Nurse. Well, you have made a simple choice; you know
not how to choose a man. Romeo? No, not he. Though his
face be better than any man's, yet his leg excels all men's; and

for a hand and a foot, and a body, though they be not to be talk'd
on, yet they are past compare. He is not the flower of courtesy,
but, I'll warrant him, as gentle as a lamb. Go thy ways, wench;
serve God. What, have you din'd at home?   46

Jul. No, no. But all this did I know before.
What says he of our marriage? What of that?

Nurse. Lord, how my head aches! What a head have I!
It beats as it would fall in twenty pieces.   50
My back o' t' other side—ah, my back, my back!
Beshrew your heart for sending me about
To catch my death with jauncing up and down!

Jul. I' faith, I am sorry that thou art not well.
Sweet, sweet, sweet nurse, tell me, what says my love?   55

Nurse. Your love says, like an honest gentleman, and a
courteous, and a kind, and a handsome; and, I warrant, a
virtuous—Where is your mother?

Jul. Where is my mother? Why, she is within.   60
Where should she be? How oddly thou repliest!
'Your love says, like an honest gentleman,
"Where is your mother?"'

Nurse.   O God's Lady dear!
Are you so hot? Marry come up, I trow.
Is this the poultice for my aching bones?   65
Henceforward do your messages yourself.

Jul. Here's such a coil! Come, what says Romeo?

Nurse. Have you got leave to go to shrift to-day?

Jul. I have.

Nurse. Then hie you hence to Friar Laurence' cell;   70
There stays a husband to make you a wife.
Now comes the wanton blood up in your cheeks:
They'll be in scarlet straight at any news.
Hie you to church; I must another way,
To fetch a ladder, by the which your love   75

Must climb a bird's nest soon when it is dark.
I am the drudge, and toil in your delight;
But you shall bear the burthen soon at night.
Go; I'll to dinner; hie you to the cell.
    Jul. Hie to high fortune! Honest nurse, farewell.   80
                                 Exeunt.

[Scene VI. Friar Laurence's *cell.*]

Enter *Friar* [*Laurence*] and *Romeo.*

    Friar. So smile the heavens upon this holy act
That after-hours with sorrow chide us not!
    Rom. Amen, amen! But come what sorrow can,
It cannot countervail the exchange of joy
That one short minute gives me in her sight.   5
Do thou but close our hands with holy words,
Then love-devouring death do what he dare—
It is enough I may but call her mine.
    Friar. These violent delights have violent ends
And in their triumph die, like fire and powder,   10
Which, as they kiss, consume. The sweetest honey
Is loathsome in his own deliciousness
And in the taste confounds the appetite.
Therefore love moderately: long love doth so;
Too swift arrives as tardy as too slow.   15

Enter *Juliet.*

Here comes the lady. O, so light a foot
Will ne'er wear out the everlasting flint.
A lover may bestride the gossamer
That idles in the wanton summer air,
And yet not fall; so light is vanity.   20

Jul. Good even to my ghostly confessor.
Friar. Romeo shall thank thee, daughter, for us both.
Jul. As much to him, else is his thanks too much.
Rom. Ah, Juliet, if the measure of thy joy
Be heap'd like mine, and that thy skill be more   25
To blazon it, then sweeten with thy breath
This neighbour air, and let rich music's tongue
Unfold the imagin'd happiness that both
Receive in either by this dear encounter.

Jul. Conceit, more rich in matter than in words,   30
Brags of his substance, not of ornament.
They are but beggars that can count their worth;
But my true love is grown to such excess
I cannot sum up sum of half my wealth.

Friar. Come, come with me, and we will make short **work**;
For, by your leaves, you shall not stay alone   36
Till Holy Church incorporate two in one.

[*Exeunt.*]

Enter *Mercutio, Benvolio,* and *Men.*

Ben. I pray thee, good Mercutio, let's retire.
The day is hot, the Capulets abroad,
And if we meet, we shall not scape a brawl,
For now, these hot days, is the mad blood stirring.   4

Mer. Thou art like one of these fellows that, when he enters
the confines of a tavern, claps me his sword upon the table and
says 'God send me no need of thee!' and by the operation of
the second cup draws him on the drawer, when indeed there
is no need.   10

Ben. Am I like such a fellow?

Mer. Come, come, thou art as hot a Jack in thy mood as
any in Italy; and as soon moved to be moody, and as soon
moody to be moved.

Ben. And what to?   15

Mer. Nay, an there were two such, we should have none
shortly, for one would kill the other. Thou! why, thou wilt
quarrel with a man that hath a hair more or a hair less in his
beard than thou hast. Thou wilt quarrel with a man for crack-
ing nuts, having no other reason but because thou hast hazel
eyes. What eye but such an eye would spy out such a quarrel?
Thy head is as full of quarrels as an egg is full of meat; and
yet thy head hath been beaten as addle as an egg for quarrelling.
Thou hast quarrell'd with a man for coughing in the street, because he hath wakened thy dog that hath lain asleep in the
sun. Didst thou not fall out with a tailor for wearing his new
doublet before Easter? with another for tying his new shoes
with old riband? And yet thou wilt tutor me from quarrelling!

Ben. An I were so apt to quarrel as thou art, any man should
buy the fee simple of my life for an hour and a quarter.   36

Mer. The fee simple? O simple!

51

Enter *Tybalt* and others.

Ben. By my head, here come the Capulets.

Mer. By my heel, I care not.

Tyb. Follow me close, for I will speak to them.   40
Gentlemen, good den. A word with one of you.

Mer. And but one word with one of us?
Couple it with something; make it a word and a blow.

Tyb. You shall find me apt enough to that, sir, an you will
give me occasion.   45

Mer. Could you not take some occasion without giving?

Tyb. Mercutio, thou consortest with Romeo.

Mer. Consort? What, dost thou make us minstrels? An
thou make minstrels of us, look to hear nothing but discords.
Here's my fiddlestick; here's that shall make you dance.
Zounds, consort!

Ben. We talk here in the public haunt of men.
Either withdraw unto some private place
And reason coldly of your grievances,   55
Or else depart. Here all eyes gaze on us.

Mer. Men's eyes were made to look, and let them gaze.
I will not budge for no man's pleasure, I.

Enter *Romeo.*

Tyb. Well, peace be with you, sir. Here comes my
man.

Mer. But I'll be hang'd, sir, if he wear your livery.   60
Marry, go before to field, he'll be your follower!
Your worship in that sense may call him man.

Tyb. Romeo, the love I bear thee can afford
No better term than this: thou art a villain.

Rom. Tybalt, the reason that I have to love thee   65
Doth much excuse the appertaining rage

To such a greeting. Villain am I none.
Therefore farewell. I see thou knowest me not.

Tyb. Boy, this shall not excuse the injuries
That thou hast done me; therefore turn and draw.   70

Rom. I do protest I never injur'd thee,
But love thee better than thou canst devise
Till thou shalt know the reason of my love;
And so, good Capulet, which name I tender
As dearly as mine own, be satisfied.   75

Mer. O calm, dishonourable, vile submission!
Alla stoccata carries it away.   [*Draws.*]
Tybalt, you ratcatcher, will you walk?

Tyb. What wouldst thou have with me?   79

Mer. Good King of Cats, nothing but one of your nine lives.
That I mean to make bold withal, and, as you shall use me hereafter, dry-beat the rest of the eight. Will you pluck your sword
out of his pilcher by the ears? Make haste, lest mine be about
your ears ere it be out.   85

Tyb. I am for you.   [*Draws.*]

Rom. Gentle Mercutio, put thy rapier up.

Mer. Come, sir, your passado!

[*They fight.*]

Rom. Draw, Benvolio; beat down their weapons.
Gentlemen, for shame! forbear this outrage!   90
Tybalt, Mercutio, the Prince expressly hath
Forbid this bandying in Verona streets.
Hold, Tybalt! Good Mercutio!

Tybalt under Romeo's arm thrusts Mercutio in, and flies
[*with his Followers*].

Mer.   I am hurt.
A plague o' both your houses! I am sped.
Is he gone and hath nothing?

Ben.   What, art thou hurt?   95

Mer. Ay, ay, a scratch, a scratch. Marry, 'tis enough.
Where is my page? Go, villain, fetch a surgeon.

[Exit Page.]

Rom. Courage, man. The hurt cannot be much.   98

Mer. No, 'tis not so deep as a well, nor so wide as a church
door; but 'tis enough, 'twill serve. Ask for me to-morrow, and
you shall find me a grave man. I am peppered, I warrant, for
this world. A plague o' both your houses! Zounds, a dog, a
rat, a mouse, a cat, to scratch a man to death! a braggart,
a rogue, a villain, that fights by the book of arithmetic!
Why the devil came you between us? I was hurt under your
arm.

Rom. I thought all for the best.

Mer. Help me into some house, Benvolio,   110
Or I shall faint. A plague o' both your houses!
They have made worms' meat of me. I have it,
And soundly too. Your houses!

Exit, [supported by Benvolio].

Rom. This gentleman, the Prince's near ally,
My very friend, hath got this mortal hurt   115
In my behalf—my reputation stain'd
With Tybalt's slander—Tybalt, that an hour
Hath been my kinsman. O sweet Juliet,
Thy beauty hath made me effeminate
And in my temper soft'ned valour's steel!   120

Enter *Benvolio*.

Ben. O Romeo, Romeo, brave Mercutio's dead!
That gallant spirit hath aspir'd the clouds,
Which too untimely here did scorn the earth.

Rom. This day's black fate on moe days doth depend;
This but begins the woe others must end.   125

Enter *Tybalt*.

Ben. Here comes the furious Tybalt back again.
Rom. Alive in triumph, and Mercutio slain?
Away to heaven respective lenity,
And fire-ey'd fury be my conduct now!
Now, Tybalt, take the 'villain' back again   130
That late thou gavest me; for Mercutio's soul
Is but a little way above our heads,
Staying for thine to keep him company.
Either thou or I, or both, must go with him.
Tyb. Thou, wretched boy, that didst consort him here,   135
Shalt with him hence.
Rom.   This shall determine that.

> *They fight. Tybalt falls.*

Ben. Romeo, away, be gone!
The citizens are up, and Tybalt slain.
Stand not amaz'd. The Prince will doom thee death
If thou art taken. Hence, be gone, away!   140
Rom. O, I am fortune's fool!
Ben.   Why dost thou stay?

> *Exit Romeo.*

Enter *Citizens*.

Citizen. Which way ran he that kill'd Mercutio?
Tybalt, that murtherer, which way ran he?
Ben. There lies that Tybalt.
Citizen.   Up, sir, go with me.
I charge thee in the Prince's name obey.   145

Enter *Prince* [attended], *Old Montague, Capulet*, their *Wives*,
and [others].

Prince. Where are the vile beginners of this fray?
Ben. O noble Prince, I can discover all

The unlucky manage of this fatal brawl.
There lies the man, slain by young Romeo,
That slew thy kinsman, brave Mercutio.   150
  Cap. Wife. Tybalt, my cousin! O my brother's child!
O Prince! O husband! O, the blood is spill'd
Of my dear kinsman! Prince, as thou art true,
For blood of ours shed blood of Montague.
O cousin, cousin!   155
  Prince. Benvolio, who began this bloody fray?
  Ben. Tybalt, here slain, whom Romeo's hand did slay.
Romeo, that spoke him fair, bid him bethink
How nice the quarrel was, and urg'd withal
Your high displeasure. All this—uttered   160
With gentle breath, calm look, knees humbly bow'd—
Could not take truce with the unruly spleen
Of Tybalt deaf to peace, but that he tilts
With piercing steel at bold Mercutio's breast;
Who, all as hot, turns deadly point to point,   165
And, with a martial scorn, with one hand beats
Cold death aside and with the other sends
It back to Tybalt, whose dexterity
Retorts it. Romeo he cries aloud,
'Hold, friends! friends, part!' and swifter than his tongue,
His agile arm beats down their fatal points,   171
And 'twixt them rushes; underneath whose arm
An envious thrust from Tybalt hit the life
Of stout Mercutio, and then Tybalt fled;
But by-and-by comes back to Romeo,   175
Who had but newly entertain'd revenge,
And to't they go like lightning; for, ere I
Could draw to part them, was stout Tybalt slain;
And, as he fell, did Romeo turn and fly.
This is the truth, or let Benvolio die.   180

Cap. Wife. He is a kinsman to the Montague;
Affection makes him false, he speaks not true.
Some twenty of them fought in this black strife,
And all those twenty could but kill one life.
I beg for justice, which thou, Prince, must give.   185
Romeo slew Tybalt; Romeo must not live.
    Prince. Romeo slew him; he slew Mercutio.
Who now the price of his dear blood doth owe?
    Mon. Not Romeo, Prince; he was Mercutio's friend;
His fault concludes but what the law should end,   190
The life of Tybalt.
    Prince.   And for that offence
Immediately we do exile him hence.
I have an interest in your hate's proceeding,
My blood for your rude brawls doth lie a-bleeding;
But I'll amerce you with so strong a fine   195
That you shall all repent the loss of mine.
I will be deaf to pleading and excuses;
Nor tears nor prayers shall purchase out abuses.
Therefore use none. Let Romeo hence in haste,
Else, when he is found, that hour is his last.   200
Bear hence this body, and attend our will.
Mercy but murders, pardoning those that kill.
                       Exeunt.

[Scene II. Capulet's *orchard*.]

Enter *Juliet* alone.

Jul. Gallop apace, you fiery-footed steeds,
Towards Phœbus' lodging! Such a wagoner
As Phaëton would whip you to the West
And bring in cloudy night immediately.

Spread thy close curtain, love-performing night,   5
That runaway eyes may wink, and Romeo
Leap to these arms untalk'd of and unseen.
Lovers can see to do their amorous rites
By their own beauties; or, if love be blind,
It best agrees with night. Come, civil night,   10
Thou sober-suited matron, all in black,
And learn me how to lose a winning match,
Play'd for a pair of stainless maidenhoods.
Hood my unmann'd blood, bating in my cheeks,
With thy black mantle till strange love, grown bold,   15
Think true love acted simple modesty.
Come, night; come, Romeo; come, thou day in night;
For thou wilt lie upon the wings of night
Whiter than new snow upon a raven's back.
Come, gentle night; come, loving, black-brow'd night;   20
Give me my Romeo; and, when he shall die,
Take him and cut him out in little stars,
And he will make the face of heaven so fine
That all the world will be in love with night
And pay no worship to the garish sun.   25
O, I have bought the mansion of a love,
But not possess'd it; and though I am sold,
Not yet enjoy'd. So tedious is this day
As is the night before some festival
To an impatient child that hath new robes   30
And may not wear them. O, here comes my nurse,

Enter *Nurse*, with cords.

And she brings news; and every tongue that speaks
But Romeo's name speaks heavenly eloquence.
Now, nurse, what news? What hast thou there? the cords
That Romeo bid thee fetch?

Nurse.   Ay, ay, the cords.   35
                                   [*Throws them down.*]
Jul. Ay me! what news? Why dost thou wring thy hands?
Nurse. Ah, weraday! he's dead, he's dead, he's dead!
We are undone, lady, we are undone!
Alack the day! he's gone, he's kill'd, he's dead!
Jul. Can heaven be so envious?
Nurse.   Romeo can,   40
Though heaven cannot. O Romeo, Romeo!
Who ever would have thought it? Romeo!
Jul. What devil art thou that dost torment me thus?
This torture should be roar'd in dismal hell.
Hath Romeo slain himself? Say thou but 'I,'   45
And that bare vowel 'I' shall poison more
Than the death-darting eye of cockatrice.
I am not I, if there be such an 'I';
Or those eyes shut that make thee answer 'I.'
If he be slain, say 'I'; or if not, 'no.'   50
Brief sounds determine of my weal or woe.
Nurse. I saw the wound, I saw it with mine eyes,
(God save the mark!) here on his manly breast.
A piteous corse, a bloody piteous corse;
Pale, pale as ashes, all bedaub'd in blood,   55
All in gore-blood. I swounded at the sight.
Jul. O, break, my heart! poor bankrout, break at once!
To prison, eyes; ne'er look on liberty!
Vile earth, to earth resign; end motion here,
And thou and Romeo press one heavy bier!   60
Nurse. O Tybalt, Tybalt, the best friend I had!
O courteous Tybalt! honest gentleman!
That ever I should live to see thee dead!
Jul. What storm is this that blows so contrary?
Is Romeo slaught'red, and is Tybalt dead?   65

My dear-lov'd cousin, and my dearer lord?
Then, dreadful trumpet, sound the general doom!
For who is living, if those two are gone?
  Nurse. Tybalt is gone, and Romeo banished;
Romeo that kill'd him, he is banished.   70
  Jul. O God! Did Romeo's hand shed Tybalt's blood?
  Nurse. It did, it did! alas the day, it did!
  Jul. O serpent heart, hid with a flow'ring face!
Did ever dragon keep so fair a cave?
Beautiful tyrant! fiend angelical!   75
Dove-feather'd raven! wolvish-ravening lamb!
Despised substance of divinest show!
Just opposite to what thou justly seem'st—
A damned saint, an honourable villain!
O nature, what hadst thou to do in hell   80
When thou didst bower the spirit of a fiend
In mortal paradise of such sweet flesh?
Was ever book containing such vile matter
So fairly bound? O, that deceit should dwell
In such a gorgeous palace!
  Nurse.   There's no trust,   85
No faith, no honesty in men; all perjur'd,
All forsworn, all naught, all dissemblers.
Ah, where's my man? Give me some aqua vitæ.
These griefs, these woes, these sorrows make me old.
Shame come to Romeo!
  Jul.   Blister'd be thy tongue   90
For such a wish! He was not born to shame.
Upon his brow shame is asham'd to sit;
For 'tis a throne where honour may be crown'd
Sole monarch of the universal earth.
O, what a beast was I to chide at him!   95
  Nurse. Will you speak well of him that kill'd your cousin?

Jul. Shall I speak ill of him that is my husband?
Ah, poor my lord, what tongue shall smooth thy name
When I, thy three-hours wife, have mangled it?
But wherefore, villain, didst thou kill my cousin?   100
That villain cousin would have kill'd my husband.
Back, foolish tears, back to your native spring!
Your tributary drops belong to woe,
Which you, mistaking, offer up to joy.
My husband lives, that Tybalt would have slain;   105
And Tybalt's dead, that would have slain my husband.
All this is comfort; wherefore weep I then?
Some word there was, worser than Tybalt's death,
That murd'red me. I would forget it fain;
But O, it presses to my memory   110
Like damned guilty deeds to sinners' minds!
'Tybalt is dead, and Romeo—banished.'
That 'banished,' that one word 'banished,'
Hath slain ten thousand Tybalts. Tybalt's death
Was woe enough, if it had ended there;   115
Or, if sour woe delights in fellowship
And needly will be rank'd with other griefs,
Why followed not, when she said 'Tybalt's dead,'
Thy father, or thy mother, nay, or both,
Which modern lamentation might have mov'd?   120
But with a rearward following Tybalt's death,
'Romeo is banished'—to speak that word
Is father, mother, Tybalt, Romeo, Juliet,
All slain, all dead. 'Romeo is banished'—
There is no end, no limit, measure, bound,   125
In that word's death; no words can that woe sound.
Where is my father and my mother, nurse?
     Nurse. Weeping and wailing over Tybalt's corse.
Will you go to them? I will bring you thither.

Jul. Wash they his wounds with tears? Mine shall be spent,
When theirs are dry, for Romeo's banishment.   131
Take up those cords. Poor ropes, you are beguil'd,
Both you and I, for Romeo is exil'd.
He made you for a highway to my bed;
But I, a maid, die maiden-widowed.   135
Come, cords; come, nurse. I'll to my wedding bed;
And death, not Romeo, take my maidenhead!
    Nurse. Hie to your chamber. I'll find Romeo
To comfort you. I wot well where he is.
Hark ye, your Romeo will be here at night.   140
I'll to him; he is hid at Laurence' cell.
    Jul. O, find him! give this ring to my true knight
And bid him come to take his last farewell.

                                                    Exeunt.

[Scene III. Friar Laurence's *cell*.]

Enter *Friar* [*Laurence*].

    Friar. Romeo, come forth; come forth, thou fearful man.
Affliction is enamour'd of thy parts,
And thou art wedded to calamity.

Enter *Romeo*.

    Rom. Father, what news? What is the Prince's doom?
What sorrow craves acquaintance at my hand   5
That I yet know not?
    Friar.   Too familiar
Is my dear son with such sour company.
I bring thee tidings of the Prince's doom.
    Rom. What less than doomsday is the Prince's doom?

Friar. A gentler judgment vanish'd from his lips—   10
Not body's death, but body's banishment.

Rom. Ha, banishment? Be merciful, say 'death';
For exile hath more terror in his look,
Much more than death. Do not say 'banishment.'

Friar. Hence from Verona art thou banished.   15
Be patient, for the world is broad and wide.

Rom. There is no world without Verona walls,
But purgatory, torture, hell itself.
Hence banished is banish'd from the world,
And world's exile is death. Then 'banishment'   20
Is death misterm'd. Calling death 'banishment,'
Thou cut'st my head off with a golden axe
And smilest upon the stroke that murders me.

Friar. O deadly sin! O rude unthankfulness!
Thy fault our law calls death; but the kind Prince,   25
Taking thy part, hath rush'd aside the law,
And turn'd that black word death to banishment.
This is dear mercy, and thou seest it not.

Rom. 'Tis torture, and not mercy. Heaven is here,
Where Juliet lives; and every cat and dog   30
And little mouse, every unworthy thing,
Live here in heaven and may look on her;
But Romeo may not. More validity,
More honourable state, more courtship lives
In carrion flies than Romeo. They may seize   35
On the white wonder of dear Juliet's hand
And steal immortal blessing from her lips,
Who, even in pure and vestal modesty,
Still blush, as thinking their own kisses sin;
But Romeo may not—he is banished.   40
This may flies do, when I from this must fly;
They are free men, but I am banished.

And sayest thou yet that exile is not death?
Hadst thou no poison mix'd, no sharp-ground knife,
No sudden mean of death, though ne'er so mean,   45
But 'banished' to kill me—'banished'?
O friar, the damned use that word in hell;
Howling attends it! How hast thou the heart,
Being a divine, a ghostly confessor,
A sin-absolver, and my friend profess'd,   50
To mangle me with that word 'banished'?
   Friar. Thou fond mad man, hear me a little speak.
   Rom. O, thou wilt speak again of banishment.
   Friar. I'll give thee armour to keep off that word;
Adversity's sweet milk, philosophy,   55
To comfort thee, though thou art banished.
   Rom. Yet 'banished'? Hang up philosophy!
Unless philosophy can make a Juliet,
Displant a town, reverse a prince's doom,
It helps not, it prevails not. Talk no more.   60
   Friar. O, then I see that madmen have no ears.
   Rom. How should they, when that wise men have no eyes?
   Friar. Let me dispute with thee of thy estate.
   Rom. Thou canst not speak of that thou dost not feel.
Wert thou as young as I, Juliet thy love,   65
An hour but married, Tybalt murdered,
Doting like me, and like me banished,
Then mightst thou speak, then mightst thou tear thy hair,
And fall upon the ground, as I do now,
Taking the measure of an unmade grave.   70
                          Knock [*within*].
   Friar. Arise; one knocks. Good Romeo, hide thyself.
   Rom. Not I; unless the breath of heartsick groans,
Mist-like infold me from the search of eyes.   *Knock.*
   Friar. Hark, how they knock! Who's there? Romeo, arise;

Thou wilt be taken.—Stay awhile!—Stand up;   *Knock*.
Run to my study.—By-and-by!—God's will,   76
What simpleness is this.—I come, I come!   *Knock*.
Who knocks so hard? Whence come you? What's your will?

   Nurse. [*within*] Let me come in, and you shall know my
    errand.
I come from Lady Juliet.

   Friar.   Welcome then.   80

Enter *Nurse*.

   Nurse. O holy friar, O, tell me, holy friar,
Where is my lady's lord, where's Romeo?

   Friar. There on the ground, with his own tears made drunk.

   Nurse. O, he is even in my mistress' case,
Just in her case!

   Friar.   O woful sympathy!   85
Piteous predicament!

   Nurse.   Even so lies she,
Blubb'ring and weeping, weeping and blubbering.
Stand up, stand up! Stand, an you be a man.
For Juliet's sake, for her sake, rise and stand!
Why should you fall into so deep an O?   90

   Rom. (*rises*) Nurse—

   Nurse. Ah sir! ah sir! Well, death's the end of all.

   Rom. Spakest thou of Juliet? How is it with her?
Doth not she think me an old murtherer,
Now I have stain'd the childhood of our joy   95
With blood remov'd but little from her own?
Where is she? and how doth she! and what says
My conceal'd lady to our cancell'd love?

   Nurse. O, she says nothing, sir, but weeps and weeps;
And now falls on her bed, and then starts up,   100

And Tybalt calls; and then on Romeo cries,
And then down falls again.

   Rom.   As if that name,
Shot from the deadly level of a gun,
Did murther her; as that name's cursed hand
Murder'd her kinsman. O, tell me, friar, tell me,   105
In what vile part of this anatomy
Doth my name lodge? Tell me, that I may sack
The hateful mansion.   [*Draws his dagger.*]

   Friar.   Hold thy desperate hand.
Art thou a man? Thy form cries out thou art;
Thy tears are womanish, thy wild acts denote   110
The unreasonable fury of a beast.
Unseemly woman in a seeming man!
Or ill-beseeming beast in seeming both!
Thou hast amaz'd me. By my holy order,
I thought thy disposition better temper'd.   115
Hast thou slain Tybalt? Wilt thou slay thyself?
And slay thy lady that in thy life lives,
By doing damned hate upon thyself?
Why railest thou on thy birth, the heaven, and earth?
Since birth and heaven and earth, all three do meet   120
In thee at once; which thou at once wouldst lose.
Fie, fie, thou shamest thy shape, thy love, thy wit,
Which, like a usurer, abound'st in all,
And usest none in that true use indeed
Which should bedeck thy shape, thy love, thy wit.   125
Thy noble shape is but a form of wax,
Digressing from the valour of a man;
Thy dear love sworn but hollow perjury,
Killing that love which thou hast vow'd to cherish;
Thy wit, that ornament to shape and love,   130
Misshapen in the conduct of them both,

Like powder in a skilless soldier's flask,
Is set afire by thine own ignorance,
And thou dismemb'red with thine own defence.
What, rouse thee, man! Thy Juliet is alive,   135
For whose dear sake thou wast but lately dead.
There art thou happy. Tybalt would kill thee,
But thou slewest Tybalt. There art thou happy too.
The law, that threat'ned death, becomes thy friend
And turns it to exile. There art thou happy.   140
A pack of blessings light upon thy back;
Happiness courts thee in her best array;
But, like a misbehav'd and sullen wench,
Thou pout'st upon thy fortune and thy love.
Take heed, take heed, for such die miserable.   145
Go get thee to thy love, as was decreed,
Ascend her chamber, hence and comfort her.
But look thou stay not till the watch be set,
For then thou canst not pass to Mantua,
Where thou shalt live till we can find a time   150
To blaze your marriage, reconcile your friends,
Beg pardon of the Prince, and call thee back
With twenty hundred thousand times more joy
Than thou went'st forth in lamentation.
Go before, nurse. Commend me to thy lady,   155
And bid her hasten all the house to bed,
Which heavy sorrow makes them apt unto.
Romeo is coming.
    Nurse. O Lord, I could have stay'd here all the night
To hear good counsel. O, what learning is!   160
My lord, I'll tell my lady you will come.
    Rom. Do so, and bid my sweet prepare to chide.
    Nurse. Here is a ring she bid me give you, sir.
Hie you, make haste, for it grows very late.   *Exit.*

Rom. How well my comfort is reviv'd by this!   165
   Friar. Go hence; good night; and here stands all your
   state:
Either be gone before the watch be set,
Or by the break of day disguis'd from hence.
Sojourn in Mantua. I'll find out your man,
And he shall signify from time to time   170
Every good hap to you that chances here.
Give me thy hand. 'Tis late. Farewell; good night.
   Rom. But that a joy past joy calls out on me,
It were a grief so brief to part with thee.
Farewell.

                                          Exeunt.

[Scene IV. Capulet's *house*]

Enter *Old Capulet*, his *Wife*, and *Paris*.

   Cap. Things have fall'n out, sir, so unluckily
That we have had no time to move our daughter.
Look you, she lov'd her kinsman Tybalt dearly,
And so did I. Well, we were born to die.
'Tis very late; she'll not come down to-night.   5
I promise you, but for your company,
I would have been abed an hour ago.
   Par. These times of woe afford no time to woo.
Madam, good night. Commend me to your daughter.
   Lady. I will, and know her mind early to-morrow;   10
To-night she's mew'd up to her heaviness.
   Cap. Sir Paris, I will make a desperate tender
Of my child's love. I think she will be rul'd
In all respects by me; nay more, I doubt it not.
Wife, go you to her ere you go to bed;   15

Acquaint her here of my son Paris' love
And bid her (mark you me?) on Wednesday next—
But, soft! what day is this?

    Par.   Monday, my lord.

    Cap. Monday! ha, ha! Well, Wednesday is **too soon.**
A Thursday let it be—a Thursday, tell her,   20
She shall be married to this noble earl.
Will you be ready? Do you like this haste?
We'll keep no great ado—a friend or two;
For hark you, Tybalt being slain so late,
It may be thought we held him carelessly,   25
Being our kinsman, if we revel much.
Therefore we'll have some half a dozen friends,
And there an end. But what say you to Thursday?

    Par. My lord, I would that Thursday were to-morrow.

    Cap. Well, get you gone. A Thursday be it then.   30
Go you to Juliet ere you go to bed;
Prepare her, wife, against this wedding day.
Farewell, my lord.—Light to my chamber, ho!
Afore me, it is so very very late
That we may call it early by-and-by.   35
Good night.

                              Exeunt.

[Scene V. Capulet's *orchard*.]

Enter *Romeo* and *Juliet* aloft, at the window.

    Jul. Wilt thou be gone? It is not yet near day.
It was the nightingale, and not the lark,
That pierc'd the fearful hollow of thine ear.
Nightly she sings on yond pomegranate tree.
Believe me, love, it was the nightingale.   5

Rom. It was the lark, the herald of the morn;
No nightingale. Look, love, what envious streaks
Do lace the severing clouds in yonder East.
Night's candles are burnt out, and jocund day
Stands tiptoe on the misty mountain tops. 10
I must be gone and live, or stay and die.

Jul. Yond light is not daylight; I know it, I.
It is some meteor that the sun exhales
To be to thee this night a torchbearer
And light thee on thy way to Mantua. 15
Therefore stay yet; thou need'st not to be gone.

Rom. Let me be ta'en, let me be put to death.
I am content, so thou wilt have it so.
I'll say yon grey is not the morning's eye,
'Tis but the pale reflex of Cynthia's brow; 20
Nor that is not the lark whose notes do beat
The vaulty heaven so high above our heads.
I have more care to stay than will to go.
Come, death, and welcome! Juliet wills it so.
How is't, my soul? Let's talk; it is not day. 25

Jul. It is, it is! Hie hence, be gone, away!
It is the lark that sings so out of tune,
Straining harsh discords and unpleasing sharps.
Some say the lark makes sweet division;
This doth not so, for she divideth us. 30
Some say the lark and loathed toad chang'd eyes;
O, now I would they had chang'd voices too,
Since arm from arm that voice doth us affray,
Hunting thee hence with hunt's-up to the day!
O, now be gone! More light and light it grows. 35

Rom. More light and light—more dark and dark our
woes!

Enter *Nurse*.

Nurse. Madam!
Jul. Nurse?
Nurse. Your lady mother is coming to your chamber.
The day is broke; be wary, look about.   40
                                                      [*Exit.*]

Jul. Then, window, let day in, and let life out.
Rom. Farewell, farewell! One kiss, and I'll descend.
                                              He goeth down.
Jul. Art thou gone so, my lord, my love, my friend?
I must hear from thee every day in the hour,
For in a minute there are many days.   45
O, by this count I shall be much in years
Ere I again behold my Romeo!
Rom. Farewell!
I will omit no opportunity
That may convey my greetings, love, to thee.   50
Jul. O, think'st thou we shall ever meet again?
Rom. I doubt it not; and all these woes shall serve
For sweet discourses in our time to come.
Jul. O God, I have an ill-divining soul!
Methinks I see thee, now thou art below,   55
As one dead in the bottom of a tomb.
Either my eyesight fails, or thou look'st pale.
Rom. And trust me, love, in my eye so do you.
Dry sorrow drinks our blood. Adieu, adieu!
                                                       Exit.
Jul. O Fortune, Fortune! all men call thee fickle.   60
If thou art fickle, what dost thou with him
That is renowm'd for faith? Be fickle, Fortune,
For then I hope thou wilt not keep him long
But send him back.

Lady. [*within*] Ho, daughter! are you up?   65
Jul. Who is't that calls? It is my lady mother.
Is she not down so late, or up so early?
What unaccustom'd cause procures her hither?

Enter *Mother.*

Lady. Why, how now, Juliet?
Jul.   Madam, I am not well.
Lady. Evermore weeping for your cousin's death?   70
What, wilt thou wash him from his grave with tears?
An if thou couldst, thou couldst not make him live.
Therefore have done. Some grief shows much of love;
But much of grief shows still some want of wit.
Jul. Yet let me weep for such a feeling loss.   75
Lady. So shall you feel the loss, but not the friend
Which you weep for.
Jul.   Feeling so the loss,
I cannot choose but ever weep the friend.
Lady. Well, girl, thou weep'st not so much for his death
As that the villain lives which slaughter'd him.   80
Jul. What villain, madam?
Lady.   That same villain Romeo.
Jul. [*aside*] Villain and he be many miles asunder.—
God pardon him! I do, with all my heart;
And yet no man like he doth grieve my heart.
Lady. That is because the traitor murderer lives.   85
Jul. Ay, madam, from the reach of these my hands.
Would none but I might venge my cousin's death!
Lady. We will have vengeance for it, fear thou not.
Then weep no more. I'll send to one in Mantua,
Where that same banish'd runagate doth live,   90
Shall give him such an unaccustom'd dram

That he shall soon keep Tybalt company;
And then I hope thou wilt be satisfied.

Jul. Indeed I never shall be satisfied
With Romeo till I behold him—dead—   95
Is my poor heart so for a kinsman vex'd.
Madam, if you could find out but a man
To bear a poison, I would temper it;
That Romeo should, upon receipt thereof,
Soon sleep in quiet. O, how my heart abhors   100
To hear him nam'd and cannot come to him,
To wreak the love I bore my cousin Tybalt
Upon his body that hath slaughter'd him!

Lady. Find thou the means, and I'll find such a man.
But now I'll tell thee joyful tidings, girl.   105

Jul. And joy comes well in such a needy time.
What are they, I beseech your ladyship?

Lady. Well, well, thou hast a careful father, child;
One who, to put thee from thy heaviness,
Hath sorted out a sudden day of joy   110
That thou expects not nor I look'd not for.

Jul. Madam, in happy time! What day is that?

Lady. Marry, my child, early next Thursday morn
The gallant, young, and noble gentleman,
The County Paris, at Saint Peter's Church,   115
Shall happily make thee there a joyful bride.

Jul. Now by Saint Peter's Church, and Peter too,
He shall not make me there a joyful bride!
I wonder at this haste, that I must wed
Ere he that should be husband comes to woo.   120
I pray you tell my lord and father, madam,
I will not marry yet; and when I do, I swear
It shall be Romeo, whom you know I hate,
Rather than Paris. These are news indeed!

Lady. Here comes your father. Tell him so yourself,   125
And see how he will take it at your hands.

Enter *Capulet* and *Nurse*.

Cap. When the sun sets the air doth drizzle dew,
But for the sunset of my brother's son
It rains downright.
How now? a conduit, girl? What, still in tears?   130
Evermore show'ring? In one little body
Thou counterfeit'st a bark, a sea, a wind:
For still thy eyes, which I may call the sea,
Do ebb and flow with tears; the bark thy body is,
Sailing in this salt flood; the winds, thy sighs,   135
Who, raging with thy tears and they with them,
Without a sudden calm will overset
Thy tempest-tossed body. How now, wife?
Have you delivered to her our decree?

Lady. Ay, sir; but she will none, she gives you thanks.
I would the fool were married to her grave!   141

Cap. Soft! take me with you, take me with you, wife.
How? Will she none? Doth she not give us thanks?
Is she not proud? Doth she not count her blest,
Unworthy as she is, that we have wrought   145
So worthy a gentleman to be her bridegroom?

Jul. Not proud you have, but thankful that you have.
Proud can I never be of what I hate,
But thankful even for hate that is meant love.

Cap. How, how, how, how, choplogic? What is this? 150
'Proud'—and 'I thank you'—and 'I thank you not'—
And yet 'not proud'? Mistress minion you,
Thank me no thankings, nor proud me no prouds,
But fettle your fine joints 'gainst Thursday next

To go with Paris to Saint Peter's Church,   155
Or I will drag thee on a hurdle thither.
Out, you green-sickness carrion! out, you baggage!
You tallow-face!
    Lady.   Fie, fie! what, are you mad?
    Jul. Good father, I beseech you on my knees,
Hear me with patience but to speak a word.   160
    Cap. Hang thee, young baggage! disobedient wretch!
I tell thee what—get thee to church a Thursday
Or never after look me in the face.
Speak not, reply not, do not answer me!
My fingers itch. Wife, we scarce thought us blest   165
That God had lent us but this only child;
But now I see this one is one too much,
And that we have a curse in having her.
Out on her, hilding!
    Nurse.   God in heaven bless her!
You are to blame, my lord, to rate her so.   170
    Cap. And why, my Lady Wisdom? Hold your tongue,
Good Prudence. Smatter with your gossips, go!
    Nurse. I speak no treason.
    Cap.   O, God-i-god-en!
    Nurse. May not one speak?
    Cap.   Peace, you mumbling fool!
Utter your gravity o'er a gossip's bowl,   175
For here we need it not.
    Lady.   You are too hot.
    Cap. God's bread! it makes me mad. Day, night, late,
    early,
At home, abroad, alone, in company,
Waking or sleeping, still my care hath been
To have her match'd; and having now provided   180
A gentleman of princely parentage,

Of fair demesnes, youthful, and nobly train'd,
Stuff'd, as they say, with honourable parts,
Proportion'd as one's thought would wish a man—
And then to have a wretched puling fool,   185
A whining mammet, in her fortune's tender,
To answer 'I'll not wed, I cannot love;
I am too young, I pray you pardon me'!
But, an you will not wed, I'll pardon you.
Graze where you will, you shall not house with me.   190
Look to't, think on't; I do not use to jest.
Thursday is near; lay hand on heart, advise:
An you be mine, I'll give you to my friend;
An you be not, hang, beg, starve, die in the streets,
For, by my soul, I'll ne'er acknowledge thee,   195
Nor what is mine shall never do thee good.
Trust to't. Bethink you. I'll not be forsworn.   *Exit.*

   Jul. Is there no pity sitting in the clouds
That sees into the bottom of my grief?
O sweet my mother, cast me not away!   200
Delay this marriage for a month, a week;
Or if you do not, make the bridal bed
In that dim monument where Tybalt lies.

   Lady. Talk not to me, for I'll not speak a word.   204
Do as thou wilt, for I have done with thee.   *Exit.*

   Jul. O God!—O nurse, how shall this be prevented?
My husband is on earth, my faith in heaven.
How shall that faith return again to earth
Unless that husband send it me from heaven
By leaving earth? Comfort me, counsel me.   210
Alack, alack, that heaven should practise stratagems
Upon so soft a subject as myself!
What say'st thou? Hast thou not a word of joy?
Some comfort, nurse.

Nurse.   Faith, here it is.
Romeo is banish'd; and all the world to nothing   215
That he dares ne'er come back to challenge you;
Or if he do, it needs must be by stealth.
Then, since the case so stands as now it doth,
I think it best you married with the County.
O, he's a lovely gentleman!   220
Romeo's a dishclout to him. An eagle, madam,
Hath not so green, so quick, so fair an eye
As Paris hath. Beshrew my very heart,
I think you are happy in this second match,
For it excels your first; or if it did not,   225
Your first is dead—or 'twere as good he were
As living here and you no use of him.
    Jul. Speak'st thou this from thy heart?
    Nurse. And from my soul too; else beshrew them both.
    Jul. Amen!   230
    Nurse. What?
    Jul. Well, thou hast comforted me marvellous much.
Go in; and tell my lady I am gone,
Having displeas'd my father, to Laurence' cell,
To make confession and to be absolv'd.   235
    Nurse. Marry, I will; and this is wisely done.   *Exit.*
    Jul. Ancient damnation! O most wicked fiend!
Is it more sin to wish me thus forsworn,
Or to dispraise my lord with that same tongue
Which she hath prais'd him with above compare   240
So many thousand times? Go, counsellor!
Thou and my bosom henceforth shall be twain.
I'll to the friar to know his remedy.
If all else fail, myself have power to die.   *Exit.*

Enter *Friar* [*Laurence*] and *County Paris*.

Friar. On Thursday, sir? The time is very short.
Par. My father Capulet will have it so,
And I am nothing slow to slack his haste.
Friar. You say you do not know the lady's mind.
Uneven is the course; I like it not.
Par. Immoderately she weeps for Tybalt's death,
And therefore have I little talk'd of love;
For Venus smiles not in a house of tears.
Now, sir, her father counts it dangerous
That she do give her sorrow so much sway,   10
And in his wisdom hastes our marriage
To stop the inundation of her tears,
Which, too much minded by herself alone,
May be put from her by society.
Now do you know the reason of this haste.   15
Friar. [*aside*] I would I knew not why it should be slow'd.—
Look, sir, here comes the lady toward my cell.

Enter *Juliet*.

Par. Happily met, my lady and my wife!
Jul. That may be, sir, when I may be a wife.
Par. That may be must be, love, on Thursday next.   20
Jul. What must be shall be.
Friar.   That's a certain text.
Par. Come you to make confession to this father?
Jul. To answer that, I should confess to you.
Par. Do not deny to him that you love me.
Jul. I will confess to you that I love him.   25

78

Par. So will ye, I am sure, that you love me.

Jul. If I do so, it will be of more price,
Being spoke behind your back, than to your face.

Par. Poor soul, thy face is much abus'd with tears.

Jul. The tears have got small victory by that,　　30
For it was bad enough before their spite.

Par. Thou wrong'st it more than tears with that report.

Jul. That is no slander, sir, which is a truth;
And what I spake, I spake it to my face.

Par. Thy face is mine, and thou hast sland'red it.　　35

Jul. It may be so, for it is not mine own.
Are you at leisure, holy father, now,
Or shall I come to you at evening mass?

Friar. My leisure serves me, pensive daughter, now.
My lord, we must entreat the time alone.　　40

Par. God shield I should disturb devotion!
Juliet, on Thursday early will I rouse ye.
Till then, adieu, and keep this holy kiss.　　*Exit.*

Jul. O, shut the door! and when thou hast done so,
Come weep with me—past hope, past cure, past help!　　45

Friar. Ah, Juliet, I already know thy grief;
It strains me past the compass of my wits.
I hear thou must, and nothing may prorogue it,
On Thursday next be married to this County.

Jul. Tell me not, friar, that thou hear'st of this,　　50
Unless thou tell me how I may prevent it.
If in thy wisdom thou canst give no help,
Do thou but call my resolution wise
And with this knife I'll help it presently.
God join'd my heart and Romeo's, thou our hands;　　55
And ere this hand, by thee to Romeo's seal'd,
Shall be the label to another deed,
Or my true heart with treacherous revolt

Turn to another, this shall slay them both.
Therefore, out of thy long-experienc'd time,   60
Give me some present counsel; or, behold,
'Twixt my extremes and me this bloody knife
Shall play the umpire, arbitrating that
Which the commission of thy years and art
Could to no issue of true honour bring.   65
Be not so long to speak. I long to die
If what thou speak'st speak not of remedy.

    Friar. Hold, daughter. I do spy a kind of hope,
Which craves as desperate an execution
As that is desperate which we would prevent.   70
If, rather than to marry County Paris,
Thou hast the strength of will to slay thyself,
Then is it likely thou wilt undertake
A thing like death to chide away this shame,
That cop'st with death himself to scape from it;   75
And, if thou dar'st, I'll give thee remedy.

    Jul. O, bid me leap, rather than marry Paris,
From off the battlements of yonder tower,
Or walk in thievish ways, or bid me lurk
Where serpents are; chain me with roaring bears,   80
Or shut me nightly in a charnel house,
O'ercover'd quite with dead men's rattling bones,
With reeky shanks and yellow chapless skulls;
Or bid me go into a new-made grave
And hide me with a dead man in his shroud—   85
Things that, to hear them told, have made me tremble—
And I will do it without fear or doubt,
To live an unstain'd wife to my sweet love.

    Friar. Hold, then. Go home, be merry, give consent
To marry Paris. Wednesday is to-morrow.   90
To-morrow night look that thou lie alone;

Let not the nurse lie with thee in thy chamber.
Take thou this vial, being then in bed,
And this distilled liquor drink thou off;
When presently through all thy veins shall run   95
A cold and drowsy humour; for no pulse
Shall keep his native progress, but surcease;
No warmth, no breath, shall testify thou livest;
The roses in thy lips and cheeks shall fade
To paly ashes, thy eyes' windows fall   100
Like death when he shuts up the day of life;
Each part, depriv'd of supple government,
Shall, stiff and stark and cold, appear like death;
And in this borrowed likeness of shrunk death
Thou shalt continue two-and-forty hours,   105
And then awake as from a pleasant sleep.
Now, when the bridegroom in the morning comes
To rouse thee from thy bed, there art thou dead.
Then, as the manner of our country is,
In thy best robes uncovered on the bier   110
Thou shalt be borne to that same ancient vault
Where all the kindred of the Capulets lie.
In the mean time, against thou shalt awake,
Shall Romeo by my letters know our drift;
And hither shall he come; and he and I   115
Will watch thy waking, and that very night
Shall Romeo bear thee hence to Mantua.
And this shall free thee from this present shame,
If no inconstant toy nor womanish fear
Abate thy valour in the acting it.   120
    Jul. Give me, give me! O, tell not me of fear!
    Friar. Hold! Get you gone, be strong and prosperous
In this resolve. I'll send a friar with speed
To Mantua, with my letters to thy lord.   124

Jul. Love give me strength! and strength shall help afford.
Farewell, dear father.

Exeunt.

[Scene II. Capulet's *house.*]

Enter *Father Capulet, Mother, Nurse,* and *Servingmen,*
two or three.

Cap. So many guests invite as here are writ.

[*Exit a Servingman.*]
Sirrah, go hire me twenty cunning cooks.

Serv. You shall have none ill, sir; for I'll try if they can lick
their fingers.

Cap. How canst thou try them so?   5

Serv. Marry, sir, 'tis an ill cook that cannot lick his own
fingers. Therefore he that cannot lick his fingers goes not with
me.

Cap. Go, begone.

Exit Servingman.
We shall be much unfurnish'd for this time.   10
What, is my daughter gone to Friar Laurence?

Nurse. Ay, forsooth.

Cap. Well, he may chance to do some good on her.
A peevish self-will'd harlotry it is.

Enter *Juliet.*

Nurse. See where she comes from shrift with merry look. 15

Cap. How now, my headstrong? Where have you been
gadding?

Jul. Where I have learnt me to repent the sin
Of disobedient opposition
To you and your behests, and am enjoin'd

By holy Laurence to fall prostrate here 20
To beg your pardon. Pardon, I beseech you!
Henceforward I am ever rul'd by you.

   Cap. Send for the County. Go tell him of this.
I'll have this knot knit up to-morrow morning.

   Jul. I met the youthful lord at Laurence' cell 25
And gave him what becomed love I might,
Not stepping o'er the bounds of modesty.

   Cap. Why, I am glad on't. This is well. Stand up.
This is as't should be. Let me see the County.
Ay, marry, go, I say, and fetch him hither. 30
Now, afore God, this reverend holy friar,
All our whole city is much bound to him.

   Jul. Nurse, will you go with me into my closet
To help me sort such needful ornaments
As you think fit to furnish me to-morrow? 35

   Mother. No, not till Thursday. There is time enough.

   Cap. Go, nurse, go with her. We'll to church to-morrow.
                             Exeunt Juliet and Nurse.

   Mother. We shall be short in our provision.
'Tis now near night.

   Cap.   Tush, I will stir about,
And all things shall be well, I warrant thee, wife. 40
Go thou to Juliet, help to deck up her.
I'll not to bed to-night; let me alone.
I'll play the housewife for this once. What, ho!
They are all forth; well, I will walk myself
To County Paris, to prepare him up 45
Against to-morrow. My heart is wondrous light,
Since this same wayward girl is so reclaim'd.

                                    Exeunt.

[Scene III. Juliet's *chamber*.]

Enter Juliet and Nurse.

Jul. Ay, those attires are best; but, gentle nurse,
I pray thee leave me to myself to-night;
For I have need of many orisons
To move the heavens to smile upon my state,
Which, well thou knowest, is cross and full of sin.   5

Enter Mother.

Mother. What, are you busy, ho? Need you my help?
Jul. No, madam; we have cull'd such necessaries
As are behooffull for our state to-morrow.
So please you, let me now be left alone,
And let the nurse this night sit up with you;   10
For I am sure you have your hands full all
In this so sudden business.
Mother.   Good night.
Get thee to bed, and rest; for thou hast need.
                    Exeunt [Mother and Nurse].
Jul. Farewell! God knows when we shall meet again.
I have a faint cold fear thrills through my veins   15
That almost freezes up the heat of life.
I'll call them back again to comfort me.
Nurse!—What should she do here?
My dismal scene I needs must act alone.
Come, vial.   20
What if this mixture do not work at all?
Shall I be married then to-morrow morning?
No, no! This shall forbid it. Lie thou there.
                    [Lays down a dagger.]

What if it be a poison which the friar
Subtilly hath minist'red to have me dead,   25
Lest in this marriage he should be dishonour'd
Because he married me before to Romeo?
I fear it is; and yet methinks it should not,
For he hath still been tried a holy man.
I will not entertain so bad a thought.   30
How if, when I am laid into the tomb,
I wake before the time that Romeo
Come to redeem me? There's a fearful point!
Shall I not then be stifled in the vault,
To whose foul mouth no healthsome air breathes in,   35
And there die strangled ere my Romeo comes?
Or, if I live, is it not very like
The horrible conceit of death and night,
Together with the terror of the place—
As in a vault, an ancient receptacle   40
Where for this many hundred years the bones
Of all my buried ancestors are pack'd;
Where bloody Tybalt, yet but green in earth,
Lies fest'ring in his shroud; where, as they say,
At some hours in the night spirits resort—   45
Alack, alack, is it not like that I,
So early waking—what with loathsome smells,
And shrieks like mandrakes torn out of the earth,
That living mortals, hearing them, run mad—
O, if I wake, shall I not be distraught,   50
Environed with all these hideous fears,
And madly play with my forefathers' joints,
And pluck the mangled Tybalt from his shroud,
And, in this rage, with some great kinsman's bone
As with a club dash out my desp'rate brains?   55
O, look! methinks I see my cousin's ghost

Seeking out Romeo, that did spit his body
Upon a rapier's point. Stay, Tybalt, stay!
Romeo, I come! this do I drink to thee.

She [*drinks and*] *falls upon her bed within the curtains.*

[Scene IV. Capulet's *house.*]

Enter *Lady of the House* and *Nurse*.

Lady. Hold, take these keys and fetch more spices, nurse.
Nurse. They call for dates and quinces in the pastry.

Enter *Old Capulet*.

Cap. Come, stir, stir, stir! The second cock hath crow'd,
The curfew bell hath rung, 'tis three o'clock.
Look to the bak'd meats, good Angelica;   5
Spare not for cost.
Nurse.   Go, you cot-quean, go,
Get you to bed! Faith, you'll be sick to-morrow
For this night's watching.
Cap. No, not a whit. What, I have watch'd ere now
All night for lesser cause, and ne'er been sick.   10
Lady. Ay, you have been a mouse-hunt in your time;
But I will watch you from such watching now.
                                   Exeunt Lady and Nurse.
Cap. A jealous hood, a jealous hood!

Enter three or four [*Fellows*], with spits and logs and baskets.

                                   Now, fellow,
What is there?
Fellow. Things for the cook, sir; but I know not what.   15

Cap. Make haste, make haste. [*Exit Fellow.*] Sirrah, fetch
    drier logs.
Call Peter; he will show thee where they are.
    Fellow. I have a head, sir, that will find out logs
And never trouble Peter for the matter.
    Cap. Mass, and well said; a merry whoreson, ha!   20
Thou shalt be loggerhead. [*Exit Fellow.*] Good faith, 'tis day.
The County will be here with music straight,
For so he said he would.   *Play music.*
                    I hear him near.
Nurse! Wife! What, ho! What, nurse, I say!

Enter *Nurse*.

Go waken Juliet; go and trim her up.   25
I'll go and chat with Paris. Hie, make haste,
Make haste! The bridegroom he is come already:
Make haste, I say.

                                    [*Exeunt.*]

[Scene V. Juliet's *chamber*.]

[Enter *Nurse*.]

Nurse. Mistress! what, mistress! Juliet! Fast, I warrant
    her, she.
Why, lamb! why, lady! Fie, you slug-abed!
Why, love, I say! madam! sweetheart! Why, bride!
What, not a word? You take your pennyworths now!
Sleep for a week; for the next night, I warrant,   5
The County Paris hath set up his rest
That you shall rest but little. God forgive me!
Marry, and amen. How sound is she asleep!

I needs must wake her. Madam, madam, madam!
Ay, let the County take you in your bed!   10
He'll fright you up, i' faith. Will it not be?

          [*Draws aside the curtains.*]

What, dress'd, and in your clothes, and down again?
I must needs wake you. Lady! lady! lady!
Alas, alas! Help, help! my lady 's dead!
O weraday that ever I was born!   15
Some aqua-vitæ, ho! My lord! my lady!

                    Enter *Mother*.

  Mother. What noise is here?
  Nurse.   O lamentable day!
  Mother. What is the matter?
  Nurse.   Look, look! O heavy day!
  Mother. O me, O me! My child, my only life!
Revive, look up, or I will die with thee!   20
Help, help! Call help.

                    Enter *Father*.

  Father. For shame, bring Juliet forth; her lord is come.
  Nurse. She's dead, deceas'd; she's dead! Alack the day!
  Mother. Alack the day, she's dead, she's dead, she's dead!
  Cap. Ha! let me see her. Out alas! she's cold,   25
Her blood is settled, and her joints are stiff;
Life and these lips have long been separated.
Death lies on her like an untimely frost
Upon the sweetest flower of all the field.
  Nurse. O lamentable day!
  Mother.   O woful time!   30
  Cap. Death, that hath ta'en her hence to make me wail,
Ties up my tongue and will not let me speak.

Enter *Friar* [*Laurence*] and the *County* [*Paris*], with *Musicians*.

  Friar. Come, is the bride ready to go to church?
  Cap. Ready to go, but never to return.
O son, the night before thy wedding day   35
Hath Death lain with thy wife. See, there she lies,
Flower as she was, deflowered by him.
Death is my son-in-law, Death is my heir;
My daughter he hath wedded. I will die
And leave him all. Life, living, all is Death's.   40
  Par. Have I thought long to see this morning's face,
And doth it give me such a sight as this?
  Mother. Accurs'd, unhappy, wretched, hateful day!
Most miserable hour that e'er time saw
In lasting labour of his pilgrimage!   45
But one, poor one, one poor and loving child,
But one thing to rejoice and solace in,
And cruel Death hath catch'd it from my sight!
  Nurse. O woe! O woful, woful, woful day!
Most lamentable day, most woful day   50
That ever ever I did yet behold!
O day! O day! O day! O hateful day!
Never was seen so black a day as this.
O woful day! O woful day!
  Par. Beguil'd, divorced, wronged, spited, slain!   55
Most detestable Death, by thee beguil'd,
By cruel cruel thee quite overthrown!
O love! O life! not life, but love in death!
  Cap. Despis'd, distressed, hated, martyr'd, kill'd!
Uncomfortable time, why cam'st thou now   60
To murther, murther our solemnity?
O child! O child! my soul, and not my child!
Dead art thou, dead! alack, my child is dead,

And with my child my joys are buried!

   Friar. Peace, ho, for shame! Confusion's cure lives not 65
In these confusions. Heaven and yourself
Had part in this fair maid! now heaven hath all,
And all the better is it for the maid.
Your part in her you could not keep from death,
But heaven keeps his part in eternal life.   70
The most you sought was her promotion,
For 'twas your heaven she should be advanc'd;
And weep ye now, seeing she is advanc'd
Above the clouds, as high as heaven itself?
O, in this love, you love your child so ill   75
That you run mad, seeing that she is well.
She's not well married that lives married long,
But she's best married that dies married young.
Dry up your tears and stick your rosemary
On this fair corse, and, as the custom is,   80
In all her best array bear her to church;
For though fond nature bids us all lament,
Yet nature's tears are reason's merriment.

   Cap. All things that we ordained festival
Turn from their office to black funeral—   85
Our instruments to melancholy bells,
Our wedding cheer to a sad burial feast;
Our solemn hymns to sullen dirges change;
Our bridal flowers serve for a buried corse;
And all things change them to the contrary.   90

   Friar. Sir, go you in; and, madam, go with him:
And go, Sir Paris. Every one prepare
To follow this fair corse unto her grave.
The heavens do low'r upon you for some ill;
Move them no more by crossing their high will.   95

               Exeunt. Manent Musicians [and Nurse].

1. Mus. Faith, we may put up our pipes and be gone.

Nurse. Honest good fellows, ah, put up, put up!
For well you know this is a pitiful case.   [*Exit.*]

1. Mus. Ay, by my troth, the case may be amended.   101

Enter *Peter*.

Pet. Musicians, O, musicians, 'Heart's ease,' 'Heart's ease'!
O, an you will have me live, play 'Heart's ease.'

1. Mus. Why 'Heart's ease'?   105

Pet. O, musicians, because my heart itself plays 'My heart
is full of woe.' O, play me some merry dump to comfort me.

1. Mus. Not a dump we! 'Tis no time to play now.   110

Pet. You will not then?

1. Mus. No.

Pet. I will then give it you soundly.

1. Mus. What will you give us?

Pet. No money, on my faith, but the gleek. I will give you
the minstrel.   116

1. Mus. Then will I give you the serving-creature.

Pet. Then will I lay the serving-creature's dagger on your
pate. I will carry no crotchets. I'll re you, I'll fa you. Do you
note me?   121

1. Mus. An you re us and fa us, you note us.

2. Mus. Pray you put up your dagger, and put out your wit.

Pet. Then have at you with my wit! I will dry-beat you with
an iron wit, and put up my iron dagger. Answer me like men.

'When griping grief the heart doth wound,
    And doleful dumps the mind oppress,
Then music with her silver sound'—   130

Why 'silver sound'? Why 'music with her silver sound'?
What say you, Simon Catling?

1. Mus. Marry, sir, because silver hath a sweet sound.   134

Pet. Pretty! What say you, Hugh Rebeck?

2. Mus. I say 'silver sound' because musicians sound for silver.

Pet. Pretty too! What say you, James Soundpost?

3. Mus. Faith, I know not what to say.   140

Pet. O, I cry you mercy! you are the singer. I will say for you. It is 'music with her silver sound' because musicians have no gold for sounding.

> 'Then music with her silver sound   145
>   With speedy help doth lend redress.'   *Exit.*

1. Mus. What a pestilent knave is this same!

2. Mus. Hang him, Jack! Come, we'll in here, tarry for the mourners, and stay dinner.

                                       Exeunt.

Enter *Romeo.*

Rom. If I may trust the flattering truth of sleep,
My dreams presage some joyful news at hand.
My bosom's lord sits lightly in his throne,
And all this day an unaccustom'd spirit
Lifts me above the ground with cheerful thoughts.   5
I dreamt my lady came and found me dead
(Strange dream that gives a dead man leave to think!)
And breath'd such life with kisses in my lips
That I reviv'd and was an emperor.
Ah me! how sweet is love itself possess'd,   10
When but love's shadows are so rich in joy!

Enter *Romeo's Man Balthasar*, booted.

News from Verona! How now, Balthasar?
Dost thou not bring me letters from the friar?
How doth my lady? Is my father well?
How fares my Juliet? That I ask again,   15
For nothing can be ill if she be well.
    Man. Then she is well, and nothing can be ill.
Her body sleeps in Capel's monument,
And her immortal part with angels lives.
I saw her laid low in her kindred's vault   20
And presently took post to tell it you.
O, pardon me for bringing these ill news,
Since you did leave it for my office, sir.
    Rom. Is it e'en so? Then I defy you, stars!
Thou knowest my lodging. Get me ink and paper   25
And hire posthorses. I will hence to-night.
    Man. I do beseech you, sir, have patience.

Your looks are pale and wild and do import
Some misadventure.

    Rom.   Tush, thou art deceiv'd.
Leave me and do the thing I bid thee do.   30
Hast thou no letters to me from the friar?

    Man. No, my good lord.

    Rom.   No matter. Get thee gone
And hire those horses. I'll be with thee straight.

                                Exit [*Balthasar*].

Well, Juliet, I will lie with thee to-night.
Let's see for means. O mischief, thou art swift   35
To enter in the thoughts of desperate men!
I do remember an apothecary,
And hereabouts 'a dwells, which late I noted
In tatt'red weeds, with overwhelming brows,
Culling of simples. Meagre were his looks,   40
Sharp misery had worn him to the bones;
And in his needy shop a tortoise hung,
An alligator stuff'd, and other skins
Of ill-shaped fishes; and about his shelves
A beggarly account of empty boxes,   45
Green earthen pots, bladders, and musty seeds,
Remnants of packthread, and old cakes of roses
Were thinly scattered, to make up a show.
Noting this penury, to myself I said,
'An if a man did need a poison now   50
Whose sale is present death in Mantua,
Here lives a caitiff wretch would sell it him.'
O, this same thought did but forerun my need,
And this same needy man must sell it me.
As I remember, this should be the house.   55
Being holiday, the beggar's shop is shut.
What, ho! apothecary!

Enter *Apothecary*.

Apoth.   Who calls so loud?
Rom. Come hither, man. I see that thou art poor.
Hold, there is forty ducats. Let me have
A dram of poison, such soon-speeding gear   60
As will disperse itself through all the veins
That the life-weary taker may fall dead,
And that the trunk may be discharg'd of breath
As violently as hasty powder fir'd
Doth hurry from the fatal cannon's womb.   65
  Apoth. Such mortal drugs I have; but Mantua's law
Is death to any he that utters them.
  Rom. Art thou so bare and full of wretchedness
And fearest to die? Famine is in thy cheeks,
Need and oppression starveth in thine eyes,   70
Contempt and beggary hangs upon thy back:
The world is not thy friend, nor the world's law;
The world affords no law to make thee rich;
Then be not poor, but break it and take this.
  Apoth. My poverty but not my will consents.   75
  Rom. I pay thy poverty and not thy will.
  Apoth. Put this in any liquid thing you will
And drink it off, and if you had the strength
Of twenty men, it would dispatch you straight.
  Rom. There is thy gold—worse poison to men's souls,   80
Doing more murther in this loathsome world,
Than these poor compounds that thou mayst not sell.
I sell thee poison; thou hast sold me none.
Farewell. Buy food and get thyself in flesh.
Come, cordial and not poison, go with me   85
To Juliet's grave; for there must I use thee.

Exeunt.

[Scene II. *Verona.* Friar Laurence's *cell.*]

Enter *Friar John* to *Friar Laurence.*

John. Holy Franciscan friar, brother, ho!

Enter *Friar Laurence.*

Laur. This same should be the voice of Friar John.
Welcome from Mantua. What says Romeo?
Or, if his mind be writ, give me his letter.
　John. Going to find a barefoot brother out,   5
One of our order, to associate me
Here in this city visiting the sick,
And finding him, the searchers of the town,
Suspecting that we both were in a house
Where the infectious pestilence did reign,   10
Seal'd up the doors, and would not let us forth,
So that my speed to Mantua there was stay'd.
　Laur. Who bare my letter, then, to Romeo?
　John. I could not send it—here it is again—
Nor get a messenger to bring it thee,   15
So fearful were they of infection.
　Laur. Unhappy fortune! By my brotherhood,
The letter was not nice, but full of charge,
Of dear import; and the neglecting it
May do much danger. Friar John, go hence,   20
Get me an iron crow and bring it straight
Unto my cell.
　John.   Brother, I'll go and bring it thee.   *Exit.*
　Laur. Now must I to the monument alone.
Within this three hours will fair Juliet wake.
She will beshrew me much that Romeo   25

Hath had no notice of these accidents;
But I will write again to Mantua,
And keep her at my cell till Romeo come—
Poor living corse, clos'd in a dead man's tomb!   *Exit.*

[Scene III. *Verona. A churchyard; in it the monument of the*
Capulets.]

Enter *Paris* and his *Page* with flowers and [a torch].

Par. Give me thy torch, boy. Hence, and stand aloof.
Yet put it out, for I would not be seen.
Under yond yew tree lay thee all along,
Holding thine ear close to the hollow ground.
So shall no foot upon the churchyard tread   5
(Being loose, unfirm, with digging up of graves)
But thou shalt hear it. Whistle then to me,
As signal that thou hear'st something approach.
Give me those flowers. Do as I bid thee, go.
    Page. [*aside*] I am almost afraid to stand alone   10
Here in the churchyard; yet I will adventure.   [*Retires.*]
    Par. Sweet flower, with flowers thy bridal bed I strew
    (O woe! thy canopy is dust and stones)
Which with sweet water nightly I will dew;
    Or, wanting that, with tears distill'd by moans.   15
The obsequies that I for thee will keep
Nightly shall be to strew thy grave and weep.
                                        Whistle Boy.
The boy gives warning something doth approach.
What cursed foot wanders this way to-night
To cross my obsequies and true love's rite?   20
What, with a torch? Muffle me, night, awhile.   [*Retires.*]

Enter *Romeo*, and *Balthasar* with a torch, a mattock, and a
crow of iron.

Rom. Give me that mattock and the wrenching iron.
Hold, take this letter. Early in the morning
See thou deliver it to my lord and father.
Give me the light. Upon thy life I charge thee,　　　　25
Whate'er thou hearest or seest, stand all aloof
And do not interrupt me in my course.
Why I descend into this bed of death
Is partly to behold my lady's face,
But chiefly to take thence from her dead finger　　　　30
A precious ring—a ring that I must use
In dear employment. Therefore hence, be gone.
But if thou, jealous, dost return to pry
In what I farther shall intend to do,
By heaven, I will tear thee joint by joint　　　　35
And strew this hungry churchyard with thy limbs.
The time and my intents are savage-wild,
More fierce and more inexorable far
Than empty tigers or the roaring sea.
　　Bal. I will be gone, sir, and not trouble you.　　　　40
　　Rom. So shalt thou show me friendship. Take thou that.
Live, and be prosperous; and farewell, good fellow.
　　Bal. [*aside*] For all this same, I'll hide me hereabout.
His looks I fear, and his intents I doubt.　　　　[*Retires.*]
　　Rom. Thou detestable maw, thou womb of death,　　　　45
Gorg'd with the dearest morsel of the earth,
Thus I enforce thy rotten jaws to open,
And in despite I'll cram thee with more food.
　　　　　　　　　　　Romeo opens the tomb.
　　Par. This is that banish'd haughty Montague
That murd'red my love's cousin—with which grief　　　　50

It is supposed the fair creature died—
And here is come to do some villanous shame
To the dead bodies. I will apprehend him.
Stop thy unhallowed toil, vile Montague!
Can vengeance be pursu'd further than death?   55
Condemned villain, I do apprehend thee.
Obey, and go with me; for thou must die.

    Rom. I must indeed; and therefore came I hither.
Good gentle youth, tempt not a desp'rate man.
Fly hence and leave me. Think upon these gone;   60
Let them affright thee. I beseech thee, youth,
Put not another sin upon my head
By urging me to fury. O, be gone!
By heaven, I love thee better than myself,
For I come hither arm'd against myself.   65
Stay not, be gone. Live, and hereafter say
A madman's mercy bid thee run away.

    Par. I do defy thy conjuration
And apprehend thee for a felon here.

    Rom. Wilt thou provoke me? Then have at thee, boy!
                          They fight.

    Page. O Lord, they fight! I will go call the watch.   71
                      [Exit. Paris falls.]

    Par. O, I am slain! If thou be merciful,
Open the tomb, lay me with Juliet.   *[Dies.]*

    Rom. In faith, I will. Let me peruse this face.
Mercutio's kinsman, noble County Paris!   75
What said my man when my betossed soul
Did not attend him as we rode? I think
He told me Paris should have married Juliet.
Said he not so? or did I dream it so?
Or am I mad, hearing him talk of Juliet,   80
To think it was so? O, give me thy hand,

One writ with me in sour misfortune's book!
I'll bury thee in a triumphant grave.
A grave? O, no, a lanthorn, slaught'red youth,
For here lies Juliet, and her beauty makes   85
This vault a feasting presence full of light.
Death, lie thou there, by a dead man interr'd.

[Lays him in the tomb.]

How oft when men are at the point of death
Have they been merry! which their keepers call
A lightning before death. O, how may I   90
Call this a lightning? O my love! my wife!
Death, that hath suck'd the honey of thy breath,
Hath had no power yet upon thy beauty.
Thou art not conquer'd. Beauty's ensign yet
Is crimson in thy lips and in thy cheeks,   95
And death's pale flag is not advanced there.
Tybalt, liest thou there in thy bloody sheet?
O, what more favour can I do to thee
Than with that hand that cut thy youth in twain
To sunder his that was thine enemy?   100
Forgive me, cousin! Ah, dear Juliet,
Why art thou yet so fair? Shall I believe
That unsubstantial Death is amorous,
And that the lean abhorred monster keeps
Thee here in dark to be his paramour?   105
For fear of that I still will stay with thee
And never from this palace of dim night
Depart again. Here, here will I remain
With worms that are thy chambermaids. O, here
Will I set up my everlasting rest   110
And shake the yoke of inauspicious stars
From this world-wearied flesh. Eyes, look your last!
Arms, take your last embrace! and, lips, O you

The doors of breath, seal with a righteous kiss
A dateless bargain to engrossing death!   115
Come, bitter conduct; come, unsavoury guide!
Thou desperate pilot, now at once run on
The dashing rocks thy seasick weary bark!
Here's to my love! [*Drinks.*] O true apothecary!
Thy drugs are quick. Thus with a kiss I die.   *Falls.*

Enter *Friar* [*Laurence*], with lanthorn, crow, and spade.

Friar. Saint Francis be my speed! how oft to-night   121
Have my old feet stumbled at graves! Who's there?
Bal. Here's one, a friend, and one that knows you well.
Friar. Bliss be upon you! Tell me, good my friend,
What torch is yond that vainly lends his light   125
To grubs and eyeless skulls? As I discern,
It burneth in the Capels' monument.
Bal. It doth so, holy sir; and there's my master,
One that you love.
Friar.   Who is it?
Bal.   Romeo.
Friar. How long hath he been there?
Bal.   Full half an hour. 130
Friar. Go with me to the vault.
Bal.   I dare not, sir.
My master knows not but I am gone hence,
And fearfully did menace me with death
If I did stay to look on his intents.
Friar. Stay then; I'll go alone. Fear comes upon me. 135
O, much I fear some ill unthrifty thing.
Bal. As I did sleep under this yew tree here,
I dreamt my master and another fought,
And that my master slew him.

Friar.   Romeo!
Alack, alack, what blood is this which stains   140
The stony entrance of this sepulchre?
What mean these masterless and gory swords
To lie discolour'd by this place of peace? [*Enters the tomb.*]
Romeo! O, pale! Who else? What, Paris too?
And steep'd in blood? Ah, what an unkind hour   145
Is guilty of this lamentable chance!
The lady stirs.

                                        Juliet rises.

Jul. O comfortable friar! where is my lord?
I do remember well where I should be,
And there I am. Where is my Romeo?   150
Friar. I hear some noise. Lady, come from that nest
Of death, contagion, and unnatural sleep.
A greater power than we can contradict
Hath thwarted our intents. Come, come away.
Thy husband in thy bosom there lies dead;   155
And Paris too. Come, I'll dispose of thee
Among a sisterhood of holy nuns.
Stay not to question, for the watch is coming.
Come, go, good Juliet. I dare no longer stay.
Jul. Go, get thee hence, for I will not away.   160
                                        Exit [*Friar*].
What's here? A cup, clos'd in my true love's hand?
Poison, I see, hath been his timeless end.
O churl! drunk all, and left no friendly drop
To help me after? I will kiss thy lips.
Haply some poison yet doth hang on them   165
To make me die with a restorative.   [*Kisses him.*]
Thy lips are warm!
Chief Watch. [*within*] Lead, boy. Which way?

Jul. Yea, noise? Then I'll be brief. O happy dagger!
                              [*Snatches Romeo's dagger.*]
This is thy sheath; there rest, and let me die.   170
                    She stabs herself and falls [on Romeo's body].

          Enter [*Paris's*] *Boy* and *Watch.*

Boy. This is the place. There, where the torch doth burn.
Chief Watch. The ground is bloody. Search about the
    churchyard.
Go, some of you; whoe'er you find attach.
                              [*Exeunt some of the Watch.*]
Pitiful sight! here lies the County slain;
And Juliet bleeding, warm, and newly dead,   175
Who here hath lain this two days buried.
Go, tell the Prince; run to the Capulets;
Raise up the Montagues; some others search.
                              [*Exeunt others of the Watch.*]
We see the ground whereon these woes do lie,
But the true ground of all these piteous woes   180
We cannot without circumstance descry.

Enter [some of the *Watch*,] with *Romeo's Man* [*Balthasar*].

2. Watch. Here's Romeo's man. We found him in the
    churchyard.
Chief Watch. Hold him in safety till the Prince come
    hither.

          Enter *Friar* [*Laurence*] and another *Watchman.*

3. Watch. Here is a friar that trembles, sighs, and weeps.
We took this mattock and this spade from him   185
As he was coming from this churchyard side.
Chief Watch. A great suspicion! Stay the friar too.

Enter the *Prince* [and *Attendants*].

Prince. What misadventure is so early up,
That calls our person from our morning rest?

Enter *Capulet* and his *Wife* [with others].

Cap. What should it be, that they so shriek abroad? 190
Wife. The people in the street cry 'Romeo,'
Some 'Juliet,' and some 'Paris'; and all run,
With open outcry, toward our monument.
Prince. What fear is this which startles in our ears?
Chief Watch. Sovereign, here lies the County Paris slain;
And Romeo dead; and Juliet, dead before, 196
Warm and new kill'd.
Prince. Search, seek, and know how this foul murder comes.
Chief Watch. Here is a friar, and slaughter'd Romeo's man,
With instruments upon them fit to open 200
These dead men's tombs.
Cap. O heavens! O wife, look how our daughter bleeds!
This dagger hath mista'en, for, lo, his house
Is empty on the back of Montague,
And it missheathed in my daughter's bosom! 205
Wife. O me! this sight of death is as a bell
That warns my old age to a sepulchre.

Enter *Montague* [and others].

Prince. Come, Montague; for thou art early up
To see thy son and heir more early down.
Mon. Alas, my liege, my wife is dead to-night! 210
Grief of my son's exile hath stopp'd her breath.
What further woe conspires against mine age?
Prince. Look, and thou shalt see.
Mon. O thou untaught! what manners is in this,
To press before thy father to a grave? 215

Prince. Seal up the mouth of outrage for a while,
Till we can clear these ambiguities
And know their spring, their head, their true descent;
And then will I be general of your woes
And lead you even to death. Meantime forbear,   220
And let mischance be slave to patience.
Bring forth the parties of suspicion.
   Friar. I am the greatest, able to do least,
Yet most suspected, as the time and place
Doth make against me, of this direful murther;   225
And here I stand, both to impeach and purge
Myself condemned and myself excus'd.
   Prince. Then say at once what thou dost know in this.
   Friar. I will be brief, for my short date of breath
Is not so long as is a tedious tale.   230
Romeo, there dead, was husband to that Juliet;
And she, there dead, that Romeo's faithful wife.
I married them; and their stol'n marriage day
Was Tybalt's doomsday, whose untimely death
Banish'd the new-made bridegroom from this city;   235
For whom, and not for Tybalt, Juliet pin'd.
You, to remove that siege of grief from her,
Betroth'd and would have married her perforce
To County Paris. Then comes she to me
And with wild looks bid me devise some mean   240
To rid her from this second marriage,
Or in my cell there would she kill herself.
Then gave I her (so tutored by my art)
A sleeping potion; which so took effect
As I intended, for it wrought on her   245
The form of death. Meantime I writ to Romeo
That he should hither come as this dire night
To help to take her from her borrowed grave,

Being the time the potion's force should cease.
But he which bore my letter, Friar John,   250
Was stay'd by accident, and yesternight
Return'd my letter back. Then all alone
At the prefixed hour of her waking
Came I to take her from her kindred's vault;
Meaning to keep her closely at my cell   255
Till I conveniently could send to Romeo.
But when I came, some minute ere the time
Of her awaking, here untimely lay
The noble Paris and true Romeo dead.
She wakes; and I entreated her come forth   260
And bear this work of heaven with patience;
But then a noise did scare me from the tomb,
And she, too desperate, would not go with me,
But, as it seems, did violence on herself.
All this I know, and to the marriage   265
Her nurse is privy; and if aught in this
Miscarried by my fault, let my old life
Be sacrific'd, some hour before his time,
Unto the rigour of severest law.
    Prince. We still have known thee for a holy man.   270
Where's Romeo's man? What can he say in this?
    Bal. I brought my master news of Juliet's death;
And then in post he came from Mantua
To this same place, to this same monument.
This letter he early bid me give his father,   275
And threat'ned me with death, going in the vault,
If I departed not and left him there.
    Prince. Give me the letter. I will look on it.
Where is the County's page that rais'd the watch?
Sirrah, what made your master in this place?   280
    Boy. He came with flowers to strew his lady's grave;

And bid me stand aloof, and so I did.
Anon comes one with light to ope the tomb;
And by-and-by my master drew on him;
And then I ran away to call the watch.   285
    Prince. This letter doth make good the friar's words,
Their course of love, the tidings of her death;
And here he writes that he did buy a poison
Of a poor pothecary, and therewithal
Came to this vault to die, and lie with Juliet.   290
Where be these enemies? Capulet, Montague,
See what a scourge is laid upon your hate,
That heaven finds means to kill your joys with love!
And I, for winking at your discords too,
Have lost a brace of kinsmen. All are punish'd.   295
    Cap. O brother Montague, give me thy hand.
This is my daughter's jointure, for no more
Can I demand.
    Mon.   But I can give thee more;
For I will raise her statue in pure gold,
That whiles Verona by that name is known,   300
There shall no figure at such rate be set
As that of true and faithful Juliet.
    Cap. As rich shall Romeo's by his lady's lie—
Poor sacrifices of our enmity!
    Prince. A glooming peace this morning with it brings. 305
    The sun for sorrow will not show his head.
Go hence, to have more talk of these sad things;
    Some shall be pardon'd, and some punished;
For never was a story of more woe
Than this of Juliet and her Romeo.   310

                                        Exeunt omnes.

NOTES

The Prologue, like the Prologue to Act II, is distinctly lyrical. It takes the form of the Shakespearean sonnet. It is spoken by the Chorus, a character whose rôle is to address the audience with interpretation and comment. Father Time in *The Winter's Tale* (iv, 1) is a good example. In *Henry V* the Chorus speaks a Prologue to each act and a final Epilogue (which is in sonnet form). Gower is the Chorus in *Pericles*. Cf. *Hamlet*, iii, 2, 255: 'You are as good as a chorus, my lord.'

3. mutiny: riot, uproar—in a more general sense than in modern usage. Cf. i, 5, 82.

4. Where . . . unclean: in which the blood of citizens stains the hands of their fellow citizens.

6. star-cross'd: thwarted by unfavourable stars; ill-fated. Cf. i, 4, 106 ff.; v, 1, 24; v, 3, 110, 111. The fatalistic interpretation of life is as inherent in this drama (though not so emphatically outspoken) as in *Macbeth*. Lest we might be tempted to regard this attitude of mind as personal to Shakespeare rather than as dramatic, we may contrast Edmund's refutation of astrology in *King Lear*, i, 2, 129 ff.

7, 8. Whose . . . strife. This foretells the reconcilement between the Montagues and the Capulets at the end of the play (v, 3, 296–304).

9. passage: course.

12. two hours'. For this estimate of the length of a performance cf. *Henry VIII*, Prologue, 12, 13; *Two Noble Kinsmen*, Prologue, 27–29. Lack of shifting scenery shortened the time of action.—**traffic:** business.

14. What . . . mend. Such apologetic promises were conventional in prologues and epilogues. Compare Puck's address to the audience at the end of *A Midsummer Night's Dream*; Epilogues to *All's Well* and *2 Henry IV*.—**miss:** fail; prove deficient.

ACT I. Scene I.

The drama begins with a typical street scene that shows the servants of the two houses in a brawl. Compare the introductory scene in *Julius Cæsar* and in *Coriolanus*. See Sprague, *Shakespeare and the Audience*, 1935, pp. 105, 109–110.

(Stage direction.) **bucklers.** Heavy swords and small shields (bucklers) were the ordinary weapons of servants; gentlemen wore rapier and dagger.

1. carry coals. A slang phrase for 'submit tamely to insults.' To lug sacks or baskets of coal was regarded as the lowest form of toil. Gregory, for the joke's sake, chooses to take Sampson's remark in a literal sense; and Sampson, thinking Gregory has misunderstood him, proceeds to explain his meaning. Cf. *Henry V*, iii, 2, 49–51: 'In Calais they stole a fire-shovel. I knew by that piece of service the men would carry coals.'

4. an: if.—**choler:** anger.—**draw:** draw our swords.

6. draw . . . collar: keep your neck out of the hangman's noose.

7. being moved: when angered.

9. moved: impelled.

10. A dog. Emphatic: 'even a *dog*.'—**moves me:** i.e., to strike.

16. take the wall. Since there were no sidewalks and there was often a gutter in the middle of the street, the edges of the street nearest the houses were obviously the cleanest and safest places for walking. Hence to *take the wall* of anybody (to insist on passing between him and the wall) was an assertion of superiority, and to *give* one *the wall* was an act of courtesy or a confession of inferior rank. Cf. *Archie Armstrong's Banquet of Jests*, 6th ed., 1640 (ed. 1872, p. 216): 'Two Gentlemen meeting, the one jostled the other from the Wall, and had almost made him to measure his length in the channell'; Heywood, *1 King Edward IV* (Pearson ed., I, 64): 'If any gallant striue to haue the wall, Ile yield it gently.'

17, 18. the weakest goes to the wall. A proverb, signifying originally that, in a crowd that is pressing forward toward some desired object, the weakest is thrust into the rear. Cf. Lyly, *Euphues* (ed. Bond, I, 201): 'The weakest must still to the wall'; Greene, *Mamillia*, Part II, 1593 (ed. Grosart, II, 241): 'The weakest is thrust to the wall, and he that worst may, holdes the candle.' The old sense comes out clearly in *Mucedorus*, 1598, iv, 3, 72 ff. (ed. Tucker Brooke, *Shakespeare Apocrypha*, p. 120):

> In time of yore, when men like brutish beasts
> Did lead their liues in loathsom celles and woodes
> And wholy gaue themselues to witlesse will,
> A rude vnruly rout, then man to man
> Became a present praie, then might preuailed,
> The weak[e]st went to walles:
> Right was vnknowen, for wrong was all in all.

See Apperson, *English Proverbs*, p. 671; Tilley, *Elizabethan Proverb Lore*, No. 674.

19. **the weaker vessels.** Cf. Lyly, *Euphues* (ed. Bond, I, 223): 'Men are always laying baytes for women, which are the weaker vessels.' See *1 Peter*, iii, 7.

27. **cruel.** The Second Quarto reads *ciuil*; corrected in the Fourth Quarto.

32. **sense:** feeling.

37. **poor-John:** dried and salted cod or hake—regarded as very poor food.—**tool:** an old slang term for 'sword.'

42. **Fear me not:** Don't worry about me—I'll not run. Gregory purposely misunderstands for the joke's sake.

44. **marry.** Originally an oath by the Virgin Mary; but weakened by usage to a mere expletive—'indeed.' Cf. i, 3, 22, 63; i, 5, 133.

45. **Let us take the law of our sides:** Let us take care to have the law on our side. Compare what Peter says to the Nurse: 'I dare draw as soon as another man, if I see occasion in a good quarrel, and the law on my side' (ii, 4, 167-169). Note also Sir Andrew Aguecheek's scruples about the law (*Twelfth Night*, iii, 4, 157-182; iv, 1, 36-39).

46. **as they list:** as they please—as an offence or as no offence.

49. **bite my thumb.** A gesture of insulting defiance. Malone cites Dekker, *The Dead Tearme*, 1608 (ed. Grosart, IV, 51): 'What Iustling, what Ieering, what byting of Thumbs to beget quarrels.' Cf. Deloney, *The Gentle Craft, ca.* 1597 (ed. Halliday, p. 73): 'When the Frenchman heard this, he stamped like a madman, and bit his thumb, saying: "Mordue, me shall be revenged, be Got!"' Evelyn in his *Diary* (October 17, 1644) describes a boatman's behaviour at Genoa: 'Here I could not but observe the suddaine and develish passion of a sea-man, who plying us was intercepted by another fellow that interpos'd his boate before him and tooke us in; for the teares gushing out of his eyes, he put his finger in his mouth and almost bit it off by the joynt, shewing it to his antagonist as an assurance to him of some bloody revenge if ever he came neere that part of the harbour again' (ed. Wheatley, 1906, I, 96, 97). Halliwell quotes Richard Peeke, *Three to One. Being an English-Spanish Combat performed the 15th day of November 1625* (ed. Arber, *An English Garner*, I [1877], 637): 'Now was I in greater danger, being, as I thought, in peace; than before when I was in battle. For a general murmur filled the air, with threatenings at me: the soldiers especially bit their thumbs, and was it possible for me to escape?'

69. **swashing blow:** a heavy downward stroke.

73. **heartless hinds:** cowardly menials.

76. **manage:** handle, wield.

79. **Have at thee:** Let me get at thee! Here goes for an attack! The standard formula of assault. Cf. iv, 5, 125; v, 3, 70.

80. **Clubs.** Clubs were the regular weapons of the London journeymen and apprentices. The cry 'Clubs!' was the citizens' watchword, whether in raising a riot or in rallying to keep the peace. See *1 Henry VI*, i, 3, 69–91; *Henry VIII*, v, 4, 49–62; *Coriolanus*, i, 1, 56, 57; *Titus Andronicus*, ii, 1, 37. Cf. Greene, *A Disputation Betweene a Hee Conny-catcher, and a Shee Conny-catcher*, 1592 (ed. Grosart, X, 215): 'The Officer . . . sayd hee was his true prisoner, and cride Clubbes: the Pren-

tises arose, and there was a great hurly burly, for they tooke
the Officers part'; Dekker, *The Shoemaker's Holiday* (Pearson
ed., I, 64): 'Downe with them, cry clubs for prentises.'—**bills:**
long, pointed weapons, often with a hook near the end.—
partisans: pikes.

81. **in his gown:** in his nightgown—i.e., a dressing gown
(such as would be thrown on by one called from sleep in haste).
Cf. *Macbeth*, ii, 2, 70, 71:

> Get on your nightgown, lest occasion call us
> And show us to be watchers.

85. **in spite of me:** with intent to defy and insult me. Cf.
Midsummer Night's Dream, iii, 2, 193, 194:

> Now I perceive they have conjoin'd all three
> To fashion this false sport in spite of me.

94. **mistempered:** tempered (composed) for an evil purpose
—with a pun on the sense of 'ill-tempered,' 'angry.'

95. **sentence:** decree.—**moved:** indignant, offended.

100. **grave:** dignified.—**beseeming:** becoming, fitting.

102. The first *cank'red* means 'eaten with rust' (from long
disuse); the second, 'malignant,' 'rancorous.'

104. **of the peace:** for breaking the peace.

108. **our.** Speaking as a sovereign, the Prince uses 'the royal
we.'

109. **Freetown.** Broke's translation of *Villafranca*.

115. **I drew:** I drew my sword.

119. **nothing.** Adverbial—'not at all.'—**withal:** thereby.

121, 122. **on part and part:** on one side and the other.—
either part: both parties.

127. **abroad:** away from my home. Cf. iii, 1, 2; iii, 5, 178;
v, 3, 190.

131. **made:** made my way.—**ware:** aware.

133. **measuring his affections:** judging his feelings. Cf. l. 154.

134, 135. **Which . . . found:** which then were most desirous
to seek the place where fewest persons were.—**Being . . . self:**

for my own society was almost more than I could endure. Benvolio, though a cheerfully sedate person, was in that mood which Jaques calls 'a most humorous sadness' (*As You Like It*, iv, 1, 19, 20)—the same mood which little Prince Arthur describes in *King John*, iv, 1, 14-16:

> I remember, when I was in France,
> Young gentlemen would be as sad as night
> Only for wantonness—

i.e., merely to indulge an idle fancy.

136. **Pursu'd . . . his:** followed the lead of *my own* fancy for solitude by refraining from any attempt to learn from him the cause of *his* fancy for the same.

137. **who:** him who.

139, 140. **With tears . . . sighs.** For similar hyperbole (sometimes sentimental or tragic, sometimes humorous or satirical) cf. l. 197; ii, 3, 73; iii, 5, 127-138; v, 3, 14, 15; *Richard II*, iii, 1, 20; iii, 3, 160-169; *Titus Andronicus*, iii, 1, 212-214, 220-230; *Antony and Cleopatra*, i, 2, 152-157; *Cymbeline*, i, 6, 66, 67.

143. **Aurora:** the goddess of the dawn.

144. **heavy:** melancholy. Cf. ll. 185, 193; i, 4, 12; ii, 2, 158; iii, 3, 157; iii, 4, 11; iii, 5, 109; iv, 5, 18.

148, 149. **humour:** mood.—**may:** can.

151. **of:** from.

152. **impórtun'd him:** questioned him insistently.

153. **many other friends:** many others who were our friends.

154. **his own affections' counsellor:** one keeping the cause of his feelings to himself. *Counsel* is the regular old word for 'secrecy' or 'a secret.' Cf. i, 3, 9; ii, 2, 53; ii, 4, 208.

155. **I will not say how true:** since perhaps he would be truer to himself (more in accord with his own best interests) if he were not so obstinately reticent.

156. **close:** reserved.

157. **sounding.** A nautical metaphor: 'investigation.' Cf. iii, 2, 126.—**discovery.** Synonymous with *sounding*.

158. **with:** by.—**envious:** malicious. Cf. iii, 1, 173; iii, 2, 47;

iii, 5, 7.—**worm:** the 'worm i' th' bud' (*Twelfth Night*, ii, 4, 114); the canker or rose caterpillar, which, being hatched inside the bud, kills it before it can blossom. Cf. ii, 3, 30; *Hamlet*, i, 3, 39, 40:

> The canker galls the infants of the spring
> Too oft before their buttons [i.e., buds] be disclos'd.

160. **sun.** The Quartos and Folios read 'same.' Theobald made the correction.

163. **So please you:** if you please—literally, so may it please you.

164. **his grievance:** the cause of his sorrow.—**or be much denied:** or have my earnest enquiries met with stubborn reticence.

165, 166. **by thy . . . shrift:** as, by waiting, to hear confession of the truth.

167. **Good morrow:** good morning. Cf. ii, 3, 31, 34.

168. **new:** recently, just now.—**Ay me!** A common interjection of lament—equivalent to *ah me!*

171. **having.** Emphatic: 'if I could only *have* it, would make,' etc.

176, 177. **in his view:** in appearance.—**in proof:** in our experience of him.

178, 179. **muffled:** since Cupid is either blind or blindfolded. Cf. i, 4, 4.—**still:** ever, always. Cf. ll. 188, 224; iii, 3, 39.—**his will:** i.e., his will to enslave us.

182. **Here's much to do with hate:** Here's a great disturbance on account of the feud—'but,' Romeo adds with a sigh, 'my unhappy love causes me even more disturbance than that.' Then he proceeds to describe love itself in a series of the whimsical contradictions customary in dealing with this subject. Petrarch set the fashion; and the Elizabethans were very fond of paradoxes.

184. **create:** created. Such participial forms are common.

185. **vanity:** emptiness, frivolity. Cf. ii, 6, 20.

188. **Still-waking:** ever-wakeful.

189. **no love:** no enjoyment.

191. **Good heart.** Here, apparently, a familiar or affectionate form of address (cf. i, 5, 88; *Tempest*, i, 1, 6, 29; *Twelfth Night*, ii, 3, 16; *Midsummer Night's Dream*, iv, 2, 26). Sometimes, however, it is a softened oath ('by God's heart'), as when the Nurse couples it with 'i' faith' (ii, 4, 184). Cf. Slender's oath 'Od's [i.e., God's] heartlings' (*Merry Wives*, iii, 4, 59); Chaucer, *Pardoner's Tale*, C 650 (ed. Robinson, p. 183): 'By Goddes precious herte.'

192. **Why . . . transgression:** Why, that is just the way in which love does wrong! Your love for me makes you sympathize with my sorrows; and the knowledge that you thus suffer with me makes my sorrows all the heavier.

194, 195. **propagate:** increase.—**to have it prest:** so as to have it burdened.—**With:** by.—**more of thine:** since thy sympathy would only add to my sorrow.

198. **Being purg'd:** when the smoke of the sighs has cleared away. Cf. ii, 3, 73, and note.

200. **discreet:** sanely discriminating.

201. **gall:** bitterness. Cf. i, 5, 94; *King Lear*, i, 4, 292.

202. **Soft!** An interjection of caution or protest: 'Wait a moment'; 'Don't be in such a hurry.' Cf. ii, 2, 2; iii, 4, 18; iii, 5, 142.

203. **An if:** if.—**you do me wrong:** for you are not treating me as a friend.

206. **in sadness:** in sober earnest—without all these fanciful phrases. Romeo purposely misunderstands *sadness*.—**that:** she whom.

208. **sadly.** Synonymous with *in sadness* (l. 206).

209. **Bid . . . will.** Romeo insists on his misinterpretation of *sadness*. To tell a sick man to make his will reminds him that death may be imminent.

210. **ill urg'd:** inopportunely mentioned—almost equivalent to 'ominous.'

212. **aim'd:** guessed. Cf. *Hamlet*, iv, 5, 9: 'They aim at it.'

215. **in . . . miss:** In that remark you certainly state a fact, but you miss the true nature of my love case.

216. **Dian's wit:** the wisdom of Diana, goddess of maidens, who is opposed to love and marriage.

217. **proof:** armour of proof—well-tested armour, protecting the wearer from Love's arrows.

219. **stay:** wait for; heed.—**siege.** For the idea that the lover lays siege to his lady-love, or to her heart, see *Hamlet*, i, 3, 122, 123, and note. Cf., for example, *Cymbeline*, iii, 4, 136, 137: 'That Cloten whose love suit hath been to me As fearful as a siege.'

223. **with . . . store:** All her store of beauty (and therefore all the beauty in the world) dies with her, for she will leave no descendants. Compare the theme of *Sonnets* i–xiv.

224. **still:** ever, always. Cf. ll. 178, 188.

228, 229. **wisely too fair . . . despair:** It shows too much saintly wisdom in so beautiful a creature to seek heavenly bliss (the reward of a votary) by dooming me to despair.

230. **forsworn to love.** Cf. Broke, fol. 4 r°: 'Or els (what booteth the to sue) loues court she hath forsworne.'

236. **To . . . more:** To look at other beautiful women is just the way to keep her surpassing loveliness still more before my mind's eye. To *call in question* is to 'make (anything) the object of thought or of notice.'

237, 238. **These happy masks . . . in mind:** The very fact that such masks are black reminds us of the beauty they hide. Cf. *Measure for Measure*, ii, 4, 79–81:

> These black masks
> Proclaim enshielded beauty ten times louder
> Than beauty could, display'd.

Ladies often wore silk masks in public. Cf. *Two Gentlemen*, iv, 4, 154–161; *Winter's Tale*, iv, 4, 223; *Othello*, iv, 2, 9.

241. **a mistress:** a lady-love.—**passing:** surpassingly, superlatively.

242. **a note:** a notice (as if in writing).

245. **I'll . . . debt:** I'll give you that instruction, or else die in the vain attempt; I'll devote my life to teaching you to forget.

Scene II.

(Stage direction.) **County:** Count. Cf. Broke, fol. 53 rº: 'Who, County paris cliped [i.e., named] was, an Earle he had to sire.'—**Clown:** merely 'servant.'

1. bound: under bonds to keep the peace. While Benvolio has been talking with Romeo, the Prince has given judgment at Freetown (i, 1, 109), requiring both Montague and Capulet to furnish sureties not to pursue their feud.

4. reckoning: reputation, estimation.

9. fourteen years. Cf. Broke, fol. 52 vº: 'Scarce saw she yet full .xvi. yeres: to yong to be a bryde.' That fourteen, and even thirteen, was regarded as a marriageable age is abundantly proved by literature and history. See, for example, *Two Noble Kinsmen*, v, 1, 107 ff.; *Winter's Tale*, ii, 1, 146, 147; Jonson, *The Magnetic Lady*, i, 1 (ed. Gifford, VI, 16):

> Her niece, Mistress Placentia Steel,
> Who strikes the fire of full fourteen to-day,
> Ripe for a husband;

Marlowe, *The Jew of Malta*, i, 2, 378–381 (ed. Bennett, p. 69); Ford, *Love's Sacrifice*, iii, 1 (ed. Gifford and Dyce, II, 58): 'Could your mouldy brain be so addle to imagine I would marry a stale widow at six-and-forty? . . . Are there not varieties enough of thirteen?' Massinger, *The Emperor of the East*, ii, 1 (ed. Gifford[2], III, 278), and *The Fatal Dowry*, iii, 1 (III, 403); Beaumont and Fletcher, *The Coxcomb*, i, 3, 5, 6 (ed. Dyce, III, 132); Fletcher, *The Humorous Lieutenant*, ii, 3 (VI, 449); *The Elder Brother*, i, 1 (X, 205); *The Nice Valour*, ii, 1 (X, 316); Dr. Thomas Tryon, *The Way to Health*, 1683, p. 628: ''Tis a very ill custom People have got to match their Daughters, almost as soon as they are out of their *Hanging-Sleeves*, and I know no excuse for it, but the *Licentiousness* of the Age, which is such, that if Parents do not provide Husbands for their Daughters at *fourteen*, they are ready to provide them themselves, or do worse.' We may note also Malevole's satire in Marston's *Malcontent*, i, 6 (ed. Wood, I, 156): 'Why, that at foure women were fools, at foureteene Drabbes, at forty bawdes, at fourescore witches.' Compare the description of 'a very, very woman' in *The Overburian Characters* (ed. Paylor, p. 4): 'She is *Mariageable* and *Fourteene* at once; and after shee doth not live but tarry.'

13. **marr'd.** Cf. ii 4, 121, 122. The antithetic use of *make* and *mar* is common in Shakespeare (as in *As You Like It*, i, 1, 31–34; *Timon*, iv, 2, 41; *Macbeth*, ii, 3, 36; *Othello*, v, 1, 4). Capulet is also thinking of the saying which Steevens quotes from Puttenham, *The Arte of English Poesie*, 1589, p. 173: 'The maide that soone married is, soone marred is,' and which Parolles adapts in *All's Well*, ii, 3, 315: 'A young man married is a man that's marr'd.'

15. **my earth:** all my earthly possessions. Capulet may intend also to suggest that Juliet is the sole object of his earthly hopes. Cf. iii, 5, 177–180.

18. **within her scope of choice:** within the limits of her choice; bounded by her wishes in choosing a husband.

19. **fair:** favourable. — **according:** consenting. — **voice.** Almost synonymous with *vote*.

25. **Earth-treading stars.** Cf. Marlowe, *Hero and Leander*, i, 97, 98:

> For every street, like to a firmament,
> Glister'd with breathing stars;

Pilgrimage to Parnassus, ll. 492, 493 (ed. Macray, p. 16):

> Then shall you have the choice of earthlie starrs
> That shine on earth as Cynthia in her skye.

26. **lusty:** lively, vigorous. Cf. i, 4, 113; ii, 4, 159.

30. **Inherit:** possess, have.

32, 33. **Which ... none.** The construction is confused, and *which* has no verb; but the sense is clear: 'And as to *her* (i.e., her whose merit most shall be; her who shall best deserve your love), when you have had a further view of many beautiful ladies, my daughter may appear to you only one of the crowd and unworthy of special admiration.'—**none**. Capulet alludes to the proverb 'One is no number.' Malone cites *Sonnet* 136: 'Among a number one is reckon'd none.' Cf. Mabbe, *Celestina* (ed. *Tudor Translations*, p. 140): 'Many more inconveniences can I tell thee of this single soale number (if one may be a number)'; Dekker, *2 Honest Whore* (Pearson ed., II, 152): 'One no number is.'

34. **sirrah**. A term of familiar address, often used to servants. See i, 5, 31, note.

39. **meddle with**: concern himself with. The jocosely grumbling Servant misapplies the familiar proverb, 'The shoemaker should not go beyond his last (Ne sutor supra crepidam).' He intimates that the task of delivering the invitations is beyond his proper business, since he does not know how to read.

45. **must**: must apply to.—**In good time!** At an opportune moment! Thus the Servant greets the approach of Benvolio and Romeo, two gentlemen who, he thinks, will help him out of his difficulty by reading the list of guests for him.

46. **one fire . . . burning.** Cf. *Two Gentlemen of Verona*, ii, 4, 192–195:

> Even as one heat another heat expels
> Or as one nail by strength drives out another,
> So the remembrance of my former love
> Is by a newer object quite forgotten;

Coriolanus, iv, 7, 54: 'One fire drives out one fire; one nail, one nail'; *King John*, iii, 1, 277, 278; *Julius Cæsar*, iii, 1, 171. See Apperson, *English Proverbs*, p. 213.

48. **holp**: helped.

49. **languish**: suffering.

52, 53. **Your plantain leaf . . . shin.** The plantain leaf 'is a blood-stauncher, and was formerly applied to green wounds' (Steevens). *Broken* means 'having the skin broken'—not, 'fractured' (cf. i, 3, 38). Steevens compares Tomkis, *Albumazar*, iv, 11 (Collier's Dodsley, VII, 194): 'Bring a fresh plantane leaf, I have broke my shin.' Cf. *Love's Labour's Lost*, iii, 1, 71–75. The two *your*'s (in 'your plaintain leaf' and 'your broken shin') are not really personal pronouns in sense. They are examples of the indefinite *your*: 'A plaintain leaf, you know, is good for a wounded shin.' Benvolio has been prescribing a cure for hopeless love. Romeo parodies him by prescribing for a trivial wound: 'If I had a broken shin, I should know how to cure it; but hopeless love is something for which neither you nor I can prescribe the remedy.'

55–57. **bound . . . tormented.** Such was the expert treatment of the insane in Shakespeare's time. See *Twelfth Night*, iii, 4, 148, 149; iv, 2, 32 ff.—**God-den . . . God gi' go-den:** good evening—contracted forms of 'God give ye good even.' Cf. ii, 4, 116, 117; iii, 1, 41; iii, 5, 173.

61. **learned it without book:** committed it to memory, learned it by heart. The Servant does not understand Romeo's words, and thinks he refers to some particular sentences that he can recognize without knowing how to read.

65. **Rest you merry!** God keep you happy! A good wish at parting. The Servant infers that Romeo cannot read, and is about to go in search of some better scholar. He does not perceive that Romeo has been jesting.

67–74. Printed in prose in the Quartos and Folios. *Anselmo* (l. 68) is Capell's conjecture for the old reading *Anselme*; *and* (l. 72) is the reading of the First Quarto. Capell suggested the insertion of 'gentle' before 'Livia.'

74. **Whither should they come?** To whose house were they to come?

84. **crush . . . wine.** A proverbially humorous invitation to drink. Cf. Chettle, *Hoffman*, iii (ed. Ackermann, p. 41): 'Wee'l crush a cup of thine owne country wine'; *Two Angry Women of Abington* (ed. Gayley, I, 573): 'Fill the potte, hostesse . . . weele crushe it'; Greene, *The Defence of Conny-catching*, 1592 (ed. Grosart, XI, 43): 'to crush a potte of ale with mee'; *George a Greene*, 1599 (Greene, ed. Grosart, XIV, 174): 'Come George, we will crush a pot before we part.'

86, 87. **ancient.** Cf. l. 20.—**Rosaline.** In the interval between scene i and scene ii, l. 46, Romeo has confided the name of his lady-love to Benvolio.

89. **with unattainted eye:** with clear sight—undisturbed by your love for Rosaline—and therefore impartially.

91. **a crow.** Cf. i, 5, 50.

94. **these:** these eyes of mine.—**drown'd:** i.e., with tears.

95. **Transparent.** This adjective sometimes means 'bright' and sometimes has the modern sense. Here both meanings are combined. Cf. *Midsummer Night's Dream*, ii, 2, 104, and note.—**heretics:** because, if my eyes pronounce any lady fairer than Rosaline, they will be false to their faith.

100–103. Cf. Broke, fol. 4 vº:

> Ere long the townishe dames together will resort:
> Some one of bewty, fauour, shape, and of so louely porte:
> With so fast fixed eye, per haps thou mayst beholde,
> That thou shalt quite forget thy loue, and passions past of olde.

Romeo follows his friend's advice: 'And euery where he would resort where Ladies wont to meete' (fol. 5 rº).

100. **scales.** Treated as a singular noun.

101. **Your lady's love:** the love that you wish your lady to have for you. 'You think her love would be a precious possession; but I will prove that it is worthless in comparison with the love of some more beautiful maiden whom I will show you at the feast.' Theobald's emendation—'Lady-love'—is certainly unnecessary.

103. **show:** appear, look.

105. **in splendour of mine own:** in the brilliant beauty of my own fair lady.

Scene III.

---

2. **year:** common as a plural; more colloquial than *years*. The word belonged in Anglo-Saxon to a large class of neuter nouns in which the plural was identical with the singular in the nominative and accusative.

3. **What!** An impatient call.—**ladybird:** a small beetle—a term of affection.

4. **God forbid!** God forbid that anything should have happened to her! Here, however, the exclamation indicates little more than impatience at Juliet's delay.

7. **matter:** business, affair.—**give leave:** leave us. Cf. ii, 5, 25.

9. **thou's** thou shalt.—**counsel:** private conversation. Cf. i, 1, 154, note.

12. **lay:** bet, wager.

13. **teen:** sorrow.

15. **Lammastide:** August 1; Anglo-Saxon *hlāfmæsse*, 'loaf-mass,' the feast of first fruits.

22. **marry:** indeed. Cf. i, 1, 44, note.

23. **the earthquake.** See Introduction.

29. **bear a brain:** have a good mind still. The phrase was in frequent use by old people as an assertion that their memory was not failing. Cf. Jonson, *Tale of a Tub*, i, 2: 'I am old Rivet still, and bear a brain.'

31. **fool.** A term of endearment, like *wretch* (l. 44), *rogue*, etc. So King Lear calls Cordelia 'my poor fool' (v, 3, 305).

32. **tetchy:** irritable.—**fall out:** quarrel. Cf. iii, 1, 32.

33. **Shake, quoth the dovehouse!** At that very moment came the earthquake, and the Nurse has an amused recollection how she ran away from the shaking dovehouse, which she personifies. Daniel compares 'Bounce, quoth the guns' (Peele, *The Old Wive's Tale*, ed. Bullen, I, 333).—**trow:** believe, think.

36. **stand high-lone:** stand erect without support or assistance. Cf. Marston, *Antonio's Revenge*, iv, 4 (ed. Wood, I, 119): 'when it [the infant] once goes high-lone.'

38. **broke her brow:** fell while trying to walk and bruised (or broke the skin of) her forehead. Cf. i, 2, 53.

40. **'A:** he.

43. **by my holidam.** Originally an oath by a holy relic or some other sacred object. *Holidam* is a form of the Anglo-Saxon *hāligdōm* (German *heiligtum*), 'sanctity,' but was often understood as 'Holy Dame,' i.e., 'Our Lady'—the Virgin Mary.

44-50. **wretch.** See l. 31, note.—**come about:** come true.—
an: if.—**stinted:** stopped crying.—**cannot choose but laugh:**
cannot help laughing. Cf. iii, 5, 78.

52. **it brow:** its brow. The usual genitive of *it* in Shakespeare
is *his* (the ancient form for both masculine and neuter), but *it's*
(or *its*) and *it* also occur several times in the Folio. *It* in this use
seems to have been common in 'baby talk,' but was not confined
thereto. Cf. *King John*, ii, 1, 160-162:

> Go to it grandam, child!
> Give grandam kingdom, and it grandam will
> Give it a plum, a cherry, and a fig.

53. **cock'rel:** young cock.

60. **the prettiest babe.** Cf. Broke, fol. 19 r°: 'A prety babe
(quoth she) it was when it was yong.'

63-65. **Marry.** See i, 1, 44, note.—**disposition:** state of mind.

76. **a man of wax:** a perfectly beautiful man—as perfect in
form and feature as a 'wax figure.' The phrase was a commonplace for such perfection. Cf. *The Fair Maide of Bristow*, sig.
A 3 v°: 'a man as twere compleat of waxe'; Nathan Field, *A
Woman is a Weathercock*, i, 2 (Collier's Dodsley, XIII, 18):

> Oh, foot! oh, leg! oh, hand! oh, body! face!
> By Jove, it is a little man of wax;

Fair Em, i, 3, 51-53 (ed. Tucker Brooke, *Shakespeare Apocrypha*, p. 290):

> A bodie were it framed of wax
> By all the cunning artists of the world,
> It could not better be proportioned.

83. **every married lineament:** all his harmonious and well-
proportioned features.

84. **one another lends content:** each feature makes every other
more pleasing by this harmony. *Content* often has a more active
sense than in modern usage. Cf. *Othello*, ii, 1, 198, 199:

> I cannot speak enough of this content;
> It stops me here; it is too much of joy.

86. **in the margent of his eyes.** His eyes are like marginal notes in a book: they interpret the meaning that is less clearly expressed by his other features. Explanatory notes (such as are now-a-days put at the foot of the page) were in Shakespeare's time usually printed in the margin (see *Hamlet*, v, 2, 162, 163). For the metaphor cf. *Love's Labour's Lost*, ii, 1, 246, 247; *Lucrece*, 99–102. Dowden cites Dekker, *The Honest Whore*, Part II (Pearson ed., II, 130):

> But why talke you all riddle thus? I read
> Strange Comments in those margines of your lookes:
> Your cheekes of late are (like bad printed Bookes)
> So dimly charactred, I scarce can spell,
> One line of loue in them.

88. **a cover:** a wife to embrace him as a cover enfolds a book.

89, 90. **much pride:** a magnificent sight.—**fair . . . hide.** In this strange passage both fish and sea are thought of as beautiful objects. So in *Much Ado*, iii, 1, 26, 27, the beauty of both fish and river is expressed—the fish has 'golden oars' with which it cuts 'the silver stream.' Desperate (and improbable) suggestions are that *lives in the sea* means 'is not yet caught,' and that there is an allusion to fishskin as book-binding material.

96. **like of:** like; be pleased with. Cf. *Much Ado*, v, 4, 59: 'I am your husband if you like of me.'

97. **I'll look . . . move:** I'll look at him with favour if what I see prompt me to love him.

99. **your consent.** Juliet, not yet in love, is content to follow her parents' wishes.

101. **curs'd:** for not being at hand to help in serving.

104. **straight:** straightway, immediately.

Scene IV.

1. **this speech.** In masquerading parties it was customary to introduce the maskers in a versified speech, explaining what characters they represent and how they come to be present. Such

a prologue Benvolio rejects as out-of-date. Steevens refers to
Timon, i, 2, 128 ff.; Collier to *Love's Labour's Lost*, v, 2, 158 ff.

4. **hoodwink'd:** blindfolded. Cf. i, 1, 178.

5. **a Tartar's painted bow.** 'The Tartarian bows . . . re-
sembled in their form the old Roman or Cupid's bow. . . .
Shakespeare used the epithet to distinguish it from the English
bow, whose shape is the segment of a circle' (Douce). Cf.
Midsummer Night's Dream, iii, 2, 101: 'Swifter than arrow
from the Tartar's bow'; Fletcher, *The Humorous Lieutenant*,
i, 1 (ed. Dyce, VI, 429): 'as arrows from a Tartar's bow.'

6. **like:** in the guise of.—**a crowkeeper:** a boy armed with
bow and arrows and stationed to guard a wheatfield from the
crows. Cf. *King Lear*, iv, 6, 87: 'That fellow handles his bow
like a crowkeeper.'

8. **After the prompter:** requiring continual prompting. So
in *Love's Labour's Lost*, v, 2, 158 ff., when Moth tries to speak
the prologue to the maskers' show, he stumbles badly and has
to be prompted.—**entrance.** Trisyllabic—*enterance*.

10. **measure them a measure:** dance for them a stately dance
(like a minuet), or a figure in such a dance. Cf. i, 5, 52.

11. **Give me a torch.** Steevens compares Dekker and Webster, *Westward Ho*, i, 2 (ed. Dyce, 1871, p. 213): 'He is just
like a torchbearer to maskers; he wears good clothes, and is
ranked in good company, but he doth nothing.'—**ambling:**
Romeo's contemptuous word for 'dancing.'

12. **heavy:** sad, melancholy. Cf. i, 1, 144, note.

18. **bound.** Some of the old dances required nimble bound-
ing (leaping upright). Mercutio puns on *bound* in the sense
of 'limit.' Romeo plays with the word in ll. 20, 21.

21. **a pitch above.** A falcon's *pitch* is the height it reaches
when it soars.

30. **A visor for a visor!** Mercutio jestingly calls his face a
visor (a mask), since masks resemble faces and one's face often
conceals one's thoughts. Cf. *Macbeth*, iii, 2, 34, 35:

> And make our faces vizards to our hearts,
> Disguising what they are.

Some editors think that Mercutio rejects a mask and that he refers to his own features as grotesque. Dowden suggests that, being an invited guest (i, 2, 70), he goes unmasked.

31. **quote:** note, observe.—**deformities:** anything unsightly in my appearance when masked.

32. **beetle brows.** Apparently Mercutio's mask has somewhat grotesque features—a red face and heavy overhanging eyebrows.—**shall:** that shall.

35. **wantons:** gay or sportive persons.

36. **senseless:** that have no feeling.—**rushes.** The floor of the ballroom (the stage) was strewn with green rushes. Cf. *Taming of the Shrew*, iv, 1, 47, 48: 'Is supper ready, the house trimm'd, rushes strew'd?'

37, 38. **proverb'd with a grandsire phrase:** furnished with an ancient proverb (given in l. 39) that justifies me in holding the light instead of taking an active part in the masquerade (cf. ll. 11-16). To *hold the candle* is to 'stand by, as a mere attendant or looker-on,' and implies inferiority in strength, skill, or rank. Cf. Henry Porter, *The Two Angry Women of Abington*, 1599, sc. xi (ed. Gayley, I, 611): 'He that worse may, must hold the candle'; Lyly, *Euphues* (ed. Bond, I, 201): 'He that worst may is alwaye enforced to holde the candell.'

39. **The game . . . done.** Cf. i, 5, 121. An old proverb advises one to cease from sport or merrymaking when it is at its height—for fear it change from jest to earnest, from play to strife, or (if a game of chance is in question) from good luck to bad. In other words, 'Let well (or well enough) alone.' The proverb is well-known in mediæval Latin: for example,

> Dum ludus bonus est, ludum dimittere fas est;
> Ni dimittatur, aliquando forte grauatur;[1]

[1] *Romanische Forschungen*, III, 286. Cf. 'Dum pulcer [i.e., pulcher] iocus est, nos hunc dimittere ius est' (*Romanische Forschungen*, III, 638; VI, 561); 'Dum iocus est, bellum cessare et omittere debes' (Egbert von Lüttich, *Fecunda Ratis*, l. 571, ed. Voigt, p. 112); 'Als dat spêl up dem besten is, so sal men aflaten. Dum non ingratus, pulchrum desistere ludo' (Tunnicius No. 42, ed. Hoffman von Fallersleben, p. 19). See W. Gottschalk, *Die Bildhaften Sprichwörter der Romanen*, III (1938), 11, 12.

and it occurs in Old French (Robert de Blois, *Floris et Liriopé*, ll. 1060, 1061; ed. Ulrich, II, 61):

> Tant com li jeus est biaz,
> Le doit on laissier par savoir.

40. dun's . . . word. 'Dun's the mouse'—which means literally 'The mouse is dun (or dark) in colour'—was a proverbial saying for 'Be quiet,' 'Keep dark,' and was therefore an appropriate word (watchword, motto) for a constable lying in wait to make an arrest, as well as for these young gentlemen, who were going in disguise to the house of Romeo's hereditary enemy. So in Dekker and Webster, *Westward Ho*, 1604 (Pearson ed., II, 352):

Honey-suckle. Serieant *Ambush*, as th' art an honest fellow, scowte in some backe roome till the watch-word be giuen for sallying forth.
Ambush. Duns the Mouse.

Malone cites *Patient Grissil*, 1603 (Sig. A 3, lf. 1 r°): 'Dun is the mouse, lie still.' Cf. Dekker, *2 Honest Whore* (Pearson ed., II, 170): 'No more words, a Mouse, Mum'; *Everie Woman in her Humor*, 1609 (ed. Bullen, *Old English Plays*, IV, 351, 352): 'Thou shalt whisper in mine eare, I will see and say little; what, I say duns the mouse'; *Roxburghe Ballads*, ed. Chappell, I, 53: 'I'le say no more but dun's the Mouse.'
41. If thou art Dun, we'll draw thee from the mire. Mercutio, having already punned once on *done* and *dun*, goes on to play with *dun* in another sense—'a dark-coloured horse.' *Dun* was common as a horse's name. Horses were often mired in the old days of bad roads, and a figurative application was easy and had become idiomatic. Cf. Otwell Johnson, letter, 1546 (*Original Letters*, ed. H. Ellis, II, 178): 'Mr. Dunne your hoerse haeth a newe master this day in Smythfeld for 1 ˢ sterling'; *Towneley Mysteries* (*Surtees Society Publications*, III [1836], 18): 'Gif Don, thyne hors, a wisp of hay'; Heywood, *1 Edward IV* (Pearson ed., I, 39): 'Driue Dun . . . faire and softly downe the hill'; *Sir John Oldcastle*, v, 3, 33, 34: 'Old

Dunne has bin moyerd [i.e., mired] in a slough in Brickhil-lane'; Chaucer, *Manciple's Prologue*, 4–6 (ed. Robinson, p. 267):

> Sires, what! Dun is in the myre!
> Is there no man, for preyere or for hyre,
> That wole awake oure felawe al bihynde?

Skelton, *Garlande of Laurell*, l. 1433: 'Dun is in the myre, dame, reche me my spur'; *The Schole House of Women*, ll. 459–461 (ed. Hazlitt, *Early Popular Poetry*, IV, 122):

> One and other little ye care,
> So ye may haue that ye desire,
> Though dun and the pack lye in the mire;

Political Poems, ed. Thomas Wright, II, 224: 'And alle gooth bacwarde, and Donne is in the myre'; Fletcher, *The Woman-Hater*, iv, 2 (ed. Dyce, I, 71): 'Dun's i' the mire; get out again how he can'; Dekker and Webster, *Westward Ho* (Pearson ed., II, 312): 'I see I'me borne still to draw Dun out ath mire for you.' William Gifford (1756–1826) in his edition of Jonson (1816) describes a game which is perhaps also in Mercutio's mind: '*Dun is in the mire*,' Gifford remarks, 'is a Christmas gambol, at which I have often played. A *log* of wood is brought into the midst of the room: this is *Dun*, (the cart-horse,) and a cry is raised, that he is *stuck* in *the mire*. Two of the company advance, either with or without ropes, to draw him out. After repeated attempts they find themselves unable to do it, and call for more assistance.—The game continues until all the company take part in it, when Dun is extricated of course' (VII, 283). For the game see Brand's *Popular Antiquities*, ed. Hazlitt, II, 287, 308. It is mentioned ('the drawing Dun out of the myer') by Rowlands, *The Letting of Humours Blood*, 1600 (Hunterian Club ed., p. 65). Cf. Shirley, *Saint Patrick for Ireland*, iii, 1 (ed. Gifford and Dyce, IV, 394):

> Then draw Dun out o' the mire,
> And throw the clog into the fire.

42. sir-reverence. An apologetic phrase (*sa' reverence, save reverence, salva reverentia*), 'respect for you being preserved,' i.e., 'spoken with no intention of offending you.' It was used (often by persons of inferior rank) in mentioning something indecent or unpleasant, to assure the person addressed that no disrespect was in the speaker's mind.[1] Mercutio implies that love is so disgraceful a fancy for a spirited youth to cherish that it ought not even to be mentioned without an apology—as if the very word *love* (which he emphasizes) were objectionable. Cf. *Greene's Tu Quoque* (Collier's Dodsley, VII, 68):

> You, as the common trick is, straight suppose
> 'Tis love (sir-reverence, which makes the word more beastly).

43–45. we burn daylight, ho! ... by day. In origin the phrase was (as Mercutio suggests) a reproof for wasting torches or candles by burning them in the daytime.[2] Its regular meaning is 'to waste the daylight hours by idleness or procrastination' (as in *Merry Wives*, ii, 1, 54). Hence Romeo objects that Mercutio's remark is not true, since it is now after dark.

46, 47. Take our good meaning. Cf. ii, 4, 131; *Midsummer Night's Dream*, ii, 2, 45: 'O, take the sense, sweet, of my innocence!'—**in that:** i.e., in 'taking our good meaning.' In understanding a person's words as he means them to be understood, Mercutio asserts, a man shows more intelligence than in merely using his sense of hearing or, indeed, all five of his senses. In short, 'To hear without an attempt to understand is stupid.'—**five wits.** The Quartos and Folios read *fine*. Corrected by Wilbraham.

---

[1] Cf. *Comedy of Errors*, iii, 2, 91–93. The synonym 'saving your (your worship's, your honour's) reverence' was common. See *Merchant of Venice*, ii, 2, 27, 138, 139; *Measure for Measure*, ii, 1, 92; *Much Ado*, iii, 4, 32; *1 Henry IV*, ii, 4, 515, 516.

[2] See addition to *The Spanish Tragedy*, iii, 12 (Kyd, ed. Boas, p. 65):

> *Hieronymo.* Light me your torches at the mid of noone.
> . . . .
> *Pedro.* Then we burne day light.

49. **no wit:** no wisdom. The play abounds in presentiments. Cf. ll. 39, 106–111; i, 5, 121, 122; ii, 2, 117–120, 139–141; ii, 6, 1–15; iii, 1, 124, 125; iii, 5, 54–59; v, 1, 1–9.

50. **to-night:** last night. Cf. ii, 4, 2.

52. **In bed.** The stock pun on *lie*, which no Elizabethan could resist. Compare Hamlet and the Sexton (v, 1, 131–138).

53. **Queen Mab.** The name seems to come from Celtic tradition, for Medb is an heroic queen in ancient Irish legendary history. Mab is the Fairy Queen in Jonson's *Althorp Entertainment*, 1603 (*A Satyre, Workes*, 1616, pp. 871, 872).

54. **the fairies' midwife.** This 'does not mean midwife *to* the fairies, but that she was the person *among* the fairies whose department it was to deliver the fancies of sleeping men of their dreams, those *children of an idle brain*' (Steevens).

55. **an agate stone:** i.e., the figure cut in the agate set in a ring.

57. **atomies:** atoms; tiny creatures.

59. **spinners':** spiders'.

62. **the moonshine's wat'ry beams.** The moon was styled 'the mother of dew' (*Batman vpon Bartholome, His Booke De Proprietatibus Rerum*, 1582, xi, 6). 'The Moone gendereth deawe in the aire, for she printeth the vertue of hir moysture in the aire, and chaungeth the ayre in a manner that is vnseene, & breedeth and gendereth deaw in the vtter part thereof' (Batman, viii, 29). Hence the moon is constantly described as 'watery'. See *Midsummer Night's Dream*, ii, 1, 162 (cf. iii, 1, 203); *Winter's Tale*, i, 2, 1; *Richard III*, ii, 2, 69.

65. **worm.** 'It was supposed . . . that when maidens were idle, worms bred in their fingers' (Nares, *Glossary*, 1822, p. 247). Nares cites Fletcher, *The Woman-Hater*, iii, 1 (ed. Dyce, I, 43):

> Keep thy hands in thy muff, and warm the idle
> Worms in thy fingers' ends.

68. **joiner:** one who makes furniture and the lighter kind of house fittings.

70. **in this state:** in this stately array; in this splendour of equipment.

72. **cursies:** curtsies.

76. **sweetmeats.** Malone thought that this refers to the 'artificial aids to perfume the breath' styled 'kissing comfits' (*Merry Wives*, v, 5, 22); but a more disagreeable interpretation is probable: cf. Dekker, *The Gull's Hornbook,* 1609 (ed. Grosart, II, 212): 'The breath of it stinks like the mouthes of Chambermaides by feeding on so many sweat meats.'

78. **smelling out a suit:** discovering some person who has a petition to the king. For a fat fee the courtier will undertake to gain the royal favour for the petitioner. Such lobbying was a notable abuse in Shakespeare's time and long before, and is frequently satirized. It is the origin of the proverb 'A friend at court is better than a penny in purse.' Cf. *Winter's Tale,* iv, 4, 766 ff., where Autolycus pretends to be a courtier and undertakes to act as 'advocate' for the Shepherd and his son.

79. **tithe-pig:** every tenth pig born—due to the parson as part of his tithes. Cf. Webster, *Duchess of Malfy,* ii, 1, 107–109 (ed. Lucas, II, 54): 'The same reason, that makes a Vicar goe to Law for a tithe-pig, and undoe his neighbours, makes them [i.e., princes] spoile a whole Province, and batter downe goodly Cities, with the Cannon.'

84, 85. **Spanish blades.** Toledo steel was famous.—**fadom:** fathoms.

87. **a prayer or two.** Cf. *Macbeth,* ii, 2, 23 ff.

89. **plats the manes.** That demons or mischievous elves disturb horses in the stable, tire them out by night-riding, and plait or tangle their manes, is a widespread modern belief, and there is abundant evidence for similar notions in mediæval and ancient times. See Kittredge, *Witchcraft in Old and New England,* p. 219 (and note 65). Matted and tangled locks of human hair —due to neglect and filthy habits—were likewise ascribed to the action of elves and hence called elflocks. Cf. *King Lear,* ii, 3, 10.

91. **misfortune bodes:** apparently because to disentangle and comb out the elflocks incensed the elves, who took their revenge by doing more serious mischief.

92. **the hag.** Mercutio thus identifies Queen Mab with the nightmare demon, fear of whom is conterminous with the bad dreams of the human race. The ancient Greek physicians explained the nightmare as due to physical causes, but the old belief was persistent. The second syllable of *nightmare* is the Anglo-Saxon *mare* ('incubus') and has nothing to do with the word *mare* which means 'a female horse.'

97, 98. **idle:** empty, silly.—**fantasy:** fancy.

103. **the dew-dropping South.** The south wind in Shakespeare's country brings rain and fog. Cf. *As You Like It*, iii, 5, 50: 'Like foggy south, puffing with wind and rain'; *Cymbeline*, iv, 2, 349: 'the spongy South.'

104. **from ourselves:** from attention to our own affairs at the moment.

106. **my mind misgives.** See l. 49, note.

107. **consequence:** future event—not, result.—**the stars.** Cf. *Prologue*, l. 6, and note.

108. **his:** its. *His* is the usual form for the neuter genitive in Shakespeare. See i, 3, 52, note.

109. **expire the term:** cause the term to come to an end.

111. **some vile forfeit.** In Shakespeare's day, a borrower, instead of paying interest, often gave a bond to repay the loan on a certain date or, in default of payment, to forfeit to the lender a much larger sum or a much more valuable piece of property. Thus, in *The Merchant of Venice*, the 'forfeit' on Antonio's bond is a pound of flesh (i, 3, 145 ff.). Cf. Bacon, *Of Usury*, 'I remember a cruel moneyed man in the country that would say, "The devil take this usury! It keeps us from forfeiture of mortgages and bonds."'

Scene V.

The feast is over and the servants are clearing the tables and making the hall ready for dancing. At l. 18 Benvolio's party of maskers enter. They are unexpected guests, for a masquerade formed no part of Capulet's programme; but they are sure of a welcome, for such a surprise was quite in accord with the manners of the time and was taken as a complimentary attention.

2. a trencher: a wooden plate or platter, which had to be scraped to clean it. Cf. *Tempest*, ii, 2, 187.

7–10. join-stools: joint-stools; stools made of parts fitted together by a joiner (cf. i, 4, 68), 'as distinguished from those of more clumsy workmanship' (*New English Dictionary*).— **court-cubbert:** court-cupboard; sideboard. Steevens quotes Chapman, *Monsieur D'Olive*, iii, 1 (Pearson ed., I, 226): 'Here shall stand my Court Cupbord, with it [i.e., its] furniture of Plate'; and *May Day* (II, 389): 'For the feast, you haue your Court cubbords planted with flagons, cannes, cups, beakers, bowles, goblets, basens and ewers.'—**Good.** Used as a noun of friendly address. Cf. *Hamlet*, i, 1, 70: 'Good now, sit down.'— **marchpane:** a kind of sweetmeat made of almonds, sugar, etc., and moulded into various shapes to ornament the table.—**loves:** lovest. Cf. iii, 5, 111.

16. the longer liver take all. A proverb, used as an encouragement to cheerfulness and a merry life. Cf. Dekker, *2 Honest Whore* (Pearson ed., II, 115): 'If I may haue meat to my mouth, and rags to my backe, and a flock-bed to snore vpon, when I die, the longer liuer take all'; *Roxburghe Ballads*, ed. Ebsworth, IV, 241:

> I'le serve my King till I am Dead,
> The longest liver then take all.

18–42. Old Capulet greets the maskers, his unexpected guests. His senility (which is the only excuse for his brutal language to Juliet in iii, 5, 150–197) is brought out to perfection in his welcome, with its mixture of would-be humour and sentimental reminiscence, and in the brief dialogue with his cousin. Our minds are carried back to the nurse's gabble in i, 3. Capulet is a great nobleman and she is a servant; but he has no more than she of 'that which should accompany old age'—dignity of mind and speech.

19. **have a bout with you:** vie with you in dancing; dance a turn with you.

20. **my mistresses!** *My masters* and *my mistresses* were used in direct address in the sense of 'gentlemen' and 'ladies.'

21. **deny:** refuse.—**makes dainty:** seems primly reluctant. Cf. *No-body and Some-body*, ll. 325–328 (ed. Simpson, I, 290):

> When the King
> Knighted the lustie gallants of the Land
> Nobody then made daintie to be knighted.

22. **Am I come near ye now?** Have I come close to hitting you? Have I scored a point? Cf. *1 Henry IV*, i, 2, 14: 'Indeed you come near me now, Hal'; Heywood, *The Wise Woman of Hogsdon*, i, 1 (Pearson ed., V, 283):

> *Chartley.* Have I toucht you?
> *Sencer.* You have come somewhat neere me, but toucht me not.

28. **A hall!** Clear the floor! The regular cry of an usher when room was wanted for dancing or the like.

29. **knaves:** fellows. *Knave*, which originally meant 'boy' (cf. German *knabe*), was often used in addressing servants, with no thought of reproach.—**tables.** The tables were set on trestles and could be turned up against the wall when not in use.

31. **sirrah.** Capulet addresses a kinsman of his own age who happens to be standing near. *Sirrah* (a form of *sir*) was a term of very familiar address. As such it was used to intimate friends (as here) or to servants (as in i, 2, 34). Sometimes it implies contempt or impatience, and in that use it may be applied to anyone whom the speaker wishes to reprove or insult.—**this unlook'd-for sport:** the arrival of the maskers.

35. **mask:** masquerade.—**By'r Lady:** an oath 'by our Lady' (the Virgin).

37. **nuptial:** nuptials, wedding.

40. **elder.** Common as the comparative of *old*; not limited (as in modern use) to special phrases (as, 'elder brother').

42. a ward: under guardianship, and therefore less than twenty-one years old. After l. 42 the First Quarto adds: 'Good youths I faith, Oh youth's a iolly thing.'

47. It seems she. See Textual Notes.

48. Like . . . ear. Holt White cites Lyly, *Euphues* (ed. Bond, II, 89): 'Tushe a faire pearle in a Murrians [i.e., a blackamoor's] eare cannot make him white.' Steevens compares *Sonnet* 27:

> Which, like a jewel hung in ghastly night,
> Makes black night beauteous and her old face new.

50. shows: appears.—**crows.** Cf. i, 2, 91.

52. measure: the movement, or figure, in the dance. Cf. i, 4, 10.

53. rude: coarse—as contrasted with the delicate beauty of Juliet's hand.

54, 55. Cf. Broke, fol. 6 v°:

> And whilest he fixd on her his partiall perced eye,
> His former loue, for which of late he ready was to dye,
> Is nowe as quite forgotte, as it had neuer been.

58. antic face: fantastic mask.

59. fleer: mock, jeer.—**solemnity:** festival, celebration.

64. in spite. Cf. i, 1, 85, and note.

67-76. In this speech Capulet shows true dignity and a sense of honour; but he instantly flares up when Tybalt opposes his will, and scolds him like a shrew.

67. Content thee: Calm thyself. Cf Broke, fol. 6 r°:

> The Capilets distayne the presence of theyr foe:
> Yet they suppresse theyr styrred yre.

68. 'A bears him like a portly gentleman: He conducts himself like a polite and dignified gentleman. *Portly* means literally 'of good port,' i.e., 'of good carriage and deportment.' It often has the sense of 'stately,' as in Marlowe, *1 Tamburlaine*, i, 2 (ed. Dyce, I, 27): 'my queen and portly emperess.' The modern sense was not unknown, however. Witness Falstaff's suggestion of a pun in describing himself: 'A goodly portly man, i' faith, and a corpulent; of a cheerful look, a pleasing eye, and a most noble carriage' (*1 Henry IV*, ii, 4, 464–466).

73. patient: calm. Cf. iii, 3, 16.

79. goodman. The title accorded to a farmer or other respectable person below the rank of gentleman. *Goodman boy* was a term of address to a presumptuous youngster. Cf. *King Lear*, ii, 2, 48, 49: 'With you, goodman boy, an you please! . . . Come on, young master!' *Sir Clyomon and Sir Clamydes*, sc. 15, l. 57 (Bullen's Peele, II, 173): 'Go to, goodman boy; chave [i.e., I have] no zervice vor no zuch flouting Jacks as you be.' —**Go to!** Go away! A phrase of expostulation or anger, like our 'Go way!' or the colloquial 'Get out!' Cf. ii, 4, 196.

81. God shall mend my soul! A pious ejaculation, here used to express impatient displeasure (like our 'Bless my soul!'). Cf. *As You Like It*, iv, 1, 192, 193: 'By my troth, and in good earnest, and so God mend me, and by all pretty oaths that are not dangerous.' Hotspur objects to 'as God shall mend me!' as too slight an oath for a lady of rank to use (*1 Henry IV*, iii, 2, 250–259). *Mend* means 'amend.'

82. mutiny: disturbance; riot; uproar. Cf. *Prologue*, l. 3.

83. You will set cock-a-hoop! You'll carry all before you! You'll be cock of the walk! The phrase *to set cock on hoop* was used to describe swaggering or unrestrained jollity. Its origin is unknown. Cf. Gabriel Harvey, *Pierce's Supererogation*, 1593 (ed. Grosart, II, 133): 'A knaue superlatiue, that setteth cocke on hoope'; Richard Williams, *Acclamatio Patriae*, ll. 106, 107 (*Ballads from Manuscripts*, ed. Morfill, II, 43):

> This is the daye wee haue longe looked for,
>   And nowe tis come, weele sett cocke on hoope.
> Tushe! feare not, hostice! weele paye thee the score!
>   Be merrye, my wenche, doe no longer droope!

See also B. J. Whiting, *Proverbs in the Earlier English Drama*, 1938, p. 338.—**you'll be the man!** You'll take command! You'll have things your own way!

86. scathe: harm, injure.—**I know what:** I know what's what; I know what I am about.

87. contráry me: set yourself up in opposition to me. Often accented in the penult.

88. Well said, my hearts! Well done, brave boys! Cf. i, 1, 191. Capulet turns for a moment from scolding Tybalt to applaud the dancers.—**princox:** a pert, saucy youngster.

90. Cheerly. An interjection—'cheer up!' 'enjoy yourselves!'

91. Patience perforce: enforced self-control. A proverbial expression. Cf. *Richard III*, i, 1, 116: '*Richard.* Meantime, have patience. *Clarence.* I must perforce'; Heywood, *A Woman Killed with Kindness* (Pearson ed., II, 138):

> Here's patience perforce,
> He needs must trot afoot that tires his horse.

—**wilful choler:** anger that wishes to have its own way.

92. their different greeting: their struggle with each other. *Different* means 'opposed,' 'hostile.'

94. convert: change (*intransitive*).—**gall.** Cf. i, 1, 201.

96. shrine: Juliet's hand, which Romeo is holding, though he does not dance (see l. 134).—**the gentle fine.** *Fine* is Warburton's conjecture for the old reading *sin* or *sinne*. Some editors retain *sin*, but at the expense of a forced interpretation.

99. Good pilgrim. Halliwell reproduces a sketch by Inigo Jones which represents a pilgrim or palmer, and he believes that this shows Romeo's attire in the masquerade. Probably, however, Juliet's use of 'pilgrim' is a mere figure of speech, suggested by Romeo's metaphor in l. 97.—**you do wrong your hand:** i.e., by calling it 'rough' and its touch 'profane.'

100. mannerly devotion. Antithetic to *profane*. Juliet coyly suggests that Romeo is not required to kiss her hand in expiation.

101. saints. Emphatic: 'even *saints*.'

102. palmers'. A palmer was a devotee who was under a vow to wander as a pilgrim from shrine to shrine for life or for a term of years. Palmers were originally so called from carrying a palm branch as a sign that they had visited the Holy Sepulchre at Jerusalem.

107. **move:** take the initiative.

108. **effect:** fulfilment. For a gentleman to kiss his partner in an Elizabethan dance was quite in accordance with etiquette. Cf. *Tempest*, i, 2, 377.

111. **urg'd:** mentioned.

112. **by th' book:** according to rule—as if you had learned a regular system of procedure from some manual of etiquette. Cf. *As You Like It*, v, 4, 93, 94: 'We quarrel in print, by the book, as you have books for good manners.'

114. **bachelor:** young gentleman.

117. **withal:** with—as often at the end of a clause. Cf. l. 145.

119. **the chinks:** plenty of coin. *Chink* and *chinks* were both colloquial in the sense of 'money.' Cf. *Wily Beguiled*, i, 1: 'Why, he that has money has heart's ease and the world in a string. O, this rich chink, and silver coin! It is the consolation of the world'; *1 Jeronimo*, i, 3, 31 (Kyd, ed. Boas, p. 305): 'gold and chinck'; *Sir Clyomon and Sir Clamydes*, sc. 6, l. 74 (Peele, ed. Bullen, II, 131): 'Well, Shift, these chinks doeth thy heart some good.'

120. **O dear account!** O heavy reckoning!—**my life ... debt:** for I am no longer my own; my life is owed to Juliet, my hereditary foe. Cf. Broke, foll. 9, 10:

> So hath he learnd her name, and knowth she is no geast,
> Her father was a Capilet, and master of the feast.
> Thus hath hys foe in choyse to geue him lyfe or death.

122. **so I fear!** See i, 4, 49, note.—**unrest.** Cf. Broke, fol. 10 rº: 'And he reproueth loue, cheefe cause of his vnrest.'

124. **banquet:** a light supper of wine and sweetmeats.—**towards:** in preparation; coming.

125. **Is it e'en so?** Do you insist on going?

126. **honest:** honourable. Cf. ii, 5, 56, 62; iii, 2, 62.

127. **More torches:** i.e., to escort the maskers to the gate.—**Come on.** Spoken to his wife and family; the maskers and other guests are departing.

128. **sirrah.** Addressed to some relative or attendant. Cf. l. 31, and note.—**fay:** faith (old French *fei,* modern *foi*).

130 ff. Cf. Broke, foll. 10 v°, 11 r°:

What twaine are those (quoth she) which prease vnto the doore,
Whose pages in theyr hand doe beare, two torches light before.
And then as eche of them had of his houshold name,
So she him namde yet once agayne the yong and wyly dame,
And tell me who is he with vysor in his hand
That yender doth in masking weede besyde the window stand.
His name is Romeus (said she) a Montegewe,
Whose fathers pride first stird the strife which both your housholdes **rewe.**
The woord of Montagew, her ioyes did ouethrow,
And straight in steade of happi hope, dyspayre began to growe.
What hap haue I quoth she, to loue my fathers foe?
What, am I wery of my wele? what, doe I wishe my woe?
But though her grieuous paynes distraind her tender hart,
Yet with an outward shewe of ioye she cloked inward smart.
And of the courtlyke dames her leaue so courtly tooke,
That none dyd gesse the sodain change by changing of her looke.

133. **Marry:** a mere expletive—much like 'why.' See i, 1, 44, note.—**be.** The subjunctive is common in indirect discourse. Cf. *Hamlet,* i, 1, 108: 'I think it be no other but e'en so.'

137. **My grave . . . bed.** Cf. iii, 5, 141.

142. **Prodigious:** monstrous. Love, which should have the form of a beautiful boy (as Cupid is painted), has in my case taken a monstrous shape—part love, part hatred. *Prodigious* properly means 'of evil omen,' and any monstrous birth was thought to portend evil.

145, 146. **withal.** Cf. l. 117.—**Anon.** In a moment! Coming! Cf. ii, 2, 137; ii, 4, 111, 225.—**the strangers:** all the guests who are not members of the family.

Act II. Prologue.

1–14. A sonnet, like the first Prologue.

2. **gapes:** is eager—as if open-mouthed to swallow the inheritance whole. Cf. *Pericles,* ii, 1, 36–38.

3. **That fair:** that fair lady, i.e., Rosaline.—**for.** Such repetition of a preposition is common in Elizabethan English.

6. **Alike bewitched:** bewitched as she that loves him is bewitched.

7. **complain:** address his pathetic words of love.

8. **fearful:** requiring extreme caution.

14. **Temp'ring . . . sweet:** mingling the utmost delight with the extreme difficulty they experience in meeting. The suggestion is that the difficulty adds delight to the interview. *Temper* often means 'mix.'—*éxtreme.* Dissyllabic adjectives are regularly accented on the first syllable when an accented syllable follows immediately. So, for example, *profound, complete, humane, distinct, conceal'd, unkind.* See Schmidt, *Shakespeare-Lexicon,* 3d ed., II, 1413–1415.

Scene I.

---

1. **forward:** i.e., away from Capulet's house.

2. **Turn back, dull earth, and find thy centre out.** Heavy things were regarded as composed chiefly of the element of earth, and as having, therefore, a natural motion toward the centre of the globe, where they will remain motionless. By 'dull earth' Romeo means his own body, which (lacking the heart) is all earth, dull and heavy in its motion away from the *centre of attraction* toward which it is naturally drawn, i.e., Juliet, with whom its heart remains. There is involved also the idea that the heart is the centre of the body. Such is, in substance, the explanation given by J. D. Rea, *Modern Philology,* XVIII (1921), 675, 676. Cf. *Troilus and Cressida,* iv, 2, 109–111:

> The strong base and building of my love
> Is as the very centre of the earth,
> Drawing all things to it.

5. **orchard:** garden—not merely a plantation of fruit trees.

6. **conjure.** Mercutio pretends to recite a spell, as if Romeo were a spirit whom he wishes to call up.

7. **Romeo! ... lover!** In conjuring up a spirit different names were recited, with the idea that the right name would cause the spirit to appear and speak. Hence Mercutio, in parodying such magic, uses various terms as synonyms for *Romeo*. Compare Hamlet, addressing his father's ghost (i, 4. 44, 45):

> I'll call thee Hamlet,
> King, father, royal Dane. O, answer me!

—**humours:** whimsies; fantastic notions.

11. **gossip.** A *gossip* was originally a sponsor (godparent). Hence the word came to mean 'a merry old woman' or (as here) 'a friendly dame.'

13. **Adam Cupid.** So called from Adam Bell, a famous archer in a famous ballad, printed in 1536 (Child, *The English and Scottish Popular Ballads*, No. 116, III, 14). *Adam* is Upton's correction of *Abraham*, the reading of the Quartos and Folios. He cites *Much Ado*, i, 1, 260, 261: 'Shoot at me; and he that hits me, let him be clapp'd on the shoulder and call'd Adam.' Steevens adds a reference to Dekker, *Satiromastix* (ed. Hawkins, III, 169): 'He shoots at thee too, Adam Bell.' Some editors regard *Abraham* as equivalent to *abram* [1]—a form of *auburn* —and think Mercutio means to call Cupid 'auburn-haired.' In support of this theory Dyce quotes *Soliman and Perseda*, v, 3, 70 (Kyd, ed. Boas, p. 223): 'That abraham-coloured Troian'; but he finally accepted the reading 'Adam.' The old reading (*Abraham*) has been stoutly defended; and it undoubtedly makes sense—'that juvenile patriarch'—for Cupid (as Rosaline reminds us in *Love's Labour's Lost*, v, 2, 11) 'hath been five thousand years a boy.' Another possibility for *young Abraham* is 'rascally young humbug,' since *Abraham man* (or *abram man*) was a slang term for a professional cheat. But *Adam* is almost certainly what Shakespeare wrote.—**trim:** accurately.

14. **King Cophetua.** In the old ballad he fell in love with a

[1] *Coriolanus*, ii, 3, 19–21: 'Not that our heads are some brown, some black, some abram.'

wandering beggar-girl and made her his queen. The song is printed in Richard Johnson's *Crowne-Garland of Goulden Roses*, ed. 1612 (Percy Society reprint, p. 45). It begins:

> I read that once, in Affrica,
>   A prince that there did raine,
> Who had to name Cophetua,
>   As poets they did faine,
>
> . . . .
>
> As he out of his window lay,
> He saw a beggar all in grey,
>   Which did increase his paine.
>
> The blinded boy, that shootes so trim,
>   From heaven down so high,
> He drew a dart, and shot at him,
>   In place where he did lye.

Cf. *Love's Labour's Lost*, iv, 1, 65 ff.

16. **The ape is dead.** Mercutio alludes to a showman's performing ape which has been trained to 'play dead' or to pretend disobedience until his master calls him with some formula or ceremony. See Strunk, *Modern Language Notes*, XXXII (1917), 215–221.—**conjure him:** in order to raise his ghost.

22. **An if:** if.

28. **fair and honest:** decent and respectable.

31. **consorted:** associated—as 'like will to like.'—**humorous:** damp, with an allusion also to the meaning 'whimsical,' 'full of fantastic notions' such as lovers entertain.

34. **medlar:** a kind of pear.

39. **truckle-bed:** trundle-bed—one which would be trundled under the larger bedstead when not in use. Mercutio speaks as if still a child whose truckle-bed might be in his parents' room.

Scene II.

---

1. **He jests . . . wound.** Romeo has overheard Mercutio's jokes at his expense.

2. **soft!** Used as an interjection to call for silence.

4. moon. In what follows the moon is identified with the goddess Diana, the patroness of maidens. Cf. i, 1, 216.

8. green: sallow. Cf. *Macbeth*, i, 7, 37: 'to look so green and pale'; Chaucer, *Troilus*, iv, 1154, 1155:

> And thus she lith with hewes pale and grene
> That whilom fressh and fairest was to sene.

17. spheres. According to the old (Ptolemaic) astronomy, each planet was set in a hollow sphere concentric with the earth, which was the centre of the system.

23. See ... hand! Cf. Broke, fol. 15 r⁰: 'In windowe on her leaning arme, her weary hed doth rest.'

31, 32. When he bestrides, etc. Cf. *Macbeth*, i, 7, 21-23:

> And pity, like a naked new-born babe,
> Striding the blast, or heaven's cherubin, hors'd
> Upon the sightless couriers of the air.

—**lazy-pacing.** So the First Quarto (*lasie pacing*). The other Quartos and the Folios read *lazie* (or *lazy*) *puffing*. The winds in old maps are often figured as winged heads puffing out air, but such an idea does not fit the context.

39. though not a Montague: even if thou wert not a Montague—for thy name is a thing external to thyself.

46. owes: owns, possesses.

48. for that name: in return for the renunciation of thy name.

53. counsel: secrets; secret thoughts. Cf. i, 1, 154, note.

57. Had I ... word. Cf. Marlowe, *Edward II* (ed. Dyce, II, 263): 'So may his limbs be torn as is this paper!'

61. dislike, displease. Cf. *like* in *if you like*, i.e., 'if it please you.'

63. orchard: garden. See ii, 1, 5.

64, 65. Cf. Broke, fol. 14 v⁰:

> Oh Romeus (of your lyfe) to lauas [i.e., lavish] sure you are:
> That in this place, and at thys tyme to hasard it you dare.
> What if your dedly foes my kynsmen, saw you here?
> Lyke Lyons wylde, your tender partes asonder would they teare.

66. **o'erperch:** fly over. Cf. Broke, fol. 24 r°:

> Approchin nere the place from whence his hart had lyfe:
> So light he wox, he lept the wall, and there he spyde his wyfe.
> Who in the window watcht the cumming of her lorde.

68. **what:** whatever.—**can.** Emphatic.

69. **let:** obstacle—as in 'without let or hindrance.'

73. **proof:** safely protected—as by 'armour of proof.'

76. **but:** unless.

78. **prorogued:** postponed, deferred. Cf. iv, 1, 48.—**wanting of.** *Of* is often used with participles.

84. **adventure.** An allusion to *adventurers*—persons who embark on long voyages to strange lands in search of treasure or rich foreign merchandise.

88. **fain:** gladly. Cf. ii, 4, 212; iii, 2, 109.—**form:** decorum, convention.

89. **compliment:** ceremony; conventional forms of speech.

92, 93. **At lovers' perjuries . . . Jove laughs.** Cf. Ovid, *Ars Amatoria*, i, 633: 'Iuppiter ex alto periuria ridet amantum'; Tibullus, iii, 6, 49, 50: 'Periuria ridet amantum Iuppiter'; Massinger, *The Fatal Dowry*, iv, 1:

> No pain is due to lovers' perjury.
> If Jove himself laughs at it, so will I.

97. **So:** provided that.

98. **fond:** unwisely affectionate. The word usually implies folly.

99. **haviour:** behaviour.—**light:** immodest.

101. **more cunning to be strange:** more skill in assuming a distant manner of speech and behaviour.

104. **My true-love passion.** The compound *true-love* is authorized by the Second Quarto ('truloue') and the Third ('trueloue'). Many editors read 'true love's,' following the First and Fifth Quartos and the Folios, but *true-love* (with the accent on the first syllable) is very expressive and avoids the question (inherent in 'true love's') whether *true* modifies

love's or *passion.*—**passion.** Used of any strong feeling or its expression. Cf. *Twelfth Night*, i, 4, 24.

106. **Which.** The antecedent is *yielding.*—**discovered:** disclosed, revealed. Cf. iii, 1, 147.

107–115. The only suggestion for this famous passage is 'And therupon he sware an othe' (Broke, fol. 15 rᵒ).

110. **That monthly changes.** Cf. *Henry V*, v, 2, 170–173: 'A good heart, Kate, is the sun and the moon; or rather, the sun, and not the moon, for it shines bright and never changes, but keeps his course truly'; *Antony and Cleopatra*, v, 2, 240, 241:

> I am marble-constant. Now the fleeting moon
> No planet is of mine.

—**her circled orb:** the sphere in which she revolves. Cf. *Much Ado*, iv, 1, 58; *Tempest*, ii, 1, 183; *As You Like It*, iii, 2, 2–4.

113. **gracious:** charming and beauteous. Cf. *Twelfth Night*, i, 5, 280, 281:

> In dimension and the shape of nature
> A gracious person.

117. **I have no joy.** See i, 4, 49, note.—**contráct.** Regularly accented on the final syllable.

118. **rash:** hasty.—**unadvis'd:** unconsidered.

124. **that:** i.e., repose and rest.

131. **frank:** free-handed, generous. Cf. *King Lear*, iii, 4, 20: 'Your old kind father, whose frank heart gave all!'

135. **both:** both my bounty (generosity) and my love.

137. **Anon.** See i, 5, 145.

139–141. See i, 4, 49, note.—**substantial** (quadrisyllable): real—as opposed to imaginary.

143, 144. Cf. Broke, foll. 15, 16:

> But if your thought be chaste, and haue on vertue ground,
> If wedlocke be the ende and marke which your desier hath found,
> Obedience set aside, vnto my parentes dew:
> The quarell eke that long agoe betwene our housholdes grewe:
> Both me and myne I will all whole to you betake:
> And following you where so you goe, my fathers house forsake.

But if by wanton loue, and by vnlawfull sute,
You thinke in ripest yeres to plucke my maydenhods dainty frute:
You are begylde, and now your Iuliet you beseekes
To cease your sute, and suffer her to liue emong her likes.

—**If that:** if. *That* is often added to particles and relative adverbs: *if that, since that, when that,* etc.—**thy bent of love:** thy aim in loving; the purpose of thy love.

145. **that I'll procure to come to thee:** for whose coming to thee I will take care (arrange, provide).

152. **By-and-by:** immediately. Cf. iii, 1, 175; iii, 3, 76; iii, 4, 35; v, 3, 284.

157, 158. **Love . . . looks.** One of Shakespeare's many references to school days. Rolfe cites *As You Like It,* ii, 7, 145–147:

> Then the whining schoolboy, with his satchel
> And shining morning face, creeping like snail
> Unwillingly to school.

—**heavy:** gloomy. Cf. *3 Henry VI,* ii, 1, 43: 'heavy looks.'

160. **tassel-gentle:** a tercel-gentle (tiercel-gentle); a male hawk.

161. **Bondage is hoarse:** The fact that I am under my father's control makes me afraid to speak aloud.—**may:** can.

179. **wanton:** a playful child—literally, a spoiled child.

181. **gyves:** fetters.

190. **ghostly father:** spiritual father; father confessor. Cf. ii, 3, 45; ii, 6, 21; iii, 3, 49.

191. **my dear hap:** the happy fortune that has befallen me.

Scene III.

2–4. **Check'ring:** variegating.—**flecked:** marked with spots and patches of light.—**Titan:** the sun god, whose chariot traverses the heavens.

5. **advance:** lift, raise. Cf. iv, 5, 73; v, 3, 96.

7. **osier cage:** basket made of willow twigs.

9. **mother . . . tomb.** Steevens compares Lucretius, v, 259:
'Omniparens eadem rerum commune sepulcrum.'

15, 16. Cf. Broke, fol. 59 vᵒ:

> What force the stones, the plants, and metals haue to woorke,
> And diuers other thinges that in the bowels of earth do loorke,
> With care I haue sought out, with payne I did them proue.

—**mickle:** great.—**the powerful grace:** 'the efficacious virtue'
(Johnson).

17, 18. **vile:** worthless.—**to the earth:** i.e., to men.

20. **from true birth:** from the real purpose of its existence.

22. **vice sometime's by action dignified:** a quality that is in
itself a fault may, under some circumstances, result in a good
action. *Vice* means 'fault' or 'faulty trait of character': it is
not so limited in sense as modern usage would suggest. Perhaps
the Friar has in mind the paradox mentioned in *Measure for
Measure*, v, 1, 444–446:

> They say best men are moulded out of faults,
> And, for the most, become much more the better
> For being a little bad.

24. **and medicine power:** and medicinal quality has power.

25. **that part:** that quality, i.e., its odour.—**cheers each part:**
revives every part of the body, like a tonic.

26. **slays . . . heart:** by dulling the heart's action it produces
insensibility.

27. **them:** themselves.—**still:** ever, always.

28. **grace:** virtue.—**rude will:** unbridled desire.

30. **canker:** a destructive caterpillar—here used metaphori-
cally for the corruption of sin. Cf. *Hamlet*, i, 3, 39: 'The canker
galls the infants of the spring'; *Two Gentlemen*, i, 1, 45, 46:

> The most forward bud
> Is eaten by the canker ere it blow.

32. **sweet:** sweetly.

33. **a distempered head.** Cf. l. 40.

37, 38. **unbruised:** unscathed; not battered by rough experiences.—**unstuff'd brain:** not clogged with cares—what Henry V calls a 'vacant mind' (iv, 1, 286).—**golden sleep.** Cf. *1 Henry IV*, ii, 3, 44: 'thy golden sleep'; *Richard III*, iv, 1, 84: 'the golden dew of sleep'; *Titus Andronicus*, ii, 3, 26: 'a golden slumber'; *Pericles*, iii, 2, 23: 'the golden slumber of repose.'

40. **with some distemp'rature:** by some mental disturbance; some trouble in your mind.

52. **thy help and holy physic:** the curative power of thy sacred art as a physician of souls.—**lies.** Singular verbs with plural subjects are common. Here *both our remedies* is equivalent to 'the remedy for both of us.' Delius compares *All's Well*, i, 3, 169: 'both our mothers,' i.e., 'the mother of us both.'

54. **steads:** is for the good of; benefits.

55. **homely:** straightforward. Synonymous with *plain.*— **drift:** the purport of thy talk; the expression of thy meaning.

56. **shrift:** absolution. The Friar means that, unless Romeo expresses his wishes clearly, he cannot expect to receive helpful advice.

60. **all combin'd:** everything has been brought into harmonious union.

63. **pass:** walk along.

65. **Saint Francis:** the founder and patron saint of the Franciscan order, to which Friar Laurence belongs.

68. **hearts . . . eyes.** On the debate between Heart and Eye see Hanford, *Modern Language Notes*, XXVI (1911), 161–165.

72. **To season:** to preserve (as in pickle)—with a play on the word in the sense of to 'flavour.'—**that of it doth not taste:** that makes no return for the tears that the lover sheds—is quite unmoved by his distress.

73. **The sun . . . clears.** The Friar jestingly implies that Romeo's sighs for love of Rosaline have clouded the air, as with a mist. Cf. i, 1, 197; *Titus Andronicus*, iii, 1, 212–214:

> Or with our sighs we'll breathe the welkin dim
> And stain the sun with fog, as sometime clouds
> When they do hug him in their melting bosoms.

79. **sentence:** judgment; settled opinion.

80. **may fall:** may be allowed to fall without being much blamed.

86. **grace:** favour.

88. **did read . . . spell:** merely repeated stock phrases learned by heart, but had no real understanding of what love means.

90–92. **In one respect:** with reference to one particular object; for the sake of accomplishing one special purpose—namely, to reconcile the two families. Cf. Broke, fol. 17 v°:

> And part because he thinkes the stormes so lately ouerpast,
> Of both the houshouldes wrath: this mariage might apease.

Juliet has the same idea in Broke, fol. 12 v°:

> For so perchaunce this new aliance may procure
> Unto our houses such a peace as euer shall endure.

93. **I stand on sudden haste:** I insist on immediate dispatch as absolutely necessary.

94. **Wisely, and slow.** Cf. ii, 6, 15. The proverb is 'Festina lente' or 'The more haste, the worse speed,' i.e., 'prosperity,' 'success.' Cf. *Jack Jugler* (ed. Child, *Four Old Plays*, p. 17): 'When a man hath most hast he spedith worst'; John Heywood, *The Four P's* (Collier's Dodsley, I, 70): 'Spede is small, whan hast is muche'; *Locrine*, i, 2, 36, 37 (ed. Tucker Brooke, *Shakespeare Apocrypha*, p. 43): 'I thinke the more haste the worst speed'; Rowley, *A Match at Midnight* (Collier's Dodsley, VII, 300): 'More haste the worse speed.'

Scene IV.

---

2. **to-night:** last night. Cf. i, 4, 50.

4. **wench.** Merely a light word for 'girl.' Cf. iii, 3, 143.

9. **answer it:** accept it. Mercutio purposely misunderstands.

11, 12. **he will answer . . . dared:** he will meet the sender in such a way as to show how courageous he is when challenged.

16, 17. **pin.** The *pin* or *clout* of a target was the black peg in the centre that served as the bull's-eye. It was surrounded by a white circle. Cf. Mabbe, *Celestina* (ed. *Tudor Translations*, p. 45): 'Many through too much eagernesse to hit the pinne, have shot farre beside the white.'—**butt-shaft:** an arrow for shooting at a target. Cf. *Love's Labour's Lost*, i, 2, 182: 'Cupid's buttshaft.' Targets were attached to the *butts*—structures of earth. Mercutio makes light of Cupid's arrow, for a butt-shaft had no barb and was easily pulled out. With similar humour Cupid's shaft is called a *birdbolt*—a light, blunt arrow for shooting at birds. Cf. *Love's Labour's Lost*, iv, 3, 23, 24: 'Proceed, sweet Cupid. Thou hast thump'd him with thy birdbolt.'

19. **Prince of Cats.** Thibaut, Thibert, or Tybert is a name for the Cat in the cycle of tales relating to Reynard the Fox.

20–23. **compliments:** ceremonies, formalities. Mercutio describes these in what follows. They include formalities in both action and speech—affectations, as he thinks them. From all that is said, however, we gather that Tybalt is an expert fencer and a dangerous antagonist with the rapier.—**as you sing pricksong:** with careful attention to accuracy, as when one sings a tune from written or printed music—not from memory or 'by the ear.' *Prick* (i.e., *dot*) refers to the notation.—**me.** This 'ethical dative' adds nothing to the sense, but gives a light touch to the phrase. Cf. l. 67; iii, 1, 6.—**minim rest:** a 'rest' or pause corresponding to a minim (the shortest note in the old music).—**button.** In fencing he will pick out a particular button on his opponent's jacket to touch with his rapier point.

26, 27. **of the very first house:** of the highest possible rank as a fencer. The phrase 'a gentleman o' the first house' is used ironically by Fletcher (*Women Pleased*, i, 3, 8; *The Woman's Prize*, iv, 1, 7) for 'an upstart.' Possibly Mercutio is punning and suggests that Tybert poses as a graduate of the very best fencing school. Staunton quotes George Silver, *Paradoxes of Defence*, 1599: Signior Rocco, as Italian fencing-master, 'disbursed a great summe of mony for the lease of a house in

Warwicke-lane, which he called his colledge.' Mercutio imitates Tybalt's affectations of voice and language and makes fun of his fondness for technical terms. The *first and second cause* refers to grounds for taking offence and sending a challenge. Tybalt is an expert in all the fantastical rules of honour which were in the newest vogue (elaborately burlesqued by Touchstone in *As You Like It*, v, 4, 48–108). *Passado* ('a step forward' accompanied by a forward thrust), *punto reverso* ('sword-point reversed,' 'backhanded thrust'), and *hay* ('home-thrust') were Italian terms, much used in England. *Hay* is really the Italian verb *ai,* 'thou hast it!' Benvolio's question in l. 28 indicates that this term, at least, was something of a novelty. Cf. Marston, *The Scourge of Villany*, xi, 52 ff. (ed. Bullen, III, 373):

> Oh come not within distance! Martius speaks,
> Who ne'er discourseth but of fencing feats,
> Of *counter times, finctures,* sly *passatas,*
> *Stamazones,* resolute *stoccatas,*
> Of the quick change with wiping *mandritta,*
> The *carricada,* with the *embrocata.*

29. **The pox of:** a plague on; plague take.—**affecting fantasticoes:** fops who put on fantastic airs; affected speakers of fantastic lingo.

30. **new tuners of accent:** fellows who speak in strange terms and with new-fashioned inflections of voice. Mercutio shows himself well-versed in the novel terms which he derides.

31, 32. **tall:** valiant.—**grandsir:** because of Benvolio's sedateness, as of one wise beyond his years.

35. **flies.** So Hamlet calls Osric a 'waterfly' (v, 2, 84). Cf. *Troilus and Cressida*, v, 1, 38, 39: 'such waterflies—diminutives of nature.'—**pardona-mi's:** because they are always 'begging pardon' in an affected tone.

36, 37. **stand . . . form:** insist so much on the new style; make such a point of it—with a pun on *stand on* in the literal sense and on *form* in the sense of 'bench.'—**bones.** No satisfactory explanation has been found. It seems unlikely that Mercutio alludes to the huge stiff breeches that might make it uncomfortable to sit on a plane surface. Dowden accepts Theobald's emendation 'their bon's! their bon's!'—'How ridiculous they make themselves in crying out *good* and being in ecstasies with every trifle.' Cf. 'bon jour' (l. 47).

39. **Without his roe:** so sad for love that there is nothing left of *Ro-meo* but *me-O!* or *O me!* Such, in effect, is Seymour's interpretation. It seems to be correct, though Dowden rejects it as a 'grotesque notion.' 'A herring without a roe'—what Falstaff styles 'a shotten herring' (*1 Henry IV*, ii, 4, 142)—is used by Thersites as a phrase of extreme contempt in *Troilus and Cressida*, v, 1, 67, 68.

40, 41. **the numbers ... in:** the verses in which Petrarch was so fluent—in his love poems to Laura.—**to:** in comparison with.

43. **a gypsy.** Mercutio was aware that *gypsy* and *Egyptian* are synonyms. Cf. *Antony and Cleopatra*, i, 1, 10; iv, 12, 28.— **hildings:** worthless creatures; jades. Cf. iii, 5, 169.

44. **not to the purpose:** not worth mentioning.

47, 48. **to ... slop:** to accord with the loose breeches you are wearing.—**fairly:** in good style.

51. **slip:** a counterfeit coin. Reed cites Greene, *A Disputation betweene a Hee Conny-catcher and a Shee Conny-catcher*, 1592 (ed. Grosart, X, 260, 261): ·'Counterfeyt peeces of mony being brasse, and couered ouer with siluer, which the common people call slips.' Mercutio has to explain his pun to his absent-minded friend, but Romeo soon wakes up and shows that he can pun with the best of them. For a similar play on words see *Troilus and Cressida*, ii, 3, 27–29: 'If I could 'a' rememb'red a gilt counterfeit, thou wouldst not have slipp'd out of my contemplation.'—**conceive:** understand.

55. **strain courtesy:** do a little violence to politeness.

58. **to cursy:** to make a curtsy.

59. **most kindly hit it:** hit the mark in giving my words an apt interpretation that is at the same time agreeable. A shadowy pun on two senses of *kindly*—'according to nature' and 'with kind disposition.'

64. **well-flower'd.** Romeo's pumps are *pinkèd*, i.e., punched or slashed in an ornamental pattern: 'If *pink* means "flower," then I may say that my pumps are ornamented with flowers' —that is, with rosettes of ribbon. Cf. *Hamlet*, iii, 2, 288, 289: 'with two Provincial roses on my raz'd shoes.'

67. **me.** Ethical dative. See l. 21.

68, 69. **the single sole of it:** i.e., of thy pump. The jest will outwear the pump and will then remain 'solely singular'—all alone by itself without the pump for a companion (with a pun on *singular* in the sense of 'unique').

70. **O single-sol'd . . . singleness!** O poor thin jest, unique in one respect only—its feebleness! *Single* for 'weak' is common. Cf. *Macbeth*, i, 3, 140: 'my single state of man.'

71. **Come between us:** i.e., to protect me. Romeo's puns make Mercutio call for help.

72, 73. **Swits and spurs!** Use switch and spurs to urge your wits to full speed. Make an effort to beat me at punning.—**cry a match:** claim the match as mine; claim the victory.

74–78. **wild-goose chase:** a wild riding race over rough country, of which the modern *steeple chase* seems to be the descendant. Romeo's 'Swits and spurs' prompted the jest. Cf. Drayton, *The Muses Elizium*, 1630, p. 22 (Spenser Society ed., p. 30):

> Our wits shall runne the Wildgoose chase,
> Spurre vp, or I will swich thee.

—**my whole five.** Cf. i, 4, 47.—**Was I with you there for the goose?** Did I score a point on you by calling you goose?

81. **I will bite thee by the ear.** An 'odd mode of expressing pleasure, which seems to be taken from the practice of animals who, in a playful mood, bite each other's ears' (Gifford).

82. **Nay, good goose, bite not!** Spare me! Proverbial as an ironical cry for mercy when one's opponent is not really formidable. Cf. Henry Porter, *The Two Angry Women of Abington*, sc. xi (ed. Gayley, *Representative Comedies*, I, 614):

> *Coomes.* Foole, ye rogue! nay, then, fall to it.
> *Nicolas.* Good goose, bite not.

83. bitter sweeting: a kind of apple. Steevens quotes *Fair Em*, ii, 1, 120, 121 (ed. Tucker Brooke, *Shakespeare Apocrypha*, p. 293):

> What, in displeasure gone,
> And left me such a bitter sweete to gnawe vpon?

and Gower, *Confessio Amantis*, viii, 190–194 (ed. Macaulay, III, 391), where love is compared to 'the bitterswete':

> For thogh it thenke [i.e., seem to] a man ferst swete,
> He schal wel finden ate laste
> That it is sour and may noght laste.

84. sharp sauce. Sharp sauces to whet the appetite were much in favour in old times, but too sour or too bitter a sauce would sting the palate or set the teeth on edge. Our adjective *saucy* preserves the figure.

86. well serv'd . . . goose? an appropriate sauce for you, my sweet (dear) goose?

87–91. cheveril: a kind of kid which stretched easily. Mercutio means that Romeo is making many jests out of one slight word—*goose*.—**for that word:** so as to make it fit that word. —**broad:** known far and wide; notorious.

95. natural: born fool; idiot.—**lolling:** sticking out his tongue.

98. bauble: the wand carried by a professional fool or jester —'a short stick ornamented at the end with the figure of a fool's head, or sometimes with that of a doll or puppet. To this instrument there was frequently annexed an inflated skin or bladder, with which the fool belaboured those who offended him, or with whom he was inclined to make sport' (Douce, *Illustrations of Shakespeare*, 1839, pp. 508, 509, with Plates ii and iii).

101. large: indecent.

106. to occupy the argument: to discourse on the subject. *Argument* often means 'subject matter.' Cf. *Macbeth*, ii, 3, 125, 126:

> Why do we hold our tongues,
> That most may claim this argument for ours?

Hamlet, iii, 2, 149, 150: 'Belike this show imports the argument of the play.'

107. **Here's goodly gear!** This is fine business!—in ironical reference to the nonsense they have been talking. At this moment the Nurse enters, walking with all the airs of a fine lady and accompanied by her servant Peter, who carries the huge fan that was fashionable in those times. Perhaps, then, Romeo's exclamation refers to her and her attendant: 'Here's a fine piece of work!' 'Here's something worth looking at!' We may take our choice.

111. **Anon:** immediately—implying readiness to carry out an order. See i, 5, 145, note.

115. **God ye good morrow:** God give ye good morning! Mercutio replies with a correction—*good-den* ('good evening'), since noon has struck. See i, 2, 57, note.

124. **quoth 'a?** Literally 'quoth he?' i.e., 'did he say?' but used much like our *indeed* in repeating something that has just been said.

129. **for fault of a worse:** for default (or lack) of a worse. Romeo substitutes *worse* for *better* in this idiomatic phrase for the jest's sake.

131. **the worst.** Because Romeo's reply, if taken literally, would indicate that he is the worst of all possible Romeos.— **took:** understood, comprehended (i.e., by the Nurse). Cf. i, 4, 46.

134. **confidence:** private conversation. This can hardly be called a blunder of the Nurse's for *conference,* though Dame Quickly uses the word in a similar way in *Merry Wives,* i, 4, 170–172: 'I will tell your worship more . . . the next time we have confidence.' Dogberry certainly means 'conference' when he says 'I would have some confidence with you that decerns [i.e., concerns] you nearly' (*Much Ado,* iii, 5, 3, 4). Walker, who cites these two passages, suggests that Benvolio's *endite* for 'invite' is in ridicule of the Nurse's 'confidence.' This is not improbable.

135. **endite:** invite. Dame Quickly uses the word in the

same sense: 'He is indited to dinner' (*2 Henry IV*, ii, 1, 30).
Cf. *Sir Gyles Goosecappe*, sig. B r⁰: 'Ile indite your La[dyship]
to supper at my lodging one of these mornings.'

136. **So ho!** A hunter's cry on first sighting a hare or fox.
Cf. *Two Gentlemen*, iii, 1, 189.

139, 140. **a lenten pie:** a rabbit pie, sparingly used in Lent
and therefore getting stale.—**something:** somewhat, rather.—
hoar: mouldy.—**spent:** used up.

151. **lady, lady, lady.** The fag-end of a ballad on the story of
Susanna and the Elders: *The Constancy of Susanna* (*Roxburghe Ballads*, ed. Chappell, I, 190–193):

> There dwelt a man in Babylon,
>   of reputation great by fame;
> He tooke to wife a faire woman,
>   Susanna she was called by name;
> A woman faire and vertuous:
>   Lady, lady,
> Why should wee not of her learne thus
>   to liue godly?

Sir Toby quotes it in *Twelfth Night*, ii, 3, 84: 'There dwelt a
man in Babylon, lady, lady!'

153, 154. **merchant:** fellow, chap (which is short for *chapman*, 'merchant').—**ropery:** an old word for 'rascally actions'
or (as here) 'rascally *talk*.' In Fletcher's comedy *The Chances*,
Gillian, the old landlady, uses it in the same way in rebuking
Don John, who has (like Mercutio) been teasing her with loose
talk: 'You'll leave this ropery when you come to my years'
(iii, 1; ed. Dyce, VII, 262). The word is not a malapropism for
roguery; it suggests the hangman's rope: such talk as 'rope-ripe'
scoundrels use, i.e., fellows who are ripe for the gallows. For
ropery the First Quarto reads *roperipe*. Steevens cites *The
Three Ladies of London*, 1584 (Bi r⁰): 'Thou art very pleasant
and ful of thy roperipe (I would say Retorick).'

159, 160. **lustier:** more vigorous.—**Jacks:** saucy rascals.—
Scurvy. A very common term of contempt.

161. **flirt-gills:** flirting trollops. *Gill-flirt* and *Gillian-flirt* are

used in the same sense. Cf. Beaumont and Fletcher, *The Knight of the Burning Pestle*, iv, 1: 'I warrant him, he'll come to some naughty end or other; for his looks say no less. . . . You heard him take me up like a flirt-gill, and sing bawdy songs upon me'; Gabriel Harvey, *Pierces Supererogation*, 1593 (ed. Grosart, II, 229): 'Yet was she not . . . such a dissolute gillian-flurtes, as this wainscot-faced Tomboy'; Fletcher, *The Chances*, iii, 1:

> Thou took'st me up at every word I spoke,
> As I had been a maukin, a flurt-gillian.

Gillian, Gill, or *Jill* (i.e., Juliana) means 'girl' or 'wench' and often expresses contempt. Cf. Fletcher, *The Night-Walker*, ii, 3 (ed. Dyce, XI, 154): 'D'ye bring your Gillians hither?' Udall, *Roister Doister*, iii, 4, 105 (ed. Manly, II, 55): 'A strawe for yond Gill!' Middleton, *A Chaste Maid in Cheapside*, iv, 3, 39 (ed. Bullen, V, 89): 'Prithee, talk of thy gills some-where else'; *Roxburghe Ballads*, ed. Chappell, II, 134: 'Every beggerly Jacke and Gill.'—**skains-mates:** cutthroat companions. A *skain* or *skeyn* was a long Irish knife. Cf. *Soliman and Perseda*, i, 3, 21, 22 (Kyd, ed. Boas, p. 169):

> Against the light foote Irish haue I serued,
> And in my skinne bare tokens of their skenes.

The Nurse means that Mercutio should keep his 'ropery' for the loose women and desperadoes with whom, as she implies, he habitually associates: she is not used to such company! Some critics have found *skains-mates* inappropriate here, thinking 'that the Nurse could not well compare herself with characters which it is presumed would scarcely be found among females of any description' (Douce), and have devised other explanations or suggested some emendation. The objection is whimsical; for, as a matter of fact, female ruffians were not unknown. Cf. Middleton, *The Roaring Girl*, Prologue, ll. 13–19 (ed. Bullen, IV, 9, 10):

> I see Attention sets wide ope her gates
> Of hearing, and with covetous listening waits,

> To know what girl this roaring girl should be,
> For of that tribe are many. One is she
> That roars at midnight in deep tavern-bowls,
> That beats the watch, and constables controls;
> Another roars i' th' daytime, swears, stabs, gives braves;

Greene, *A Disputation Betweene a Hee Conny-catcher and a Shee Conny-catcher*, 1592 (ed. Harrison, p. 40): 'Mistresse Nan . . . hath sworne to weare a long Hamborough knife to stabbe mee.' Skains were well-known weapons in England. Thus in an account of an affray at Exeter (about 1450) between sheriff's officers (sergeants) and cathedral attendants, we read in the Mayor's complaint that the latter had not only 'long knyvis' but also 'yryssh skenes drawyn yn theire hondis to have sleyn the saide sergeantis' (*Letters and Papers of John Stillingford*, Camden Society, New Series, 1871, II, 78). Cf. Dekker's account of the English Gypsies in his *Lanthorne and Candlelight*, 1609, Chap. viii (ed. Grosart, III, 261): 'The bloudy tragedies of al these, are only acted by the Women, who carrying long kniues or Skeanes vnder their mantles, do thus play their parts.'

161. Before 'And thou' the First Quarto has the stage direction: 'She turnes to Peter her man.'

168, 169. **quarrel:** cause.—**the law.** Cf. i, 1, 44–56.

174. **lead her into a fool's paradise:** Cf. Clement Robinson, *A Handful of Pleasant Delights*, 1584 (ed. Rollins, p. 34):

> For when they see they may her win,
> They leaue then where they did begin.
> They prate and make the matter nice,
> And leaue her in fooles paradice;

Robert Tailor, *The Hog hath Lost his Pearl*, 1613, ii (Collier's Dodsley, VI, 351): 'My lord, not to hold you any longer in a fool's paradise, nor to blind you with the hopes I never intend to accomplish, know, I neither do, can, or will love you'; Marston, *The Malcontent*, v, 4 (ed. Wood, I, 213): 'Promise of matrimony by a young gallant, to bring a virgin Lady into a fooles paradise.' See Apperson, *English Proverbs*, p. 225.

179–181. **double:** with duplicity; deceitfully.—**weak:** unmanly; unworthy of a gentleman. The Nurse takes her turn at fine affectations in language.

182. **commend me to thy lady.** To *commend* is to 'hand over,' so that this phrase (which was the usual formula in sending one's respects or regards) means literally 'present me as her humble servant.' Cf. l. 223; iii, 3, 155; iii, 4, 9.

192–194. **shrift:** confession. Cf. Broke, fol. 18 v°:

> On Saterday quod he, if Iuliet come to shrift,
> She shalbe shriued and maried, how lyke you noorse this drift?

194. **Here is for thy pains.** Romeo offers the Nurse a tip, which she accepts after a polite refusal. Cf. Broke, fol. 19 v°:

> Then he .vi. crownes of gold out of his pocket drew:
> And gaue them her, a slight reward (quod he) and so adiew.

196. **Go to!** Come, come!—in protest against her refusal of the tip. The phrase means literally 'Go hence,' 'Go away'; thus it came to be used like our colloquial 'Go way!'—but with more dignity—to express indignation, expostulation, or incredulity. Cf. i, 5, 79.

200. **a tackled stair.** So in Broke, fol. 22 v°:

> Of corde I will bespeake, a ladder by that time:
> By which, this night, while other sleepe, I will your window clime.

In fol. 23 v° Broke calls it 'a corden ladder.' Cf. *Two Gentlemen*, ii, 6, 33, 34:

> This night he meaneth with a corded ladder
> To climb celestial Silvia's chamber window.

201. **topgallant:** the very summit. A *topgallant* is a mast above the topmast.

202. **convoy:** means of conveyance.

203. **quit thy pains:** reward thy efforts.

204. **mistress.** Trisyllabic. Cf. iii, 5, 152.

208. **Two may keep counsel,** etc. *May* means 'can' (its original sense); *counsel* is 'secrecy' or 'a secret.' For the proverb cf.

Gabriel Harvey, *Pierces Supererogation*, 1593 (ed. Grosart, II, 312): 'Two frendes, or bretheren may keepe counsell, when one of the two is away'; Whetstone, *1 Promos and Cassandra*, iv, 5: 'The prouerbe sayth, two may keepe counsell if that one be gone'; *Titus Andronicus*, iv, 2, 144. See Apperson, *English Proverbs*, p. 655; Tilley, *Elizabethan Proverb Lore*, No. 361.

211. **a little prating thing.** Cf. Broke, fol. 19 r°:

> A prety babe (quoth she) it was when it was yong,
> Lord how it could full pretely haue prated with it tong.

212-217. **lay knife aboard:** literally, 'to carve for himself,' 'take a slice of the roast.' Cf. Nashe, *Lenten Stuffe*, 1599 (ed. Grosart, II, 253): '*Hydra* herring will haue euery thing Sybarite dainty, where he lays knife aboord.'—**lieve:** lief, gladly.—**properer:** handsomer.—**clout:** piece of cloth.—**versal world:** universal world; universe. Cf. iii, 2, 94.—**a letter:** one and the same letter.

219. **that's the dog's name.** *R* was styled *littera canina*, 'the dog's letter,' because of its snarling sound. Warburton refers to Ben Jonson's *English Grammar*: 'R. Is the dog's letter and hurreth in the sound.' Cf. Persius, i, 109, 110: 'Sonat hic de nare canina Littera.' Todd quotes Nashe, *Summer's Last Will and Testament* (ed. McKerrow, III, 254): 'They arre and barke at night against the Moone.' Cf. *The Jests of Scoggin* (ed. Hazlitt, *Shakespeare Jest-Books*, II, 127): 'The gentleman did come, and scrape and whine at the door like a dog. Scogin arose and went to the doore, and said: arre, arre, like another dog.' The Nurse refuses to believe that Romeo's name begins in such an ugly fashion.

221. **sententious.** The Nurse's mistake for *sentences*, i.e., 'clever sayings.' Rosemary, which was supposed to strengthen the memory, stood for *remembrance* in the Elizabethan language of flowers. Cf. *Hamlet*, iv, 5, 175, 176: 'There's rosemary, that's for remembrance. Pray you, love, remember.' The Nurse, who is comically eager to repay Romeo for his liberal tip, pretends that she has heard Juliet linking the words

Romeo and *rosemary* in pretty sentimental phrases.—**of it:** about it.—**that:** so that.

225. **Anon.** See i, 5, 145, note.

Scene V.

---

6. **low'ring:** shadowy.

7. **doves.** The chariot of Venus was drawn by doves, which, as especially affectionate birds, were sacred to her. Cf. *Venus and Adonis*, 153, 1190; *Lucrece*, 58; *Midsummer Night's Dream*, i, 1, 171; *Tempest*, iv, 1, 94.

11. **hours.** Dissyllabic. Cf. iii, 1, 200; v, 3, 253. Often spelled *hower*.

12. **affections:** natural feelings.

14. **bandy:** bat to and fro (as a ball in tennis).

16. **old ... dead:** old folks, many of them, *play dead* in their movements—move as if they were trying to imitate dead men. But the line is very likely misprinted. For *many feign* the emendation *move i' faith* has been suggested by Dyce.

22. **them.** *News* was originally plural (i.e., 'new things'): cf. iii, 5, 124; v, 1, 22. In l. 35 it is singular.

25. **give me leave:** let me alone; leave me to myself. Cf. i, 3, 7.

26. **a jaunce:** a jolting; a fatiguing walk.

27. **I would ... news:** I would gladly exchange with you— my bones for your news.

36, 37. **I'll stay the circumstance:** I'll wait patiently for the details if you'll only tell me the main fact. Cf. v, 3, 181.— **satisfied:** informed.

38, 39. **you know not how to choose a man.** The Nurse speaks ironically: she is approving Juliet's choice. Cf. *Captain Thomas Stukeley* (ed. Simpson, I, 162):

> Well, Nell, well,
> You cannot choose a man, not you! by yea and nay
> I grow in good opinion of him.

Note Broke, fol. 19 v°:

> For thou mayst hold thy selfe the happiest vnder sonne:
> That in so little while, so well so worthy a knight hast wonne.
> The best yshapde is he, and hath the fayrest face,
> Of all this towne, and there is none hath halfe so good a grace,
> So gentle of his speche, and of his counsell wise:
> And still with many prayses more she heaued him to the skies.

44. **the flower of courtesy.** Cf. ii, 4, 61.

45. **Go thy ways:** literally, 'go on thy way,' 'go along'; but used merely as a vague phrase: 'well, well.'—**wench:** girl. Cf. ii, 4, 4; iii, 3, 143.

50. **as:** as if.

52. **Beshrew:** literally, 'curse,' but regularly used in a light sense. Cf. iii, 5, 223, 229.

53. **jauncing:** jolting. See l. 26. Cf. *Seneca's Ten Tragedies* (ed. *Tudor Translations*, II, 217): 'while he from wonted wayes his Jades [i.e., horses] doth jaunce.'

56. **honest:** honourable.

64. **Marry come up.** An exclamation of impatient protest. For *marry* see i, 1, 44, note.—**I trow:** I believe; sure enough!

67. **coil:** disturbance, fuss, racket.

68. **shrift:** confession.

72, 73. **wanton:** uncontrolled; easily excited.—**They'll . . . news.** The Nurse teases Juliet for blushing: 'Any sudden news always makes your cheeks scarlet in a second!'—**straight:** straightway. Cf. i, 3, 104.

74. **must:** must go.

78. **soon at night:** this very night. In Elizabethan usage *to-night* often means 'last night' (cf. i, 4, 50) and *soon at night* regularly indicates the night that is coming. Cf. *Othello*, iii, 4, 198: 'Say if I shall see you soon at night.'

80. **Honest:** trusty.

Scene VI.

1-15. See i, 4, 49, note.

3, 4. **come . . . can:** no matter what sorrow may be able to do.—**what:** whatever.—**countervail:** counterbalance.—**the exchange of joy:** the joy that I receive (in advance) in exchange for any woe that may come in the future.

9. **These . . . ends.** Cf. ii, 2, 117, 118.

12. **his:** its—the regular old neuter genitive of *it*. See i, 3, 52, note.

13. **confounds:** destroys.

14. **long love doth so:** Love must be moderate if it is to last long. Friar Laurence is thinking of the proverb: 'Hot love soon cold.' Cf. Fletcher, *The Maid in the Mill*, iii, 3 (ed. Dyce, IX, 256): 'This is hot love, that vanisheth like vapours'; *The Nut-Brown Maid* (Balliol MS., st. 21, ed. Hales and Furnivall, *Bishop Percy's Folio Manuscript*, III, 181): 'It is said of olde, Son whot, sone colde'; *Roxburghe Ballads*, ed. Ebsworth, VII, 105: 'The hottest love is soonest cold.'

15. **Too swift . . . too slow.** Cf. ii, 3, 94, and note.

16, 17. **O, so light a foot . . . flint:** She is so exalted by the joy of love that she barely touches the flinty pathway as she trips along. This interpretation fits the lines that follow and accords with the reading of the First Quarto:

> So light of foote nere hurts the troden flower:
> Of loue and ioy, see see the soueraigne power.

Contrast *2 Henry VI*, ii, 4, 8-9, 34, where Duke Humphrey says of the Duchess, who is doing penance:

> Uneath [i.e., hardly] may she endure the flinty streets
> To tread them with her tender-feeling feet;

and the Duchess herself laments: 'The ruthless flint doth cut my tender feet.' Dowden's explanation—that the Friar is thinking of 'the hardness and sharpness of the path of life'— is ingenious, but seems out of harmony with the context.

18, 19. **the gossamer . . . air:** the light thread of spider's web that floats idly, the sport of summer air.—**wanton:** sportive.

20. **vanity:** literally, 'emptiness'—hence, 'lack of substantial quality,' 'triviality.' The Friar is thinking of the transitory nature of all human joys. Compare the use of *vanity* in *Ecclesiastes*, i, 2.

21. **ghostly:** spiritual. Cf. ii, 2, 190; ii, 3, 45.—**cónfessor.** Cf. iii, 3, 49.

23. **As much:** good even also.

25. **that:** if. Often used instead of repeating a particle.

26. **blazon:** describe. To *blazon* is, specifically, to 'describe a coat of arms in accurate heraldic terms.'

29. **encounter:** meeting.

30, 31. **Conceit:** understanding; full conception or realization of anything.—**Brags . . . ornament:** When a person has a full conception of his happiness, all language is too poor to express the truth; he is satisfied to *feel* the joy and does not pride himself on adorning it with words.

32. **their worth:** what they are worth; their possessions. Steevens compares *Antony and Cleopatra*, i, 1, 15: 'There's beggary in the love that can be reckon'd.'

Act III. Scene I.

2. **The day is hot.** 'It is observed, that in Italy almost all assassinations are committed during the heat of summer' (Johnson). Reed quotes Sir Thomas Smith's *Common-welth of England*, ii, 21 (ed. 1589, p. 92): 'In the warme time the people for the most parte be more vnrulie.'—**abroad:** out; in the streets —literally, away from home. Cf. i, 1, 127; v, 3, 190.

5 ff. Mercutio amuses himself by describing the opposite of Benvolio's character.

8, 9. **by . . . cup:** as soon as his second drink has had time to affect him.—**draws him:** draws his sword.—**the drawer:** the waiter who draws and serves the wine.

12-14. **Jack:** fellow. Cf. ii, 4, 159; iv, 5, 148.—**moved to be moody:** incited to anger.—**moody to be moved:** irascible; prone to angry outbursts.

32-36. **fall out:** quarrel. Cf. i, 3, 32.—**doublet:** a kind of jacket.—**riband:** ribbon.—**apt:** ready, prompt. Used in a more active sense than is now common. Cf. l. 44.—**fee simple:** absolute ownership.—**for an hour and a quarter:** if he would insure my life for that period.

39. **By my heel.** A scornful oath. Cf. *Much Ado*, iii, 4, 50, 51: 'I scorn that with my heels'; *Merchant of Venice*, ii, 2, 9, 10: 'Do not run; scorn running with thy heels.'

41. **good den:** good evening. See i, 2, 57, note.

48. **Consort?** A troop of minstrels was called a *consort*. Mercutio chooses to take Tybalt's word in an insulting sense. Cf. iv, 5, 116, note.

50. **Here's my fiddlestick:** laying his hand on his sword. He does not draw yet. See l. 78.

52. **Zounds.** A strong oath: 'by God's wounds,' i.e., the wounds that Christ suffered on the cross. Cf. l. 104.

55. **coldly:** coolly.

58. **not ... no.** Such double negatives are common. In Old English, as in Greek, the repetition strengthens the negative.

60. **livery:** as if Tybalt by *man* had meant 'servant.'

64. **villain:** low fellow (not in the modern sense).

66, 67. **Doth ... greeting:** goes far to justify on my part the absence of the rage that such a greeting would normally excite.—**appertaining:** appropriate, fitting.

72. **devise:** imagine.

74. **tender:** hold, value.

77. **Alla stoccata.** Mercutio nicknames **Tybalt** by applying to him a technical term in fencing ('at the thrust'), as if he had called him 'this fencing expert.' Cf. *Merry Wives*, ii, 1, 233, 234: 'your passes, stoccadoes, and I know not what'; Mabbe, *Celestina* (ed. *Tudor Translations*, p. 260): 'giving them a fearefull stocada, or mortall wound'; Nashe, *The Unfortunate Traveller*, 1594 (ed. McKerrow, II, 207): 'You may straight

crie *Sic respondeo*, and giue him the stockado'; Dekker, *Jests*, 1607 (ed. Grosart, II, 304): 'sends his stoccado cleanly into your bosome.'—**carries it away**: wins the day; gets the victory. See ii, 4, 18-27, and notes.

78. **you ratcatcher.** Cf. ii, 4, 19.—**walk**: step aside a moment.

80-82. **Good King of Cats ... the eight**: Being a cat, I suppose you have nine lives. One of them I mean to take; and then, according as you treat me well or ill, I'll spare your eight other lives or thrash you until you have lost them all.—**withal**: with—as often at the end of a clause.—**as**: according as.—**dry-beat**: thrash. Cf. iv, 5, 126.

83. **pilcher**: an outer garment of leather—here used in scornful jest for 'scabbard.' Cf. *fiddlestick* for 'rapier' in l. 50.

88. **Come ... passado!** Come, sir, show your thrust that you are so fond of talking about! See ii, 4, 27.

90. **outrage.** Trisyllabic.

92. **bandying**: brawling. Cf. ii, 5, 14, note.

94. **sped**: finished, done for.

97. **villain**: fellow.

106. **fights by the book of arithmetic.** Cf. Webster, *Duchess of Malfy*, ii, 3, 27 (ed. Lucas, II, 81): 'Then he'l fight by the booke.'

112. **worms' meat**: food for worms.—**I have it.** Cf. note on 'the hay' (ii, 4, 27).

114. **ally**: kinsman, relative.

120. **temper**: my (effeminate) disposition. The figure comes from tempering or hardening a sword blade by dipping it in a mixture of oil and water. Romeo means that his valour has been softened (not hardened) by immersion, as it were, in his mood of effeminacy.

121. **brave**: noble. The word means, in Elizabethan English, 'fine,' 'splendid'; it is not confined to valour.

122. **aspir'd**: risen above.

124. **This ... depend**: The fate which governed to-day's tragedy will work out its final issue in the future. Cf. i, 4, 49, note.—**moe.** Not a form of *more*, but an independent forma-

tion from the same root.—**depend:** impend. Cf. *Troilus and Cressida*, ii, 3, 22.

128, 129. **respective lenity:** considerate mildness.—**conduct:** guide, leader.

135. **consort.** Tybalt repeats the word at which Mercutio had taken offence (ll. 47, 48).

138. **up:** up in arms; roused to keep the peace and make an arrest.

139. **amaz'd:** in a maze; dazed; in utter confusion—almost equivalent to 'paralyzed.' Cf. iii, 3, 114. *Midsummer Night's Dream*, iii, 2, 344: 'I am amaz'd, and know not what to say.'

141. **I am fortune's fool!** I am befooled by fortune; I am reduced by fortune to the condition of the fool in a household—the helpless victim of mockery and abuse. Cf. *King Lear*, iv, 6, 194, 195: 'I am even The natural fool of fortune'; *Hamlet*, i, 4, 54: 'we fools of nature.'—**stay:** linger.

144. **Up:** Come along.

147, 148. **discover:** disclose, reveal.—**manage:** course; rise and progress.

150-154. Cf. Broke, fol. 29 vº:

> The fray hath end, the Capilets do bring the brethles corce,
> Before the prince: and craue, that cruell dedly payne
> May be the guerdon of his falt, that hath their kinsman slaine.

157-180. Benvolio's account of the affray is substantially true, but he errs in representing Tybalt as attacking Mercutio. In Broke's poem Mercutio has no part in the affray in which Tybalt is killed. 'A band of Capilets' happen to meet 'a band of Montagewes.' The Capulets make the attack, led by Tybalt. Romeo hears the noise, hastens up, and tries to stop the fight. Tybalt attacks him savagely and is killed. 'The lookers on do say, the fight begonne was by Tybalt' (foll. 27-29).

159. **nice:** trivial, trifling.—**the quarrel:** the cause of the quarrel.—**urg'd:** mentioned.—**withal:** at the same time.

162. **take truce with:** come to terms with; pacify.—**spleen:** quarrelsome temper; irascibility. Cf. *1 Henry VI*, iv, 6, 13:

'Quicken'd with youthful spleen and warlike rage'; *Captain Thomas Stukeley* (ed. Simpson, *The School of Shakspere*, I, 199): 'Undaunted spirit and uncontrolled spleen.' The spleen was thought to be the bodily organ whose action gave the impulse to various sudden emotional outbursts, such as anger, nervousness, or uncontrollable laughter (the French *fou rire*).

163, 164. **he tilts . . . breast.** 'The small portion of untruth in Benvolio's narration [is] finely conceived' (Coleridge, *Shakespeare Criticism*, ed. Raysor, I, 10).—**tilts:** thrusts—as if he were a knight in full career at a tournament.

170. **Hold, friends! friends, part!** Cf. Broke, fol. 28 v°: 'Part frendes (sayd he) part frendes, helpe frendes to part the fray.'

173. **envious:** malignant; full of enmity. See i, 1, 158, note.

174. **stout:** valiant.

175. **by-and-by:** presently; in a very short time. See ii, 2, 152, note.

176. **entertain'd revenge:** yielded to the impulse for vengeance.

177. **to't they go like lightning.** Cf. Broke, fol. 29 v°: 'Euen as two thunderboltes, throwne downe out of the skye, . . . So met these two.'

182. **Affection:** partiality.

192, 193. **we.** The royal *we*, which the Prince uses in speaking officially (cf. l. 201). In the next sentence he changes to the personal *I*: 'I am personally involved in the actions of your feud.'—**exíle.** A common Elizabethan accentuation. Cf. iii, 2, 133; iii, 3, 20, 140; v, 3, 211.

194. **My blood:** since Mercutio was my kinsman.

195, 196. **amerce:** penalize.—**mine:** my blood.

198. **purchase out:** buy immunity for.

200. **hour.** Dissyllabic. Cf. ii, 5, 11; v, 3, 253.

Scene II.

1, 2. fiery-footed steeds: the horses that draw the chariot of Phœbus, the sun god. His *lodging* is below the horizon at sunset. Malone compares Marlowe, *Edward II*, iv, 3 (ed. Charlton and Waller, pp. 160, 161):

> Gallop apace, bright Phœbus, through the sky,
> And dusky night, in rusty iron car,
> Between you both shorten the time, I pray,
> That I may see that most desired day.

—**wagoner:** charioteer.

3. Phaëton. See Ovid, *Metamorphoses*, i, 746-778; ii, 1-339. Cf. *3 Henry VI*, ii, 6, 11-13:

> O Phœbus, hadst thou never given consent
> That Phaëton should check thy fiery steeds,
> Thy burning car never had scorch'd the earth!

6. runaway eyes: eyes that will not stay at home and attend to their own affairs, but are always gadding about, and thus see many things that do not concern them.—**wink:** be closed— since they cannot see in the dark. The Quartos and Folios read *runnawayes*, *run-awayes*, *run-awaies*, or *run-aways*. Many pages have been filled with conjectural emendations or with attempts to explain *runaway's* or *runaways'*. *Runaway* is Blackstone's reading, but his explanation is unsatisfactory. He takes *runaway eyes* to mean 'starlight.' If *runaways'* is accepted, the best interpretation is: 'vagabonds',' 'strollers',' i.e., the eyes of persons who wander about the city instead of staying at home and minding their own business.

10. civil: decorous, sober (in attire and demeanour).

12. learn: teach. Cf. iv, 2, 17.

14. Hood . . . cheeks. A metaphor from falconry. To *bate* is to 'flap the wings.' Dyce quotes Randle Holme, *Academy of Armory*, Book ii, chap. 11, p. 238: 'Bate . . . is when the Hawk fluttereth with her Wings either from Pearch or Fist, as it were striveing to get away.'—**unmann'd:** not yet trained to recognize the falconer and obey his voice; untamed. Cf. *Taming of the Shrew*, iv, 1, 196, 197:

> Another way I have to man my haggard [i.e., my wild hawk],
> To make her come, and know her keeper's call.

A wild or excited hawk was reduced to quiet by having a hood drawn over its head: so night is to spread its veil over Juliet's blushes.

15. **strange:** unfamiliar. Cf. *Macbeth*, i, 3, 145: 'our strange garments.'

25. **garish:** gaudy, gorgeous.

37. **weraday!** well-a-day! alas! A corruption of *wellaway* (Anglo-Saxon *wā lā wā*, 'woe lo woe').

40. **envious:** malicious. Cf. i, 1, 158, note.

45. **I:** ay—usually written *I* in Shakespeare's time.

47. **cockatrice:** the basilisk—a fabulous serpent which killed with the venomous glance of its eyes. Cf. *Twelfth Night*, iii, 4, 214, 215: 'They will kill one another by the look, like cockatrices'; *2 Henry VI*, iii, 2, 52, 53:

> Come, basilisk,
> And kill the innocent gazer with thy sight.

Sir Thomas Browne has a long chapter on this creature in his *Pseudodoxia Epidemica, Vulgar Errors*, iii, 7 (cited by Nares).

49. **those eyes:** i.e., thine eyes.

53. **God save the mark!** God avert the evil omen! Used, like the Latin *absit omen*, when something unlucky or disastrous is mentioned. The Nurse utters this proverbial phrase to avert ill fortune as she points at her own breast. 'God bless the mark!' is also common (*Merchant of Venice*, ii, 2, 25). The origin of the expressions is unknown.

56. **gore-blood:** clotted blood.—**swounded:** swooned.

57. **bankrout:** bankrupt.—**break.** This involves a pun on *break* in the sense of 'declare one's self insolvent.' Cf. *Merchant of Venice*, iii, 1, 120; *As You Like It*, ii, 1, 57.

59. **Vile earth.** Addressed to her own body.—Vile: worthless.
—**to earth resign:** give thyself up to earth; return to earth.
Cf. *Ecclesiastes*, xii, 7: 'Then shall the dust return to the earth
as it was.'

62. **honest:** honourable. Cf. i, **5,** 126, note.

67. **dreadful trumpet:** 'the last trump' (*1 Corinthians*, xv,
52). Cf. *2 Henry VI*, v, 2, 43: 'Now let the general trumpet
blow his blast.'

73. **O serpent . . . face!** Cf. *Macbeth*, i, 5, 66, 67. For other
varieties of the Virgilian 'latet anguis in herba' (*Eclogues*, iii,
93) see Apperson, *English Proverbs*, p. 583; Tilley, *Elizabethan
Proverb Lore*, No. 570; Rollins's note on Richard Edwardes,
The Paradise of Dainty Devices, p. 196.

74. **keep:** inhabit (and guard). For caves stored with treasure and guarded by a dragon (as in *Beowulf*) or some other
demonic creature see Kittredge, *Witchcraft in Old and New
England*, Chap. XII, pp. 204 ff. (and note 8, p. 517).

75. **tyrant:** ruffian. Cf. i, 1, 26.

77. **Despised . . . show:** despicable reality masked under a
divine appearance.

78. **Just:** exact.—**justly:** truly.

80. **nature.** Personified as the creative force, as very often.

87. **All . . . dissemblers.** The first *all* is prolonged with a
change of pitch and thus counts as a dissyllable; *forsworn* is a
trisyllable (as if *forsworen*).—**naught:** wicked.

88. **aqua vitæ:** *eau de vie*, brandy. The Nurse calls to Peter,
who is her special attendant.

90. **Blister'd be thy tongue.** A proverbial punishment for
slander. Cf. Greene, *Alphonsus*, iv, 2 (ed. Collins, I, 118): 'A
blister build upon that traytors tongue!' Lyly, *Sapho and
Phao*, i, 2 (ed. Fairholt, I, 161): 'Report hath not alwaies a
blister on her tongue,' i.e., 'is not always a slanderer.'

98, 99. Cf. Broke, foll. 32, 33:

> Ah cruell murthering tong, murthrer of others fame:
> How durst thou once attempt to tooch the honor of his name?
> . . . .

Whether shall he (alas) poore banishd man now flye:
What place of succor shall he seeke beneath the starry skye?
Since she pursueth him and him defames by wrong:
That in distres should be his fort, and onelie rampier strong.

—**poor my lord.** *My lord* and other vocatives, as if single words, are often preceded by an adjective. Cf. iii, 5, 200; v, 3, 124.—**smooth:** speak well of. *Smooth* also carries the meaning 'stroke soothingly'—in antithesis to *mangle*.

102-104. **Back, foolish tears . . . joy.** Cf. *Macbeth*, i, 4, 33-35:

> My plenteous joys,
> Wanton in fulness, seek to hide themselves
> In drops of sorrow.

Shakespeare's characters never tire of commenting on the paradox of weeping for joy. See *Tempest*, iii, 1, 73, 74; *All's Well*, iv, 3, 78, 79; *Winter's Tale*, v, 2, 49-51; *King John*, v, 7, 108, 109; *King Lear*, i, 4, 191-194.

109. **fain:** gladly. Cf. ii, 2, 88; ii, 4, 212.

110. **presses:** forces its way.

116. **if sour woe delights in fellowship.** The proverb 'Misery loves company' means that it is a consolation to one who is in distress to have associates in that distress. Juliet bitterly perverts the sense by personifying Woe, as if one woe delighted in the society of other woes. For the proverb cf. Chaucer, *Troilus*, i, 708, 709:

> Men seyn, 'to wreche is consolacioun
> To have another felawe in his peyne';

Marlowe, *Faustus*, sc. v, l. 42 (ed. A. W. Ward, p. 15): 'Solamen miseris socios habuisse doloris.' The Canon's Yeoman in Chaucer distorts the proverb (*Canterbury Tales*, G, 746, 747, ed. Robinson, p. 258):

> For unto shrewes [i.e., bad men] joye it is and ese
> To have hir felawes in peyne and disese.

See also Skeat, *Early English Proverbs*, p. 63; Tilley, *Elizabethan Proverb Lore*, No. 446.

117. **needly . . . griefs:** insists on having other griefs to accompany it.

120. **modern:** ordinary, commonplace.

121. **a rearward:** literally, a rear guard—a troop that closes up the rear of an army.

126. **In that word's death:** in the death involved in that word 'banished.'—**sound:** plumb the depths of (cf. i, 1, 157). But there may be a play upon words; for *sound* means also to 'utter,' to 'express.'

127. **is.** A singular verb often has two subjects, especially when the verb precedes.

129. **bring:** conduct.

133. **exíl'd.** A common accentuation. Cf. iii, 1, 192, note.

139. **wot:** know.

141. **I'll . . . cell.** Cf. Broke, fol. 35 rº: 'Straight would I hye where he doth lurke to frier Laurence cell.'

Scene III.

---

1. **fearful:** timorous. Cf. iii, 5, 3.

2. **enamour'd of thy parts:** in love with thy attractive qualities. Cf. iii, 5, 183.

4. **doom:** judgment, final decision.

7. **sour.** Cf. iii, 2, 116; v, 3, 82.

10. **vanish'd:** was breathed. The phrase suggests that words are breath and have no permanent existence. Doubtless *vanish'd* was preferred to some more obvious verb for the sake of its jingle with *banishment*. Such tricks of phrase abound in this drama.

11 ff. Broke's poem makes much of Romeo's transports of despair and of the Friar's rebuke (foll. 36 vº ff.).

16. **be patient:** be calm; show fortitude. Cf. i, 5, 73.—**the world is broad and wide:** cf. Broke, fol. 41 rº:

> Unto a valiant hart, there is no banishment,
> All countreys are his natiue soyle beneath the firmament.

17. **without:** outside of.

20. **world's exíle:** exile from this world. For the accent of *exile* cf. iii, 1, 192: iii, 2, 133. *World's* is an objective genitive.

26. **rush'd:** thrust violently.

28. **dear mercy.** *Dear* is regularly used to emphasize the meaning of the noun that follows. Cf. 'dear faith' (*Twelfth Night*, i, 4, 25); 'dear vows' (*Troilus and Cressida*, iv, 4, 39); 'dear thanks' (*Timon*, iv, 3, 192); 'your dearest speed' (*1 Henry IV*, v, 5, 36); 'my dearest foe' (*Hamlet*, i, 2, 182).

33. **validity:** value, dignity, worth. Cf. *All's Well*, v, 3, 192; *Twelfth Night*, i, 1, 12; *King Lear*, i, 1, 83.

34. **state:** rank.—**more courtship:** more of the life and condition of a courtier.

39. **Still:** ever. Cf. i, 1, 178, 188, 224.—**their own kisses:** the kisses which her lips give each other.

45. **mean:** means. Cf. v, 3, 240.

49. **ghostly cónfessor.** Cf. ii, 2, 190; ii, 3, 45; ii, 6, 21.

52. **fond:** foolish. Cf. iv, 5, 82.

55. **Adversity's sweet milk, philosophy.** Cf. Broke, fol. 39 v°:

> Vertue is alwayes thrall, to troubles and annoye,
> But wisdome in aduersitie, findes cause of quiet ioy.

56. **comfort:** sustain.

57. **Yet.** Emphatic: 'Still that fatal word?' Cf. *Macbeth*, v, 1, 35.

60. **prevails:** avails.

62. **when that:** when. See ii, 2, 143, note.

63. **dispute:** discuss.—**of thy estate:** concerning thy situation.

64. **that:** that which, what.

69. **And fall upon the ground.** Cf. Broke, fol. 36 v°:

> And as the smitten deere, in brakes is waltring found:
> So waltreth he, and with his brest doth beate the troden grounde.

70. **Taking . . . grave.** Cf. *As You Like It*, ii, 6, 2: 'Here lie I down and measure out my grave.'

73. **Mist-like.** Cf. i, 1, 140; ii, 3, 73.

76. **By-and-by:** in a moment! (addressed to the person knock-
ing).—**God's will.** An oath merely.

85, 86. **case:** condition, state.—**woful sympathy:** agreement
in sorrow; a like condition of woe.—**predicament:** situation.

90. **an O:** a lamentation.

94. **old.** This adjective merely strengthens the meaning of
the noun. So 'old swearing' for 'hard swearing' (*Merchant of
Venice*, iv, 2, 15); 'old tumbling' (Fletcher, *The Pilgrim*, iii,
7; ed. Dyce, VIII, 56); 'old turning the key' (*Macbeth*, ii, 3, 2).

98. **cónceal'd.** For the accent see ii, Prologue, 14, note.—
cancell'd: made of no effect.

103. **level:** aim or direct line of aim. Cf. *Pericles*, ii, 3, 114:
'That's the mark I know you level at.'

106. **this anatomy:** this frame of mine.

107, 108. **sack:** rifle.—**mansion:** abiding place. After 'mansion' the First Quarto has the stage direction: 'He offers to
stab himselfe, and Nurse snatches the dagger away.'

109 ff. **Art thou a man? . . . seeming both.** Cf. Broke, fol.
38 vº:

> Art thou quoth he a man? Thy shape saith, so thou art:
> Thy crying and thy weping eyes, denote a womans hart.
> For manly reason is quite from thy mynd outchased,
> And in her stead affections lewd, and fansies highly placed.
> So that, I stoode in doute this howre (at the least)
> If thou a man, or woman wert, or els a brutish beast.

113. **ill-beseeming:** befitting neither man nor woman.

114. **amaz'd.** Cf. iii, 1, 139.

115. **better temper'd:** composed of better qualities. To *temper* means literally to 'mix.'

119. **Why railest thou on thy birth, the heaven, and earth?**
Cf. Broke, foll. 37, 38:

> First, nature did he blame, the author of his lyfe,
> In which his ioyes had been so scant, and sorowes aye so ryfe:
> The tyme and place of byrth he fiersly did reproue,
> He cryed out (with open mouth) against the starres aboue:
> . . . .
> He blamed all the world.

Malone thinks that Shakespeare's Romeo 'has not here railed on his birth, &c.' But in effect he does rail on his birth in ll. 104–108; on heaven's mercy (note the Friar's comment in l. 24); and on earth—the whole world except Verona—in ll. 17, 18.

121. **lose:** abandon—i.e., by the sin of suicide.

123–125. **Which:** who.—**in all:** in all three.—**in that true use.** Friar Laurence puns on *use* in the ordinary sense and *use* in the sense of 'interest on money.' To take interest on a loan was regarded as sinful or, at best, discreditable. The usurer has abundance of money, and puts it to bad use: Romeo has abundance of manly beauty, of love, and of intellect, but he uses no one of them in a befitting way.—**bedeck:** adorn; do honour to. —**wit:** intellect.

126, 127. **is but a form of wax,** etc.: might as well be a wax figure, for it abandons that quality which makes a man a man —valour.

131. **Misshapen . . . both:** losing its proper form—i.e., changing from wisdom to madness—in its task of guiding thy shape and thy love.

132. **Like powder . . . flask.** Powder flask and lighted match were parts of a soldier's equipment in the old days of matchlock guns, before flint-locks were invented.

134. **with thine own defence:** by that which should be a defensive weapon; i.e., by thy intellect, which, in thy ignorant use of it, has become 'the unreasonable fury of a beast' (l. 111).

136. **dead.** See ll. 69, 70.

137. **There.** Emphatic: 'in that regard,' 'in that respect.'

146. **decreed:** decided.

148. **set:** posted (at the city gates).

151. **blaze:** proclaim, make public.—**your friends:** i.e., your families—the Montagues and the Capulets. *Your* is plural, referring to both Romeo and Juliet. Cf. ii, 3, 90–92.

155. **Commend me:** give my respects. See ii, 4, 182, note.

157. **apt.** Cf. iii, 1, 35, 44.

166. **here stands all your state:** the condition of your affairs is such that you must act precisely as follows.

Scene IV.

2. **move:** speak to; make a proposition to. Capulet means that there has been no opportunity to speak with Juliet on this subject since the feast (see i, 3, 80, 105).

9. **Commend me.** Cf. ii, 4, 182, note.

11. **mew'd . . . heaviness:** shut up, with grief as her only companion. The mews were the caged buildings where falcons were kept.

12. **make a desperate tender:** take the whole risk of making an offer. It is only fair to old Capulet to remember that Juliet, before she saw Romeo, had received with dutiful humility her mother's suggestion of marriage with Paris (i, 3, 97–99).

16. **son:** son-in-law. It was very common to use this term (by anticipation) before the marriage. Cf. iv, 1, 2.

18. **soft!** wait a moment! Cf. i, 1, 202; ii, 2, 2; iii, 5, 142.

20. **A Thursday:** on Thursday.

23. **keep no great ado:** have no great festivity at the wedding.

27. **half a dozen friends.** See iv, 2, 2, and note.

32. **against:** in anticipation of. Cf. iv, 1, 113; iv, 2, 46.

33. **Light . . . ho!** A call to a servant. Cf. *Hamlet*, iii, 2, 280, 281.

34, 35. **Afore me:** upon my word—a light oath. As *before God!* means 'I swear, taking God to witness,' so *afore me* or *before me* means 'I swear, taking myself to witness.' Cf. *Twelfth Night*, ii, 3, 194; *Othello*, iv, 1, 149; *Pericles*, ii, 1, 84.— **it is . . . by-and-by.** A proverbial expression. Cf. Fletcher and Middleton, *The Widow*, iii, 2, 1, 2 (ed. Bullen, V, 174):

> *Philippa.* What time of night is't?
> *Violetta.*   Time of night do you call't?
>   It is so late 'tis almost early, mistress.

—**by-and-by:** in a moment. Cf. ii, 2, 152, note. It is about twelve o'clock midnight.

Scene V.

3. **fearful:** timorous. Cf. iii, 3, 1.

7. **envious:** malicious. Cf. i, 1, 158, note.

8. **lace:** i.e., with streaks of light. Cf. *Julius Cæsar*, ii, 1, 103, 104:

> Yon grey lines
> That fret the clouds are messengers of day,

where *fret* means 'interlace.' So in Fletcher, *The Maid's Tragedy*, i, 2 (Masque):

> Those eastern streaks
> That warn us hence before the morning breaks.

9. **Night's candles.** Cf. *Merchant of Venice*, v, 1, 220: 'By these blessed candles of the night'; *Macbeth*, ii, 1, 4, 5: 'There's husbandry in heaven; Their candles are all out.'

13. **exhales.** The substance of a meteor was thought to be a gas given out (exhaled) by the sky or some heavenly body. Hence meteors were called exhalations. Cf. *1 Henry IV*, ii, 4, 351, 352: 'Do you see these meteors? Do you behold these exhalations?' v, 1, 19: 'an exhal'd meteor'; *Julius Cæsar*, ii, 1, 44: 'the exhalations, whizzing in the air.'

18. **so:** if.

19. **yon grey.** Cf. ii, 3, 1: 'the grey-ey'd morn.'

20. **the pale . . . brow:** the pale reflection of the moon's forehead.

22. **vaulty:** vaulted.

23. **care:** eager desire.

29. **division:** modulation; harmonious variation. Cf. Heywood, *A Woman Killed with Kindness* (Pearson ed., II, 148):

> Her Lute: Oh God, vpon this instrument
> Her fingers haue run quicke diuision,
> Sweeter then that which now diuides our hearts.

31. **chang'd eyes:** exchanged eyes. The eyes of the toad are

large and beautiful; those of the lark are insignificant. Hence arose the old saying that Juliet quotes.

33. **affray:** frighten. *Afraid* is the past participle of this verb.

34. **with . . . day:** by the morning song which the lark sings to summon the daylight. The *hunt's-up* was a song calling upon the sleeper to arise and join the hunters:

> The hunt is up! the hunt is up!
> And now it is almost day.

See Chappell, *Popular Music of the Olden Time*, I, 60–62; van Duyse, *Het Oude Nederlandsche Lied*, II (1905), 1300–1303; *As You Like It*, iii, 3, 101–103, note.

43. **friend.** *Friend* for 'lover' and *lover* for 'friend' were common Elizabethan meanings.

44. **day in the hour.** The next line explains Juliet's phrase.

46. **this count:** this way of reckoning time.—**much in years:** advanced in age.

54. **ill-divining.** See i, 4, 49, note.

59. **Dry:** thirsty. Grief was thought to exhaust the blood. Cf. *Pericles*, iv, 1, 23, 24: 'Do not Consume your blood with sorrowing'; Fletcher, *The Humorous Lieutenant*, iv, 4 (ed. Dyce, VI, 506): 'Oh, fear and sorrow's dry'; Marlowe and Nashe, *Dido, Queen of Carthage*, ii, 1, 3–6 (ed. Dyce, II, 378):

> Oh, my Achates, Theban Niobe,
> Who for her sons' death wept out life and breath,
> And, dry with grief, was turn'd into a stone,
> Had not such passions in her head as I!

Sir Thomas Eliot, *The Castel of Helth*, 1541, iii, 12 (sig. D ii): 'There is nothynge more ennemye to lyfe than sorowe, callyd also heuynes, for it exhausteth bothe naturall heate and moysture of the bodye, and dothe extenuate or make the body leane, dulleth the wytte, and darkeneth the spirites, letteth [i.e., hinders] the vse and iudgement of reason, and oppresseth memorye.' See Apperson, *English Proverbs*, p. 589. Every sigh was supposed to draw away a drop of blood from the heart. Cf. *Midsummer Night's Dream*, iii, 2, 97, and note.

61. **what dost thou with him?** what business have you with Romeo?

62. **renowm'd:** renowned.

67, 68. **not down:** not gone to bed.—**late ... early.** Cf. iii, 4, 34, 35.—**procures:** brings.

71. **What ... tears?** Cf. Broke, fol. 34 v°: 'Tibalt your frend is ded, what weene you by your teares To call him backe agayne?' and fol. 50 v°: 'You can not call him backe with teares, and shrikinges shrill.'

72. **An if:** if.

74. **wit:** wisdom, common sense.

75. **feeling:** heartfelt. Cf. *Winter's Tale*, iv, 2, 8, 9: 'to whose feeling sorrows I might be some allay'; *King Lear*, iv, 6, 226: 'known and feeling sorrows.'

78. **I cannot choose but ... weep:** I cannot help weeping for.

82. **Villain . . . asunder.** Let no one associate his name, however remotely, with the word 'villain.'

84. **like he:** as he does.

90. **runagate:** renegade, fugitive, runaway. Cf. *Cymbeline*, iv, 2, 62: 'I cannot find those runagates.'

91. **Shall:** who shall.

94–96. The trick in these lines consists in the ambiguity of *dead*, which Lady Capulet understands to go with *him*, but which Juliet construes with 'is my poor heart.'

98, 99. **temper:** mix, compound.—**That:** so that.

100. **sleep.** Lady Capulet understands this of the sleep of death.

101. **and cannot:** i.e., when I cannot.

103. **his body that:** the body of him who.

108. **careful:** solicitous for your welfare. See ll. 177–180. Cf. Broke, fol. 53 v°: 'her carefull louing father.'

109. **heaviness:** grief.

110. **sorted out:** picked out, selected (from among these days of mourning).—**sudden:** immediate.

111. **expects.** A common form of the second person singular. Cf. i, 5, 10; *Hamlet*, i, 4, 53.

112. **in happy time!** very opportunely!—a customary phrase to welcome a piece of good fortune.

124. **news.** A plural, as very commonly. Cf. ii, 5, 22; v, 1, 22.

130. **a conduit.** Conduits often had the human figure. Cf. Broke, fol. 42 r°: 'the conduits of his teares'; fol. 51 r°: 'conduites of the eyne.'—**still:** always.

132. **counterfeit'st:** dost imitate.

137. **Without . . . calm:** unless there is a calm soon.

139. **delivered:** reported.—**decree:** decision.

140. **she will none:** she will none of it; she won't *have* it.

141. **married to her grave.** This sounds very dreadful to our ears, but we should remember that it was a conventional phrase in Shakespeare's time and should make allowance for Juliet's mother accordingly. Cf. i, 5, 137; Sidney, *Arcadia*, i, 5, 5 (ed. 1590, fol. 20 v°): 'Shee . . . assured her mother, she would first be bedded in her graue, then wedded to Demagoras'; Fletcher, *The Night-Walker*, i, 3 (ed. Dyce, XI, 137): 'You had better marry her to her grave a great deal; There will be peace and rest'; Henry Porter, *The Two Angry Women of Abington*, 1599 (ed. Gayley, *Representative Comedies*, I, 590): 'Ile rather have her married to her grave'; William Haughton, *Englishmen for My Money*, 1616 (sig. K 2 r°): 'Would you wed your Daughter to a Graue?' *England's Helicon*, 1600, ed. Rollins, I, 102): 'With the earth would I were wed.'

142. **Soft! take me with you:** Wait a moment! let me understand you. A common idiom—literally, 'Don't go so fast that I can't keep up with you.'

145, 146. **wrought:** procured.—**worthy:** noble.

150. **choplogic:** subtle arguer; hair-splitter. The word is always used contemptuously. To *chop* is to 'exchange'; hence a *choplogic* is 'one who exchanges logic for logic,' 'one who bandies arguments or sophisms with another.'

152. **Mistress.** Trisyllabic. Cf. ii, 4, 204.—**minion:** darling—hence, ironically (as here), 'spoiled darling,' 'proud minx,' or the like. Capulet scolds so indecently that his wife (and even the Nurse) reproves him.

154. **fettle . . . joints:** get your fine self ready. To *fettle* is to 'adjust.'—**'gainst:** in preparation for.

156. **hurdle:** a rough sledge on which condemned criminals were dragged to the place of execution.

157. **green-sickness** (*adj.*): chlorotic.

158. **tallow-face!** No doubt Juliet is pale enough.

160. **patience:** calmness.

165. **itch:** i.e., to strike you.

169. **hilding:** worthless creature; jade. Cf. ii, 4, 43.

170. **to blame:** blameworthy.—**rate:** berate, scold.

172. **Smatter . . . gossips:** Keep your mumbling chatter for your old women friends. Cf. *Ballads from Manuscripts,* ed. Furnivall, I, 228:

> Thus the people smatter,
> That dayly talke and clatter.

173. **God-i-god-en!** God give you good evening! Here used merely as a taunting remark. Cf. i, 2, 57, 58; ii, 4, 116; iii, 1, 41.

174. **speak.** Prolonged in pronunciation with a change of pitch—counting therefore as a dissyllable.

177. **God's bread!** An oath by the sacred host or consecrated wafer.

177–183. Cf. Broke, fol. 55:

> I with long and earnest sute, prouided haue for thee,
> One of the gretest lordes, that woonts about this towne,
> And for his many vertues sake, a man of grete renowne;

and fol. 53 vº:

> The person of the man, the fewters of his face,
> His youthfull yeres, his fayrenes, and his port and semely grace:
> With curious woordes she payntes before her daughters eyes,
> And then with store of vertues prayse, she heaues him to the skyes.
> She vaunts his race, and gyftes, that Fortune did him geue:
> Wherby (she saith) both she and hers, in great delight shall liue.

178–182. **abroad:** away from home. Cf. i, 1, 127; iii, 1, 2; v, 3, 190.—**still:** always.—**care.** Cf. l. 108.—**demesnes:** domains, landed property.

183. **parts:** qualities. Cf. iii, 3, 2.

185, 186. Cf. Broke, fol. 55 v°:

> Thou plaiest in this case,
> The daintie foole, and stubburne gyrle, for want of skill,
> Thou dost refuse thy offred weale, and disobey my will.

—**puling:** whimpering, whining.—**mammet:** doll, baby. Cf. Dekker, *The Gentle Craft* (Pearson ed., I, 36): 'Now mammet you haue well behau'd yourself' says the Lord Mayor to his daughter, who objects to a suitor.—**in . . . tender:** when good fortune is offered her.

189. **I'll pardon you.** To *pardon* sometimes means to 'excuse one's absence' or to 'give one permission to depart.' (See *Two Gentlemen*, iii, 2, 98; *Merchant of Venice*, iv, 1, 402; *Taming of the Shrew*, Induction, ii, 121; *Hamlet*, iii, 2, 329.) In repeating Juliet's 'pardon' with ironical emphasis Capulet suggests this sense of the word, which he enforces in the next lines.

192. **advise:** think it over; consider.

194. We should remember that Capulet is raging—not making soberly literal threats.

197. **be forsworn:** break my oath.

200. **sweet my mother.** See iii, 2, 98, note.

207. **my faith in heaven:** my plighted faith (my marriage vow) is registered above.

211. **stratagems:** dreadful deeds, atrocities. Cf. *Merchant of Venice*, v, 1, 85: 'treasons, stratagems, and spoils.'

215. **all . . . nothing:** the chances are everything to nothing.

216. **to challenge you:** to claim you as his wife.

221. **dishclout:** dishcloth. Cf. Broke, fol. 64 v°:

> County Paris now she praiseth ten times more,
> By wrong, then she her selfe by right, had Romeus praysde before.

222. **green.** Clear hazel eyes with a shade of green were much admired. Cf. *Midsummer Night's Dream*, v, 1, 342.

223. **Beshrew:** curse. Lightly used, however. Cf. l. 229; ii. 5, 52; v, 2, 25.

237. **Ancient damnation!** You damned old crone! You old devil! Abstract nouns are often used to designate persons.[1] This particular noun was popular as a term of abuse. Cf. Marston, *The Malcontent*, v, 2, 190, 191 (ed. Bullen, I, 303): 'Ye ancient damnation'; Heywood, *The English Traveller* (Pearson ed., IV, 20): 'that old damnation'; Dekker and Webster, *Westward Ho*, ii, 2 (ed. Dyce, 1871, p. 220): 'thou stale damnation'; Marston, *The Malcontent*, ii, 3, 204 (ed. Bullen, I, 252): 'friendly damnation'; the same, *The Dutch Courtezan*, i, 2, 26 (II, 15): 'I rail at thee, necessary damnation?' *1 Jeronimo*, i, 3, 14, 15 (Kyd, ed. Boas, p. 304): 'How might I crosse it, my sweet mischiefe? Hunny damnation, how?'

242. **my bosom:** my confidences; my secret counsels. Cf. *Julius Cæsar*, ii, 1, 305; v, 1, 7; *King Lear*, iv, 5, 26; *Othello*, iii, 1, 58.—**twain:** separate.

ACT IV. Scene I.

---

2. **father.** Cf. iii, 4, 16.

3. **I am nothing slow to slack his haste:** I am not at all reluctant, so as to check his haste. 'His haste shall not be abated by my slowness' (Johnson).

5. **Uneven:** full of obstacles. Cf. *2 Henry IV*, ii, 3, 2: 'Give even way unto my rough affairs'; *Midsummer Night's Dream*, iii, 2, 417: 'Fallen am I in dark uneven way.'

11. **marriage.** Trisyllabic, as in v, 3, 241.

13. **minded ... alone:** dwelt upon if she is solitary.

[1]Cf. 'these woes,' i.e., 'these woful objects' (v, 3, 179); 'Bring in the admiration' i.e., 'this wonderful person' (*All's Well*, ii, 1, 91); 'Get thee to yond same sovereign cruelty' (*Twelfth Night*, ii, 4, 83); 'and you, enchantment' (*Winter's Tale*, iv, 4, 445); 'like a sickness' (*Midsummer Night's Dream*, iv, 1, 176); 'Let me embrace thine age' (*Tempest*, v, 1, 121); 'Age, thou hast lost thy labour' (*Winter's Tale*, iv, 4, 787); 'Now, blasphemy' (*Tempest*, v, 1, 218); 'Bravely, my diligence' (*Tempest*, v, 1, 241).

19. That may . . . wife. A riddling answer: 'I may perhaps be your wife when that is possible.'

21. What must be shall be. Cf. Beaumont and Fletcher, *The Scornful Lady*, iii, 1 (ed. Dyce, III, 56): 'What must be, must be'; Marmion, *The Antiquary*, iv (Collier's Dodsley, X, 67): 'Well, you are a tyrant, lead on: what must be, must be'; Teshe, *The Order of the Garter*, l. 170 (*Ballads from Manuscripts*, II, 121): 'Che sara, sara. What shalbe, shalbe.'

23. To answer that: if I should answer that question.

27. price: value.

31. bad enough. Conventional self-depreciation in declining a compliment. Cf. *As You Like It*, iii, 3, 33 (and note); *Love's Labour's Lost*, ii, 1, 13, 14.—**before their spite:** before they spitefully damaged it.

34. to my face. With an obvious pun.

38. evening mass. Simpson has shown that 'the custom of having evening mass lingered in Verona for nearly three centuries after Shakespeare's time' (*New Shakspere Society Transactions*, 1875-76, pp. 148-150).

40. entreat . . . alone: ask you to allow us to have the present moment to ourselves.

41. shield: prevent, forbid.

46. thy grief: the special cause of thy grief (for Paris has just told him of the intended marriage).

47. It . . . wits: It forces me beyond the limits of my mind; drives me to my wit's end, and beyond; my utmost wisdom cannot devise a remedy.

48. prorogue: postpone. Cf. ii, 2, 78.

54. presently: instantly. Cf. ll. 61, 95; v, 1, 21.

57. label. The seal of a deed or other document was often attached to a label (strip of parchment) which was fastened to the document and hung down below the lower edge. Malone cites *Richard II*, v, 2, 56.

59. both: both my hand and my heart.

60, 61. time: life.—**present:** immediate.

62. extremes: extreme straits; supreme difficulties. Cf. ii,

Prologue, 14; *3 Henry VI*, i, 1, 215: 'Who can be patient in such extremes?'

64. the . . . art: the authority conferred upon thee by age and experienced wisdom.

75. cop'st: dealest. To *cope* or *cope with* is to 'deal or negoti- ate or associate with' in any way. Cf. *Hamlet*, iii, 2, 59, 60; *Winter's Tale*, iv, 4, 433-435. Juliet has called the knife an 'umpire'—one who 'arbitrates' (l. 63). The Friar uses the figure of entering into negotiations with Death.

78. yonder. With a gesture. *Yonder* (the reading of the First Quarto) is much more vivid than *any* (the reading of all the other Quartos and the Folios).

79. in thievish ways: in paths infested with robbers. *Thief* was common in this stronger sense.

81. charnel house: a vault or small building attached to a church and used as a depository for such skulls and bones as came to light in digging new graves. Cf. *Macbeth*, iii, 4, 71.

83. reeky: reeking.—**chapless:** without the (lower) jaw. Cf. *Hamlet*, v, 1, 96, 213.

87. doubt: hesitation.

89. merry: cheerful. Less strong than in modern usage.

96, 97. humour: current—literally, moisture.—**native:** natu- ral.—**surcease:** shall cease; shall die away.

101. shuts up: brings to a close.—**day:** daylight.

102. supple government: the vital controlling power that makes the body supple.

105. two-and-forty. The exactness of this figure (instead of a round number like eight-and-forty) gives us confidence in the Friar's prescription. See Introduction.

107. morning. It was customary for the intending bride- groom to wake the bride on the wedding day by music under her window.

110. uncovered: with the face bare. Cf. Broke, fol. 71 r°:

An other vse there is, that who soever dyes,
Borne to their church with open face, vpon the beere he lyes
In wonted weede [i.e., clothing] attyrde, not wrapt in winding sheete.

After l. 110 all the Quartos (except the First) and all the Folios insert 'Be borne to buriall in thy kindreds graue.' See Textual Notes.

113. **against:** against the time that; in anticipation of the time that. Cf. iii, 4, 32; iv, 2, 46.

114. **letters.** Plural in the singular sense (like the Latin *litterae*).—**drift:** purpose, intention.

119. **no inconstant toy:** no whim or fancy that interferes with your firmness. Cf. Broke, fol. 60 vᵒ: 'Cast of from thee at once, the weede of wommanish dread'; and fol. 61 vᵒ: 'That no inconstant ;oy thee let [i.e., hinder], thy promesse to fulfill.'

121. **O, tell not me of fear!** O, do not speak of my being afraid!

Scene II.

---

2. **Sirrah.** See note on i, 5, 31.—**twenty . . . cooks.** Capulet's 'We'll keep no great ado' and 'some half a dozen friends' (iii, 4, 23 ff.) should not be taken literally. He was merely playing the conventional trick of self-depreciation.—**cunning:** skilful.

6, 7. **'tis . . . fingers.** An old saying. If a cook did not lick his fingers, it was a sign that he had no faith in the excellence of his own viands. Cf. Puttenham, *The Arte of English Poesie*, 1589, p. 157 (quoted by Steevens): 'A bad Cooke that cannot his owne fingers lick.' The proverb is often used (though not so here) to suggest embezzlement or sly profiting on the part of the manager of any business. Thus in Capt. Nathaniel Boteler's *Dialogues* (ed. Perrin, Navy Records Society, 1929, p. 15): 'I doubt not, but these Cooks know well enough how to lick their own fingers; and I assure myself that their fat fees make them gainers.' Cf. Greene, *A Quip for an Upstart Courtier*, 1592 (ed. Grosart, XI, 240): 'I hope there is no Taylor so precise but he can playe the cooke and licke his owne fingers: though he looke vp to Heauen, yet hee can cast large shreds of such rich stuffs into hell vnder his shop boord'; Middleton, *Women Beware Women*, i, 2, 44, 45:

> And if we lick a finger then sometimes,
> We're not to blame, your best cooks use it.

14. peevish: childish, silly. Cf. *Julius Cæsar*, v, 1, 61: 'a peevish schoolboy.'—**harlotry:** good-for-nothing. Cf. *1 Henry IV*, iii, 1, 198.—**it:** used of persons to express the familiarity either of affection or of contempt. Here it expresses affection, for old Capulet has got over his fit of senile frenzy.

15. merry: cheerful. See iv, 1, 89. Cf. Broke, fol. 62 r°: 'with pleasant face, and with vnwonted chere.'

17. learnt me: taught myself. Cf. iii, 2, 12.

26. becomed: becoming.—**might:** could.

31, 32. this reverend ... bound to him. Cf. Broke, fol. 63 r°:

> In all our common weale, scarce one is to be founde,
> But is for somme good torne vnto this holy father bounde.

33. closet: private sitting room.

38. provision: furnishings and outfit of every sort.

45, 46. up: completely.—**Against.** Cf. iii, 4, 32; iv, 1, 113.

Scene III.

1–5. Cf. Broke, fol. 65 v°:

> Dere frend (quoth she) you knowe, to morow is the day
> Of new contract, wherfore this night, my purpose is to pray,
> Vnto the heauenly myndes, that dwell aboue the skyes,
> And order all the course of thinges, as they can best deuise,
> That they so smyle vpon the doinges of to morow,
> That all my remnant of my lyfe, may be exempt from sorow:
> Wherfore I pray you leaue me here alone this night.

4, 5. state: condition.—**cross:** full of contrarieties; perverse.

8, 9. behooffull: advantageous, fitting.—**state:** ceremony, festival.—**So please you.** See i, 1, 163, note.

15. faint: causing faintness.

21. What ... at all? Cf. Broke, fol. 66 v°:

> What doe I knowe (quoth she) if that this powder shall
> Sooner or later then it should or els not woorke at all?

25. minist'red: provided.

29. tried: proved by experience.

30. I ... thought. This line is omitted in the Folios and in all the Quartos except the First.

31–59. Dekker must have been under the spell of this amazing soliloquy when he described plague-stricken London in *The Wonderfull Yeare*, 1603 (ed. Harrison, p. 38):

> What an vnmatchable torment were it for a man to be bard vp euery night in a vast silent Charnell-house? hung (to make it more hideous) with lamps dimly & slowly burning, in hollow and glimmering corners: where all the pauement should in stead of greene rushes, be strewde with blasted Rosemary: withered Hyacinthes, fatall Cipresse and Ewe, thickly mingled with heapes of dead mens bones: the bare ribbes of a father that begat him, lying there: here the Chaplesse hollow scull of a mother that bore him: round about him a thousand Coarses, some standing bolt vpright in their knotted winding sheetes: others halfe mouldred in rotten coffins, that should suddenly yawne wide open, filling his nosthrils with noysome stench, and his eyes with the sight of nothing but crawling wormes. And to keepe such a poore wretch waking, he should heare no noise but of Toads croaking, Screech-Owles howling, Mandrakes shriking: were not this an infernall prison? Would not the strongest-harted man (beset with such a ghastly horror) looke wilde? and runne madde? and die? And euen such a formidable shape did the diseased Citie appeare in.

Cf. Broke, fol. 66 v°:

> Or how shall I . . .
> Endure the lothsome stinke of such an heaped store
> Of carkases, not yet consumde and bones that long before
> Intombed were, where I my sleping place shall haue,
> Where all my auncesters do rest, my kindreds common graue.
> Shall not the fryer and my Romeus when they come,
> Fynde me (if I awake before) ystifled in the tombe?

38. The ... night: the horrible thoughts which death and night will put into my head.

39, 40. the terror ... As in a vault: the terror which the place itself will cause me, being, as I shall be, in a vault.—**As.** Equivalent to 'as being.'—**réceptàcle.** For the accentuation cf. *Titus Andronicus*, i, 1, 92: 'O sacred receptacle of my joys.'

43. **green in earth:** freshly laid in the grave.

44. **fest'ring:** decaying.

48. **mandrakes.** The plant mandragora has a root resembling the human body in shape. It was valued for medicinal properties. To uproot it, however, was thought to be dangerous, for its shriek when torn from the ground was fatal to the hearer or, at least, drove him mad. Hence, according to the usual story, it was customary to loosen the earth about the root and attach a dog to the plant for the final tug.[1] Cf. *2 Henry VI*, iii, 2, 310: 'Would curses kill as doth the mandrake's groan'; Webster, *The White Devil*, v, 6, 67, 68 (ed. Lucas, I, 186):

> Millions are now in graves, which at last day
> Like Mandrakes shall rise shreeking;

Sir Thomas Browne, *Vulgar Errors*, ii, 6 (ed. Wilkin, 1852, I, 197): 'The third [assertion] affirmeth the roots of mandrakes do make a noise, or give a shriek, upon eradication; which is indeed ridiculous, and false below confute; arising, perhaps, from a small and stridulous noise, which being firmly rooted, it maketh upon divulsion of parts.'

49. **That . . . hearing them:** hearing which. *That* and a personal pronoun, taken together, are equivalent to a relative. So *that he* often means 'who.'

50. **distraught:** distracted.

54. **rage:** frenzy.

---

[1] See the fifth-century treatise of the so-called Apuleius Platonicus, *De Medicaminibus Herbarum*, ed. Mancini, 1903, pp. 48–51 (John Goodyer's translation of the same, 1655, ed. Gunther, 1934, pp. 473, 474; *Leechdoms*, ed. Cockayne, I, 244–247); J. F. Payne, *English Medicine in the Anglo-Saxon Times*, 1904, pp. 72–76 (figures 3–6 show the dog pulling up the mandrake), and *Transactions of the Bibliographical Society*, VI, 71; J. Henry Middleton, *Illuminated Manuscripts*, 1892, p. 51, fig. 7; Sir Christopher Heydon, *A Defence of Iudiciall Astrologie*, 1603, pp. 416–418; Increase Mather, *Illustrious Providences*, 1684, Chap. viii, pp. 253, 254.

58, 59. **Stay: stop.—within the curtains.** These (also called the 'traverse') shut off the back stage. Cf. iv, 5, 95, note.

Scene IV.

1. **Hold.** An interjection meaning little more than 'here!'

2. **the pastry:** the pastry cook's room.

3. **The second cock.** The times of cockcrow were conventionally fixed as follows: first cock, midnight; second cock, 3 A.M.; third cock, an hour before day. Cf. *Macbeth*, ii, 3, 26.

4. **The curfew bell.** The same bell that rings at night gives the morning signal.

5. **bak'd meats:** pasties, meat pies. Cf. *Hamlet*, i, 2, 180, 181:

> The funeral bak'd meats
> Did coldly furnish forth the marriage tables.

—Angelica. The Nurse, not Lady Capulet.

6. **cot-quean:** a man who meddles with the household affairs that are a woman's business. An old New England name for such a person is *hen-hussy*, corresponding to the English dialect word *hen-huswife* (*Dialect Notes*, I [1896], 74; *English Dialect Dictionary*, III, 141). Dyce compares Fletcher, *Love's Cure*, ii, 2, 3 ff.: 'What should you do in the kitchen? ... Don Lucio? Don Quot-quean, Don Spinster! wear a petticoat still, and put on your smock a Monday!'

8. **watching:** lack of sleep.

11. **a mouse-hunt:** a mouse-hunter (like a cat); a night-prowler in your rakish youth.

13. **jealous hood:** one who wears jealousy all the time as if it were a hood. Cf. Greene, *Mamillia*, Part II, 1593 (ed. Grosart, II, 292): 'Be she as chaste as *Lucretia*,—yet her honor, honestie and good name shall not onely be suspended but greatly suspected: yea, in so much that the olde man himselfe to keepe his doting wits warme, will couer his head with a ielous cap, being very credulous to beleeue ech flying tale, and

suspicious euermore to iudge the woorst.' *Hood* is an independent word, not the suffix *-hood* seen in *womanhood, childhood*, etc.

20. **whoreson.** Used, without any specific meaning, for
'rogue,' 'rascal,' 'fellow.'

21. **loggerhead:** blockhead. *Logger* is a synonym for *log*.
Capulet explains the Servant's jest. Cf. *Love's Labour's Lost*,
iv, 3, 204; *1 Henry IV*, ii, 4, 4; *Taming of the Shrew*, iv, 1, 128:
'You loggerheaded and unpolish'd grooms!'; Richard Edwardes, *Damon and Pithias* (Collier's Dodsley, I, 227): 'the
logger-headed knave.'

Scene V.

1. **Fast:** fast asleep.—**warrant.** Monosyllabic (*warr'nt*).

2. **slug-abed:** lazy sleepyhead.

4. **pennyworths:** allowances (of sleep).

6. **set up his rest:** firmly resolved; determined. A figure from
the game of primero, meaning, literally, to 'make one's bet in
reliance upon the cards in one's hand.' Cf. Anthony Bacon,
1593 (Spedding, *Bacon's Letters and Life*, I, 254): 'The Earl
of Essex was here yesterday three hours, and hath ... promised
to set up, as they say, his whole rest of favour and credit for
my brother's preferment before Mr. Cooke.' See v, 3, 110.

11. **Will it not be?** Is it impossible to wake you?

12. **down:** abed.

15. **weraday.** See iii, 2, 37.

16. **aqua vitæ.** See iii, 2, 88.

18. **heavy:** sorrowful. See i, 1, 144, note.

25. **Out.** An interjection of lament. Originally the Anglo-
Saxon rallying cry; then, a call for help.

37. **deflowered:** ravished.

40. **living:** my possessions.

41. **thought long.** An old idiom for 'look forward with
impatient longing.'

45. **In lasting . . . pilgrimage:** in all his toilsome pilgrimage, long as it has lasted.

47. **solace:** take comfort.

56. **détestàble.** The regular accent in Shakespeare. Cf. v, 3, 45.

60. **Uncomfortable:** discomforting, distressful. Adjectives in *-able* often have an active sense. Cf. v, 3, 148.

61. **solemnity:** festal rites. Cf. i, 5, 59.

65. **Confusion's:** disaster's, calamity's.

72, 73. **advanc'd:** i.e., in rank—by marriage to the County Paris.—**advanc'd:** raised. Cf. ii, 3, 5; v, 3, 96.

76. **well:** in blessed condition, in heaven—common in this sense. Cf. v, 1, 17; *Macbeth*, iv, 3, 177; *Antony and Cleopatra*, ii, 5, 32, 33: 'We use To say the dead are well.'

79. **rosemary:** a symbol of remembrance. Its smell was thought to refresh the memory. Cf. *Hamlet*, iv, 5, 175, 176.

80, 81. **as the custom . . . church.** For the custom see *Hamlet*, v, 1, 255–257, and note.

82, 83. **though . . . merriment:** though human nature, which is weak in judgment, prompts us all to lament, yet reason bids us rejoice—for 'to die is gain' (*Philippians*, i, 21).

84–90. Cf. Broke, fol. 70 vᵒ:

> Now is the parents myrth quite chaunged into mone,
> And now to sorow is retornde the ioye of euery one.
> And now the weding weedes for mourning weedes they chaunge,
> And Hymene into a Dyrge, alas it seemeth straunge.
> In steade of mariage gloues, now funerall gloues they haue,
> And whom they should see maried, they follow to the graue.

—**ordainèd festival:** arranged for festal purposes. *Festival* is an adjective.—**cheer:** viands.—**sullen:** deep-voiced and dismal.

94. **for some ill:** because of some sin that you have committed.

95. Before the Musicians speak the First Quarto has the stage direction: 'They all but the Nurse goe foorth, casting Rosemary on her and shutting the Curtens.' Cf. iv, 3, 59, note.

96–149. This long passage of low comedy has shocked some critics, and scenes iv and v were omitted by Goethe in his arrangement of Romeo and Juliet for the Weimar theatre in 1811. There is no occasion, however, for regarding it as un-Shakespearean. Something was needed to allow for an interval of time between Act iv and Act v, and whatever was used for that purpose was required not to advance the action. A comic interlude was the conventional thing for such a purpose. Compare the Porter's speech in *Macbeth*, ii, 3. High comedy would not serve, for the Elizabethan audience felt the need of utter relaxation from tragic stress and strain.

99–101. **case.** The Nurse means 'situation,' 'state of things'; but the Musician thinks she is referring to the shabby case in which he keeps his instrument.—**amended:** repaired.

101. For *Enter Peter* the Second and Third Quartos have *Enter Will Kemp*. Kempe was a famous comic actor and one of Shakespeare's partners. We know from speech headings in *Much Ado*, iv, 2 (First Folio) that he played Dogberry.

102. **Heart's ease.** The old play *Misogonus* (cited by Collier) contains 'a songe to the tune of hartes ease' (ii, 2, 69 ff.; ed. Brandl, pp. 439, 440). See E. W. Naylor, *Shakespeare and Music*, 1896, p. 193.

106, 107. **My heart is full of woe.** Steevens identified the anonymous song which Peter mentions. The first stanza runs as follows (*Shakespeare Society Papers*, I, 13):

> Complaine, my lute, complaine on him,
>   That stayes so long away;
> He promis'd to be here ere this,
>   But still unkind doth stay.
> But now the proverbe true I finde,
> Once out of sight then out of minde.
> Hey, hoe! my heart is full of woe!

109. **merry dump.** A *dump* sometimes means 'a dance tune'; but a dump was a slow dance, or a dismal tune. Cf. *Two Gentlemen*, iii, 2, 83–86:

> Visit by night your lady's chamber window
> With some sweet consort. To their instruments
> Tune a deploring dump. The night's dead silence
> Will well become such sweet-complaining grievance.

When the word designates a poem, the implication is mournful. Nothing could be gloomier, for instance, than 'The Sheepheard's Dumpe' (*England's Helicon*, 1600, ed. Rollins, I, 101), which begins:

> Like desart Woods, with darksome shades obscured,
> Where dreadfull beasts, where hatefull horror raigneth,
> Such is my wounded hart, whom sorrow paineth.

Peter's request, then, is paradoxical.

115. **the gleek:** the scornful speech; the jibe. Cf. *1 Henry VI*, iii, 2, 123: 'Now where's the Bastard's braves and Charles his glikes?' *Henry V*, v, 1, 78, 79: 'gleeking and galling at this gentleman.'

115, 116. **give you the minstrel:** call you 'minstrel'—a contemptuous term—instead of 'musician.' Many minstrels were vagabonds. Cf. iii, 1, 48.

117. **serving-creature:** a contemptuous term for 'servant.' Cf. *Arden of Feversham*, iv, 1, 67 (ed. Tucker Brooke, *Shakespeare Apocrypha*, p. 23): 'a seruing creature like your selfe.'

120–122. **carry no crotchets:** put up with none of your notions. Peter puns on two senses of *crotchet*: (1) 'a quarter note in music'; (2) 'a whim,' 'caprice,' 'notion.'—**re ... fa.** Peter uses these names of musical notes as verbs in a grotesque threat.—**note me:** observe and understand what I say.—**you note us:** you make musical notes of us. *Us* is emphatic.

123. **put out:** show, display,—not, extinguish. The Musician has no objection to a combat of wits.

124, 125. **have at you.** A challenging phrase, giving notice of an attack. Cf. i, 1, 79; v, 3, 70.—**dry-beat:** beat thoroughly, thrash. Cf. iii, 1, 82. The word means literally 'to beat without drawing blood,' as with the flat of one's sword or with a cudgel. Cf. Howell, *Lexicon Tetraglotton*, 1660, Section xliv: 'To dry baste with the flat: . . . Donner des coups de plat d'espée'; Mabbe, *Celestina* (ed. *Tudor Translations*, p. 260): 'dry beatings, without drawing of bloud'; Greene, *Mamillia*, Part II, 1593 (ed. Grosart, II, 150): 'These dry blowes could

draw no bloud.'—**iron wit.** Peter seems to mean 'a wit as
strong as iron'; but the phrase conveys to the hearer a suggestion of heaviness of mind; and this suggestion is intensified by
dry-beat, for *dry* often means 'stupid.' Cf. *As You Like It*, ii, 7,
38–40:

> In his brain,
> Which is as dry as the remainder biscuit
> After a voyage.

—**put up:** sheathe.

128. **When griping grief,** etc. A poem entitled 'In commendation of Musick,' by Richard Edwardes (*The Paradyse of
Daynty Deuises,* 1576, ed. Rollins, p. 63; cf. the editor's note,
pp. 227, 228), begins:

Where gripyng grief the hart would wound & dolfull domps the mind[1]
  oppresse
Then Musick with her siluer sound, is wont with spede to giue redresse,
Of troubled minde for euery sore, swete Musick hath a salue therfore.

129. **dumps:** griefs, sorrows. Cf. *Taming of the Shrew*, ii, 1,
286: 'Why, how now, daughter Katherine? in your dumps?'
Titus Andronicus, i, 1, 391: 'these dreary dumps.'

132. **Catling:** 'a small lute-string made of *catgut*' (Steevens).

135. **Rebeck:** a kind of stringed instrument.

139. **Soundpost:** 'a small peg of wood fixed beneath the
bridge of a violin or similar instrument' (*New English Dictionary*).

141. **I cry you mercy!** I beg your pardon! i.e., for calling
upon you to *say,* when your business is to *sing.*

147. **pestilent:** plaguy—a common term of abuse.

148. **Jack.** Cf. ii, 4, 159; iii, 1, 12.

149. **stay dinner:** wait until we have had our dinner.

[1]The first edition (1576) has 'thē' (i.e., 'them') for 'the mind.' Corrected in the edition of 1578.

Act V. Scene I.

1–9. Skeat (Chaucer, II, 500) compares the passage in which Troilus has a like fallacious forecast of good fortune: *Troilus,* v, 1164–1169:

> It is naught al for nought
> That in myn herte I now rejoysse thus.
> It is ayeyns som good I have a thought.
> Not I nat how, but, syn that I was wrought,
> Ne felte I swich a comfort, dar I seye.
> She comth to-nyght, my lif that dorst I leye!

1. trust . . . sleep: put trust in the favourable reports of sleep *as being true.* But Romeo knows that dreams are said to 'go by contraries.' Cf. *Julius Cæsar,* iii, 3, 1, 2, and note.

8. breath'd . . . lips. Malone cites Marlowe, *Hero and Leander,* ii, 3 ('He kiss'd her and breath'd life into her lips') and reminds us that Shakespeare quotes a line from this poem in *As You Like It,* iii, 5, 81, 82:

> Dead shepherd, now I find thy saw of might,
> 'Who ever lov'd that lov'd not at first sight?'

17. well: in bliss, in heaven. See iv, 5, 76, and note. Cf. *Macbeth,* iv, 3, 177–179, for this ambiguous use of *well* in breaking bad news.

21. took post: hired posthorses (for swift travel).

22. these ill news. Cf. ii, 5, 22; iii, 5, 124.

23. office: duty.

24. stars. Cf. Prologue, l. 6; i, 4, 107.

27. have patience: be calm; show fortitude. Cf. i, 5, 73, 91; iii, 3, 16; v, 3, 221, 261. *Patience* is a trisyllable.

28, 29. do import Some misadventure: signify some mischance that is to happen. The Servant expresses, in guarded terms, his fear that Romeo may commit suicide.—**deceiv'd:** mistaken.

38. 'a: he.

39. **weeds:** clothes.—**overwhelming brows:** eyebrows jutting out over his sunken eyes.

40. **Culling of simples:** sorting out medicinal herbs—called *simples* because used in *compounding* medicines.

41–48. Cf. Broke, fol. 72 r°:

> An Apothecary sate vnbusied at his doore,
> Whom by his heauy countenaunce he gessed to be poore,
> And in his shop he saw his boxes were but fewe,
> And in his window (of his wares) there was so small a shew.

42–44. **tortoise . . . alligator . . . fishes.** Such curiosities were regularly displayed in apothecaries' shops. Steevens assures us that he had 'met with the alligator, tortoise, &c., hanging up in the shop of an ancient apothecary at Limehouse, as well as in places more remote' from London. He refers to Plate iii in Hogarth's *Marriage à la Mode*. Malone cites Nashe, *Have with You to Saffron-Walden*, 1596 (ed. Grosart, III, 97, 98): 'The next rat he seazd on hee made an Anatomie of, . . . and after hanged her ouer his head in his studie, in stead of an Apothecaries Crocodile, or dride Alligatur.'

45. **account:** reckoning, amount, number.

47. **packthread:** twine for packs (parcels).

51. **present:** instant.

52. **caitiff:** miserable. Cf. French *chétif*, from Latin *captivus*. The word was used in a general sense to express pity, contempt, or resentment.

59. **forty ducats.** A gold ducat is usually estimated as worth about ten shillings; but the purchasing power of money is so different from what it was in old times that such figures are not very illuminating.

60. **dram:** draught, drink.—**soon-speeding gear:** quickly efficacious stuff. Cf. Broke, fol. 72 v°: 'Fayre syr (quoth he) be sure, this is the speeding gere.'

62. **That:** so that.

67. **any he.** Cf. 'I am that he, that unfortunate he' (*As You Like It*, iii, 2, 414, 415); 'the proudest he That stops my way in Padua' (*Taming of the Shrew*, iii, 2, 236, 237); 'The fair,

the chaste, and unexpressive she' (*As You Like It*, iii, 2, 10);
'You are the cruell'st she alive' (*Twelfth Night*, i, 5, 259).—
utters: dispenses, sells.

68. **bare:** poverty-stricken.

70. **Need . . . eyes.** This powerful line has not escaped
prosaic criticism. Otway, reproducing it in his *Caius Marius*,
substituted *stareth* for *starveth*, and Rowe accepted the emendation. But the meaning is plain enough: 'Your eyes betray
your abject poverty; they show that you are starved and down-
trodden.'

77-79. **Put this . . . straight.** Steevens compares Chaucer,
Pardoner's Tale, C, 859 ff. (ed. Robinson, p. 186):

> The pothecarie answerde, 'And thou shalt have
> A thyng that, also God my soule save,
> In al this world ther is no creature,
> That eten or dronken hath of this confiture
> Noght but the montance of a corn of whete,
> That he ne shal his lif anon forlete;
> Ye, sterve he shal, and that is lesse while
> Than thou wolt goon a paas nat but a mile,
> This poysoun is so strong and violent.'

85. **cordial:** a restorative—literally, a stimulant for the heart.

Scene II.

5-12. Cf. Broke, fol. 70 rº:

> And for because in Italy it is a wonted gyse,
> That fryers in the towne should seeldome walke alone,
> But of theyr couent ay should be accompanide with one:
> Of his profession, straight a house he findeth out,
> In minde to take some frier with him, to walke the towne about.
> But entred once, he might not issue out againe,
> For that a brother of the house, a day before or twayne,
> Dyed of the plage (a sikenes which they greatly feare and hate)
> So were the brethren charged to kepe within there couen gate
> Bard of their felowship, that in the towne do woone,
> The towne folke eke commaunded are, the friers howse to shoone:
> Till thei that had the care of helth, their freedome should renew.

6. **to associate me:** to be my companion. The rule of the order forbade him to travel without another friar in his company.

8. **searchers:** officers whose duty was to investigate cases of the plague.

9. **a house:** a monastery or friary.

10. **pestilence:** the plague.

11. **Seal'd up the doors.** This was the regular procedure in London.

17. **brotherhood:** i.e., my position as friar.

18. **nice:** trivial; of slight consequence.—**charge:** weighty matters.

19. **of dear import:** of vast importance.—**the neglecting it:** the omission to deliver it.

21. **crow:** short crowbar.

24. **Within this three hours.** Cf. iv, 1, 105; v, 3, 176.

25. **beshrew:** reprove—literally, curse. See ii, 5, 52; iii, 5, 223, 229.

26. **accidents:** happenings.

Scene III.

3. **all along:** at full length.

14. **sweet water:** perfumed water.

20. **cross:** thwart; interfere with.

22. **mattock:** a kind of pickaxe.

32. **dear:** momentous.

33-36. **But if . . . limbs.** Cf. Broke, fol. 73 v°:

> Se that thou get thee hence, and on the payne of death,
> I charge thee that thou comme not nere, while I abyde beneath.

—**jealous:** suspicious.

41. **Take thou that.** Giving him a purse of gold.

44. **doubt:** suspect.

45. **détestàble.** Cf. iv, 5, 56.—**maw:** gullet.—**womb:** belly.

48. in despite: to spite thee—by making thee eat when thou art already gorged with food.—*opens the tomb.* How this was managed on Shakespeare's stage must remain uncertain. Perhaps there was some structure on the backstage; perhaps the actor opened a trapdoor in the main stage.

52, 53. to do . . . bodies. This seems to have been suggested to Shakespeare by the suspicion of the Watch in Broke, fol. 78 v⁰:

> They did suppose, inchaunters to be comme,
> That with prepared instrumentes had opened wide the tombe,
> In purpose to abuse the bodies of the ded,
> Which by theyr science ayde abusde do stand them oft in sted.

Cf. *Macbeth*, i, 3, 28, 29; iv, 1, 26–31.—**apprehend:** arrest.

63. fury: insane rage, frenzy.

68. defy: reject, repudiate.—**thy conjuration:** thy adjuration; thy solemn bidding.

70. provoke: challenge.—**have at thee.** Cf. i, 1, 79; iv, 5, 124.

76. betossed: agitated, distracted.

78. should have: was to have.

82. sour. Cf. iii, 2, 116; iii, 3, 7.

83. triumphant: magnificent.

84. a lanthorn: a lantern; 'a spacious . . . turret full of windows' (Steevens).

86. presence: presence chamber; room of state (where a king appears on state occasions).

84–86. Cf. *Titus Andronicus* ii, 3, 226–230:

> Upon his bloody finger he doth wear
> A precious ring that lightens all this hole,
> Which, like a taper in some monument,
> Doth shine upon the dead man's earthly cheeks
> And shows the ragged entrails of the pit.

87. Death. See iii, 5, 237, note.

88–91. How oft . . . merry! A frequent observation, which may be left to the psychologists to explain. One who is unusually cheerful is often said by the Scots to be *fey,* i.e., doomed to speedy death. Cf. *Julius Cæsar*, iii, 3, 1, 2, and note.—**their keepers:** their jailers. Romeo is thinking of condemned prisoners.—**a lightning before death.** An idiomatic phrase for the phenomenon mentioned. Steevens cites Munday and Chettle, *The Death of Robert Earl of Huntington*, ii, 2 (Collier's Dodsley, XIII, 47):

> I thought it was a lightening before death,
> Too sudden to be certain.

See Apperson, *English Proverbs*, p. 365.—**O, how . . . lightning?** For he is not merry, but overwhelmed with desperate grief.

96. **advanced:** raised. Cf. ii, 3, 5; iv, 5, 73.

98-100. **what more favour . . . enemy?** Cf. Broke, fol. 75 r°:

> What more amendes, or cruell wreke desirest thou?
> To see on me, then this which here is shewd forth to the nowe:
> Who reft by force of armes from thee thy liuing breath,
> The same with his owne hand thow seest, doth poyson him selfe
>   to death.
> And for he caused thee in tombe too soone to lye,
> Too soone also yonger then thow himselfe he layeth by.

99. **cut . . . twain:** cut the thread of thy life in thy early years.

106. **still:** ever, always.

110. **set . . . rest:** take up my abode forever. To *set up one's rest* means regularly to 'make a firm resolution.' Cf. iv, 5, 6; *Merchant of Venice*, ii, 2, 110: 'I have set up my rest to run away.' Romeo plays with the phrase. Cf. Nashe, *Have with You to Saffron Walden*, 1596 (ed. Grosart, III, 149): 'No roofe had he to hide his noddle in, or whither he might go to set vp his rest.'

111. **stars.** Cf. *Prologue*, l. 6; i, 4, 107; v, 1, 24.

115. **A dateless bargain to engrossing death:** a sale (of myself) for ever to all-devouring death. To *engross* means literally to 'purchase in large quantities—*in gross.*'

116. **conduct:** guide. He speaks to Death.

117. **pilot.** He speaks to himself. In desperation, he is taking his instructions for pilotage from Death.

121. **Saint Francis:** his patron saint.—**be my speed:** prosper me.

122. **stumbled at graves!** To stumble was regarded as a bad omen—especially, to stumble at the threshold and, worst of all, to stumble at a grave mound. Cf. *3 Henry VI*, iv, 7, 11, 12:

> For many men that stumble at the threshold
> Are well foretold that danger lurks within;

Richard III, iii, 4, 83–85:

> Three times to-day my footcloth horse did stumble,
> And startled when he look'd upon the Tower,
> As loath to bear me to the slaughterhouse.

See Grose's *Popular Antiquities*, ed. Hazlitt, III, 221, 222.

124. **good my friend.** This order (instead of *my good friend*) is common, especially in *good my lord*. The phrase *my friend* is treated as a compound substantive. Cf. iii, 2, 98; iii, 5, 200.

125. **vainly:** uselessly; to no purpose.

136. **unthrifty:** unfortunate.

145, 146. **Ah, what an unkind hour . . . chance!** The doctrine is essentially fatalistic, as if every hour were predestined to good or evil fortune; but here the *hour* is personified, as if it acted with intentional unkindness.—**únkind.** For the accent see the note on ii, Prologue, 14.

148. **comfortable:** helpful. Juliet awakes, as Friar Laurence has told her she would, 'as from a pleasant sleep' (iv, 1, 106), and her first words are a blessing on the Friar, whose presence she of course does not suspect. Adjectives in *-able* often have an active sense: as, *disputable* (inclined to discuss); *medicinable* (medicinal); *capable* (capacious).

149. **should be:** was to be (according to the Friar's plan).

156, 157. **I'll dispose . . . nuns.** Cf. Broke, fol. 76 r°:

> And sayth that he will soone prouyde
> In somme religious house for her a quiet place,
> Where she may spend the rest of lyfe.

159. **I dare no longer stay.** Cf. Broke, fol. 77 v°:

> The fryer and the seruant fled and left her there alone.
> For they a sodayne noyse, fast by the place did heare,
> And lest they might be taken there, greatly the[y] stoode in feare.

162. **timeless:** untimely.

163. **churl:** niggard.

164. **To help me after:** to help me to follow thee in death.

165. **Haply:** perchance.

166. **with:** by means of.—**a restorative.** For such his kiss would be under other conditions.

169. **happy:** opportune; fortunately discovered.

170. **rest.** So the First Quarto. The other Quartos and the Folios read 'rust,' which is eloquently defended by Grant White: 'She sees her dead Romeo's dagger, which would otherwise rust in its sheath, rusting in her heart.'

173. **attach:** arrest.

176. **two days buried.** This fits the 'two-and-forty hours' (iv, 1, 105).

179. **these woes:** these woful objects. Cf. iii, 5, 237, note.

180. **ground.** This is an admirable example of the Elizabethan habit of punning, even in the most serious discourse.

181. **circumstance:** details; detailed information. Cf. ii, 5, 36.

189. **our.** The royal *we*. Cf. i, 1, 109.

190. **shriek abroad:** run about the streets shrieking. See i, 1, 127; iii, 1, 2; iii, 5, 178.

194. **startles:** springs up; rises with startling sound.

203. **mista'en:** mistaken; made a mistake.—**his house:** its proper habitation; its proper sheath.

204. **on the back.** 'The dagger,' Steevens notes, 'was anciently worn behind the back.' He cites Wager, *The Longer Thou Livest, the More Fool Thou Art*, sig. D:

> Thou must weare thy sworde by thy side,
> And thy daggar handsumly at thy backe.

211. **exíle.** Cf. iii, 1, 192; iii, 2, 133; iii, 3, 20, 140.

216. **outrage:** passionate outcry; violent lamentation. Cf. *1 Henry VI*, iv, 1, 126: 'clamorous outrage.'

218. **spring, head, descent.** Synonymous: 'source,' 'origin.'

221. **And let . . . patience:** And let your misfortunes be controlled by calm endurance.

222. **of suspicion:** suspected. Cf. 'thieves of mercy' for 'merciful robbers' (*Hamlet*, iv, 6, 21).

224. **as:** considering how.

226. **impeach:** accuse.—**purge:** clear, exonerate.

227. **excus'd:** exculpated; found innocent.

229 ff. 'It is much to be lamented,' Dr. Johnson remarks, 'that the poet did not conclude the dialogue with the action, and avoid a narrative of events which the audience already knew.' But—whatever the audience knows—it was certainly imperative that the Prince, the Montagues, and the Capulets should learn facts that are known to Friar Laurence only. Otherwise the conclusion (ll. 296 ff.) would be impossible.

229. **my short date of breath:** the short term of my life.

240. **mean:** means. Cf. iii, 3, 45.

241. **marriage.** Trisyllabic. Cf. iv, 1, 11.

243. **my art:** i.e., as a physician.

247. **as this dire night.** *As* (adding no visible meaning) is common with expressions of time (as in our *as yet* for 'yet'). Cf. *Julius Cæsar*, v, 1, 71, 72:

> This is my birthday: as this very day
> Was Cassius born.

251. **stay'd by accident:** delayed by chance.

253. **hour.** Dissyllabic. Cf. ii, 5, 11; iii, 1, 200.

255. **closely:** in concealment.

257. **some minute:** a minute or so. Cf. l. 268: 'some hour.'

261. **patience:** fortitude or submission.

266. **privy (to):** secretly informed of.

267. **Miscarried:** went wrong, went amiss.

270. **still:** ever.

273. **in post.** Cf. v, 1, 25, 26.

280. **what . . . master:** What was your master doing?
281–285. The style is beautifully simple, as befits the Boy.
284. **by-and-by:** immediately. Cf. ii, 2, 152, note.
289. **therewithal:** with this (i.e., the poison).
293. **with:** by means of.
294. **winking at:** shutting my eyes to.
297. **This . . . jointure.** In a marriage contract the sum reserved for the wife if she survive her husband is called her *jointure*. Capulet asks only his enemy's hand-clasp as the jointure of Juliet.
299–303. Cf. Broke, fol. 84 v°:

> The bodies dead remoued from vaulte where they did dye,
> In statelie tombe, on pillers great, of marble rayse they hye.
> On euery syde aboue, were set and eke beneath,
> Great store of cunning Epitaphes, in honor of theyr death.
> And euen at this day the tombe is to be seene.
> So that among the monumentes that in Verona been,
> Ther is no monument more worthy of the sight
> Then is the tombe of Iuliet, and Romeus her knight.

300. **whiles:** while, as long as.
301. **at . . . set:** be valued at such a high rate.
303. **As rich:** i.e., also of gold.—**Romeo's:** i.e., his statue.
304. **of.** In modern English, 'to.'
305–310. The Prince's formal speech serves as a kind of Epilogue. It resembles the Prologue in style and metre. In Elizabethan tragedy it is the rule for that one of the survivors who is highest in rank to speak the closing words.
308. **Some . . . punished.** In Broke's poem (foll. 83, 84) the Nurse is banished because she had concealed from Juliet's parents the marriage, 'which might haue wroght much good, had it in time been knowne' (cf. ii, 3, 90–92); Peter is set free because he had only obeyed his master's orders; the Apothecary is hanged; Friar Laurence is 'discharged quite' with 'no marke of defame,' because he had often done the state service. He voluntarily entered a hermitage two miles from Verona: 'Fyue yeres he liued an Hermite, and an Hermite dyd he dye.'

TEXTUAL NOTES

[Qq indicates the exact agreement of four Quartos—Q₃ (1599), Q₃ (1609), Q₄ (undated), and Q₅ (1637). Q₂ without mention of the others indicates the agreement of the same four except in some detail of spelling. Q₁ (1597) is occasionally cited. Ff indicates the exact agreement of all four Folios—F₁ (1623), F₂ (1632), F₃ (1664), and F₄ (1685). F₁ without mention of the others indicates agreement of the four except in some detail of spelling. The figures 1 and 2 after an editor's name indicate first and second edition. Conjectures are marked 'conj.'; omissions, 'om.']

Act i, Prologue, 1–14 omitted in Ff.
Scene 1, 27 cruel] ciuil (Q₂); ciuill (Q₃ F₁); cruell (Q₄ Q₅).
32 in (Q₁ Q₄ Q₅ F₂ F₃ F₄)] om. Q₂ Q₃ F₁.
37 two (Q₁)] om. Qq Ff.
69 swashing (Q₄ Q₅)] washing (Q₂ Q₃ Ff).
79 (stage direction)] *Fight* (Ff); om. Qq.
81 *Citizens*] om. Qq Ff; Clark and Wright conj.
99 Verona's] *Neronas* (Q₂); corrected in Q₃.
127 drave (Q₅ F₂ F₃ F₄)] driue (Q₂); draue (Q₃ Q₄ F₁).
129 the city's] the Citties (Q₁); this Citie (Q₂); this City (Q₃ Q₄ Q₅ Ff).
148 portentous (F₂ F₃ F₄)] portendous (Q₂ Q₃ Q₅ F₁); protendous (Q₄); portentious (Q₁).
154 his (Q₃ Q₄ Q₅ Ff)] is (Q₂).
160 sun (Pope₂; Theobald)] same (Qq Ff).
184 create (Q₁ F₂ F₃ F₄)] created (Qq F₁).
186 well-seeming (F₃ F₄)] welseeing (Q₂ F₁); wellseeing (Q₃); welseeming (Q₄ F₂); well seeming (Q₅).
197 rais'd] raisde (Q₁); made (Qq Ff).
199 lovers'] a louers (Q₁); louing (Q₂ F₁).
209 Bid . . . will] Bid a sickman in sadnes make his will (Q₁); Bid a sicke man in sadnesse make his will (Q₄ Q₅); A sicke man in sadnesse makes his will (Q₂ Q₃ F₁); A sicke [sick (F₃ F₄)] man in good sadnesse [sadness (F₃ F₄)] makes his will (F₂ F₃ F₄).
210 Ah (Q₁)] A (Qq F₁); O (F₂ F₃ F₄).
218 unharm'd] vnharm'd (Q₁); vncharmd (Q₂ Q₃ Q₄); vncharm'd (F₁); uncharm'd (Q₅ F₂ F₃ F₄).
225 makes (Q₄ Q₅ F₂ F₃ F₄)] make (Q₂ Q₃ F₁).

Scene 2, 14 The earth hath (Q₄ Q₅)] Earth hath (Q₂ Q₃ F₁); Earth up hath (F₂ F₃ F₄).
18 agree (Q₃ Q₄ Q₅ Ff)] agreed (Q₂).
29 female (Q₁)] fennell (Q₂ Q₃); Fennell (Q₄ Q₅ F₁); Female (F₂ F₃ F₄).
32 Which . . . one] Which one more view [veiw (Q₃)], of many, mine being one, (Q₂ Q₃ Ff); Which on more view of many, mine being one, (Q₄ Q₅).

38 written here? It] written. Here it (Qq F₃ F₄); written. Heere it (F₁); written. Heert it (F₂).

68 Anselmo (Capell conj.; Dyce₂)] Anselme (Q₁ Qq F₁ F₂); Anselm (F₃ F₄).

69 Vitruvio (F₃ F₄)] Vtruuio (Q₁ Q₂ Q₃ Q₄ F₁); Utruvio (Q₅); Vtruvio (F₂).

72 and (Q₁)] om. Qq Ff.

77, 78 *Ro.* Whither to supper? *Ser.* To (Q₂); Whither to supper. *Ser?* To (Q₃); *Ro.* Whither to supper. *Ser.* To (Q₄); *Rom.* Whither? to supper? *Ser.* To (Q₅ F₁). Corrected by Theobald (Warburton).

85 *Exit* (Ff)] om. Qq.

87 lov'st] loues (Q₁ Q₂ Q₃ Q₄ F₁); lovest (Q₅ F₂ F₃ F₄).

93 fires (Pope)] fier (Q₂ Q₃); fire (Q₄ Q₅ F₁ F₂ F₃); Fire (F₄).

103 seems] seemes (Q₁ Q₂); shewes (Q₃ Q₄ Q₅ F₁ F₂); shews (F₃ F₄).

Scene 3, 14 She is (Steevens 1793)] shee's (Q₁ Q₅ F₁); shees (Q₂ Q₃ Q₄ F₂); she's (F₃ F₄).

17 shall (Q₃ Q₄ Q₅ Ff)] stal (Q₂).

36 high-lone] high lone (Q₁); hylone (Q₂); a lone (Q₃); alone (Q₄ Q₅ Ff).

43 holidam (Q₅)] holydam (Q₂ Q₃); holy dam (Q₄); holy-dam (F₁ F₂ F₃); Holy-dam (F₄).

52 it brow (Qq F₁ F₂)] its brow (F₃); its Brow (F₄).

65 disposition (Ff)] dispositions (Qq).

66 honour (Pope)] honor (Q₁); houre (Qq F₁).

71 mothers. By my count, I] mothers by my count. I (Q₂ Q₃); mothers by my count, I (Q₄); mothers by my count: I (Q₅); Mothers. By my count I (F₁); Mothers. By my count, I (F₂ F₃ F₄).

99 make it (Q₁ Q₄ Q₅ F₂ F₃ F₄)] make (Q₂ Q₃ F₁).

Scene 4, 7, 8 Nor . . . entrance (Pope from Q₁)] om. Qq Ff.

23 *Mer.* (Q₅)] *Horatio* (Q₂ Q₃); *Mercu.* (Q₄); *Hora.* (Ff).

31 quote (Q₃ Q₄ Q₅ Ff)] coate (Q₁); cote (Q₂).

39 done (Q₁ F₁ F₂ F₃)] dum (Q₂); dun (Q₃ Q₄ Q₅); Dun (F₄).

42 Of this sir-reverence love] Of this surreuerence loue (Q₁); Or saue you reuerence loue (Q₂); Or [Or, (F₄)] saue [save (F₂ F₃ F₄)] your reuerence [reverence (F₂ F₃); reverence, (F₄)] loue [love (F₂ F₃); Love (F₄)] (Ff).

45 We . . . day (Capell)] We burne our lights by night, like Lampes by day (Q₁); We waste [wast (Q₃)] our lights in vaine, lights lights by day (Q₂ Q₃ Q₅); We waste our lights in vaine, Lights Lights by day (Q₄); We wast our lights in vaine, lights, by day (F₁).

47 five (Wilbraham conj.; Malone)] fine (Qq Ff).

57 atomies (Q₃ Q₄ Q₅)] Atomi (Q₁); ottamie (Q₂); Atomies (Ff).

58 Athwart] A thwart (Q₁); ouer (Q₂ Q₃ Q₄ F₁); over (Q₅ F₂ F₃ F₄).

61 spider's] spider (Q₂ Q₃); Spider (Q₄); spiders (Q₅); Spiders (Ff).

63 film] filmes (Q₁); Philome (Qq F₁); filme (F₂ F₃ F₄).
66 maid] maide (Q₁); man (Qq F₁); woman (F₂ F₃); Woman (F₄).
72 O'er] O're (Q₁); On [on (Q₅)] (Qq Ff).
76 breaths (Rowe)] breathes (Q₁); breath (Qq F₁).
81 dreams he] dreames he (Q₁); he dreams (Q₂ Q₃ F₂ F₃ F₄); he dreames
(Q₄ Q₅ F₁).
90 elflocks] Elfelocks (Q₁); Elklocks (Q₂ Q₃ F₁); Elflocks (Q₄ F₂ F₃ F₄);
Elflockes (Q₅).
103 face (Q₁)] side (Qq Ff).
113 sail] saile (Q₁); sute (Qq Ff).

Scene 5, 19 have a bout] haue about (Q₁); walke about (Qq F₁).
20 Ah ha, my] ah ha my (Q₁); Ah my (Qq F₁); Ah me (F₂ F₃ F₄).
28 (stage direction)] After l. 27 in Qq Ff.
48 Like (Q₁ F₂ F₃ F₄)] As (Qq F₁).
96 fine (Warburton conj.; Theobald)] sinne *or* sin (Qq Ff).
97 ready (Q₁ Q₅ F₂ F₃ F₄)] did readie (Q₂ Q₄); did ready (Q₃ F₁).
134 there (Q₁)] here (Qq Ff).
144 this . . . this (Ff)] tis . . . tis (Qq).

Act ii, Prologue, 4 match'd (F₄)] match (Q₂); matcht (Q₃ Q₄ Q₅ F₁ F₂
F₃).

Scene 1, 6 Nay, . . . too] continued to Benvolio in Q₂ Q₃ Ff; given to
Mercutio in Q₁ Q₄ Q₅.
9 one rhyme] one rime (Q₁ Q₃ Q₄ F₁); on rime (Q₂); one ryme (Q₅);
one time (F₂ F₃ F₄).
10 pronounce] Pronounce (Q₁); pronounce (Q₄ Q₅); prouaunt, (Q₂
Q₃); Prouant, (F₁); Couply (F₂ F₃ F₄).
10 dove] Doue (Q₁); day (Q₂ Q₃ F₁ F₂ F₃); die (Q₄); dye (Q₅); Day
(F₄).
12 heir] heire (Q₁ Q₄ Q₅); her (Q₂ Q₃ Ff).
13 Adam Cupid] (Upton conj.; Steevens 1778)] *Abraham: Cupid* (Q₁
Q₂ Q₃); *Abraham Cupid* (Q₄ Q₅ Ff); auborn Cupid (Theobald conj.);
auburn Cupid (Dyce₁); abram Cupid (Dyce conj.).
13 trim (Q₁)] true (Qq Ff).
38 et cetera, thou a] *Et cætera*, thou a (Q₁); or thou a (Q₂ Q₃ Ff); &
[and (Q₅)] catera, and thou a (Q₄ Q₅).

Scene 2, 16 do (Q₃ Ff)] to (Q₂); doe (Q₄ Q₅).
20 eyes (Q₁)] eye (Qq F₁ F₂ F₃); Eye (F₄).
29 white-upturned] Hyphen supplied by Theobald₂.
31 lazy-pacing (Pope)] lasie pacing (Q₁); lazie [lazy (F₂ F₃ F₄)] puffing
(Qq Ff).

41, 42 nor any . . . name! (Malone)] ô (*or* O) be some other name Belonging to a man. (Qq Ff); nor any other part. (Q₁).

44 name (Q₁)] word (Qq Ff).

45 were (Q₃ Q₄ Q₅ Ff)] wene (Q₂).

48 that (Q₁)] thy (Qq Ff).

59 that (Q₁)] thy (Qq Ff).

59 utterance] vtterance (Q₁); vttering (Q₃ F₁).

61 saint] Saint (Q₁); maide (Q₂); Maid (Ff).

61 dislike (Qq Ff)] displease (Q₁).

69 let (Q₁)] stop (Qq Ff).

75 sight (Q₁)] eies (Q₂); eyes (F₁).

83 vast shore wash'd] vast shore, washt (Q₁); vast shore washeth (Q₂); **vast** shore washet (Q₃); vast shore washt (Q₄ Q₅); vast-shore-washet (F₁); **vast-shore:** washd (F₂); vast-shore: wash'd (F₃); vast-shore, wash'd (F₄).

84 would (Q₁)] should (Qq Ff).

99 haviour (F₂ F₃ F₄)] hauiour (Q₁); behauior (Q₂); be hauiour (Q₃); behauiour (F₁ Q₄); behauiour (Q₅).

101 more cunning (Q₁)] coying (Q₂ Q₃ F₁); more coying (Q₄ Q₅); more coyning (F₂ F₃ F₄).

104 true-love] truloue (Q₂); trueloue (Q₃); true loue (Q₄); true loues (Q₁); true loues (Q₅); true Loues (F₁).

107 swear] sweare (Q₁); vow (Qq Ff).

110 circled (Q₁ Q₃ Q₄ Q₅ Ff)] circle (Q₂).

136 (stage direction)] *Cals* [*Calls* (F₄)] *within* (Ff); om. Qq.

141 (stage direction)] om. Qq F₁; *Enter.* (F₂ F₃ F₄).

153 suit (Q₅)] strife (Q₂ Q₃ Ff); sute (Q₄). Broke has 'To cease your sute' (fol. 16 r⁰).

155 *Exit* (Ff)] om. Qq.

163, 164 than mine With] then With (Q₂ Q₃ F₁); then myne With (Q₄); than mine, With (Q₅); then with The (F₂ F₃); than with The (F₄).

164 Romeo's name] *Romeos* name (Q₁); *Romeo* (Qq Ff).

165 Romeo!] *Romeo?* (Q₁); om. Qq Ff.

169 dear] Neece (Q₂ Q₃ F₁); Deere (Q₄ Q₅); sweete (F₂); sweet (F₃); Sweet (F₄).

169 At what (Q₁)] What (Qq Ff).

171 years (F₃ F₄)] yeare (Q₂); yeares (Q₃ Q₄ F₁ F₂); yeeres (Q₅).

180 That . . . her (Pope)] That . . . his (Qq Ff); Who . . . her (Q₁; Capell).

182 silk] silke (Q₁); silken (Qq Ff).

182 loving-jealous] Hyphen inserted by Theobald.

187 *Exit* (Pope)] om. Qq F₁; after l. 188 (F₂ F₃ F₄).

188 Sleep . . . breast] Given to Romeo in Q₁ Q₄ Q₅; to Juliet in the rest.

189 In Q₂ Q₃ F₁, ll. 1–4 of sc. 3 are inserted between l. 189 and l. 190 and are repeated at the beginning of sc. 3. Q₄ Q₅ have the right arrangement. F₂ F₃ F₄ follow the arrangement of F₁ through l. 191 but begin the Friar's speech with l. 5.

190 father's cell] fathers Cell (Q₁); Friers close cell [*or* Cell] (Qq F₂ F₃ F₄); Fries close Cell (F₁).

Scene 3, 2 Check'ring (F₃ F₄)] Checkring (Q₁ Q₃ Q₄ Q₅ F₁ F₂); Checking (Q₂ here, but 'Checkring' above).
3 flecked darkness] flecked darkenes (Q₁); fleckeld darknesse (Q₂ here, but 'darknesse fleckted' above; Q₃ Q₄ Q₅); fleckled darknesse (F₁); darknesse fleckel'd (F₂); darkness fleckel'd (F₃); Darkness fleckel'd (F₄).
4 day's . . . wheels] daies path, and *Titans* fierie wheeles (Q₁); daies path, and *Titans* burning wheeles (Q₂ here, but 'daies pathway, made by *Tytans* wheeles' above); daies [dayes (Q₄ Q₅)] path, and *Titans* burning wheeles (Q₃ Q₄ Q₅ F₁); dayes pathway, made by *Titans* wheeles (F₂ F₃); days path-way, made by *Titan*'s Wheels (F₄).
8 precious-juiced] Hyphen inserted by Pope.
22 sometime's (Capell)] sometimes (Q₁); sometime (Qq Ff).
23 small (Q₁)] weake *or* weak (Qq Ff).
26 slays (F₄)] slaies (Q₁); staies (Q₂); slayes (Q₃ Q₄ Q₅ F₁ F₂ F₃).
30 Qq Ff mark the entrance of Romeo after l. 22; corrected by Pope.
74 ring yet in mine] ring yet in my (Q₁); yet ringing in mine (Q₃); yet ringing in my (Q₃ F₁); yet ring in my (Q₄ F₂ F₃ F₄); yet ring in mine (Q₅).
85 chide not (Q₁)] chide me not (Qq Ff).
85 She whom] she whom (Q₁); her (Qq Ff).

Scene 4, 14 shot (Q₁)] run *or* runne (Qq Ff).
18 *Ben.* (Q₁ Ff)] *Ro.* or *Rom.* (Qq).
19 I can tell you (Q₁)] om. Qq Ff.
21, 22 rests me his minim rest, one (Malone)] rests me his minum rest one (Q₁); he rests, his minum rests, one (Q₂); he rests his minum [*minum* (Q₄ Q₅)] rests, one (Q₃ Q₄ Q₅); he rests his minum, one (Ff).
29 fantasticoes (Q₁)] phantacies (Q₂ Q₃ Q₄ F₁ F₂); phantasies (Q₅ F₃ F₄).
32 grandsir (Q₃ Q₄)] graundsir (Q₁ Q₂); Grand-sire (Q₅); Grandsire (F₁ F₂ F₃); Grandsir (F₄).
35 pardona-mi's] pardonmees (Q₁); pardons mees (Q₂); pardon mees (Q₃); pardona-mees (Q₄ Q₅); pardon mee's (F₁); pardon-mee's (F₂); pardon-me's (F₃ F₄).
37 bones . . . bones (Qq Ff)] *bon's* . . . *bon's* (Theobald).
41 was but (Q₁)] was (Qq Ff).
67 Well said (Q₁)] Sure wit (Qq Ff).
71 wits faint (Q₅)] wits faints (Q₂ Q₃ Q₄ F₁); wit faints (F₂ F₃ F₄); wits faile (Q₁).
74 our wits (Qq Ff)] thy wits (Q₁; Capell).
108 *Mer.* (Q₁)] om. Qq Ff.
109 *Ben.* (Q₁)] *Mer.* (Qq Ff).
113, 114 the fairer face of the two] the fairer face (Qq Ff); the fairer of the two (Q₁).

121 made for himself] made for himselfe (Q₁); made, himself (Q₂ F₂); made, himselfe (F₁ F₂ Q₃ Q₄ Q₅); made himself (F₄); for himselfe (Q₁).

135 endite (Qq F₁)] inuite (Q₁); envite (F₂); invite (F₃ F₄).

140 (stage direction)] *He walkes by them, and sings.* (Q₁); om. Qq Ff.

152 Marry, farewell!] Marry farewell. (Q₁); om. Qq Ff.

153 ropery (F₂ F₃)] roperie (Qq F₁); Roguery (F₄); roperipe (Q₁).

161 skains-mates] skaines mates (Q₁ Qq F₁ F₂); skains mates (F₃); skains-Mates (F₄).

161 After 'skaines mates' Q₁ has *She turnes to Peter her man.*

174 into (Q₁)] in (Qq Ff).

209 I warrant (F₂ F₃ F₄)] Warrant (Qq F₁).

226 Peter . . . apace (Clark and Wright)] *Peter*, take my fanne, and goe before (Q₁); Before [Before, (F₄)] and apace (Qq Ff).

Scene 5, 5 glide (F₄)] glides (Qq F₁ F₂ F₃).

11 Is three (Q₃ Q₄ Q₅)] Is there (Q₂); I three (Ff).

16 old folks, many feign] old folks, many fain (Q₂); old folkes, many faine (Q₃ Q₄); old folkes many faine (Q₅); old folkes, Many faine (F₁); old folks, marry, feign (Johnson); old folks move, i' faith (Dyce conj.; Hudson).

26 jaunce] iaunce (Q₂ Q₃); iaunt (Q₄ F₁ F₂); jaunt (Q₅ F₃); Jaunt (F₄).

26 had (Q₃ Q₄ Q₅ Ff)] om Q₂.

53 jauncing] iaunsing (Q₂ Q₃); iaunting (Q₄ F₁ F₂); jaunting (Q₅ F₃ F₄).

Scene 6, 16, 17 Here . . . flint] See where she comes. | So light of foote nere hurts the troden flower: | Of loue and ioy, see see the soueraigne power. (Q₁).

18 gossamer] gossamours (Q₂ Q₃); Gossamours (Q₄ Q₅ F₁ F₂ F₃); Gossamour (F₄).

27 music's] musicke (Q₂ Q₃); Musickes (Q₄ Q₅ F₃); musickes (F₁ F₂); Musicks (F₄).

37 *Exeunt* (F₂ F₃ F₄)] om. Qq F₁.

ACT iii, Scene 1, 2 Capulets] *Capels* (Q₂ Q₃); *Capulets* (Q₄ Q₅ Ff); *Capels* are (Q₁).

37 (stage direction)] *Enter* Tybalt, Petruchio, *and others.* (Q₂ F₁).

38 come (Q₅ F₂ F₃ F₄)] comes (Q₂ Q₃ Q₄ F₁).

55 And (Capell)] Or (Qq Ff).

77 Alla stoccata (Knight)] *Alla stucatho* (Qq F₁); *Allastucatho* (F₂ F₃ F₄).

93 *with his Followers*] supplied by Clark and Wright.

94 o' both your (Dyce)] on your (Q₁); a both (Qq); a both the (F₁); of both the (F₂ F₃ F₄).

113 soundly too. Your houses!] soundly, to your houses. (Q₂); soundly,

to your houses. (Q₂); soundly to your houses— (Q₄ Q₅); soundly to your Houses. (F₁); soundly too [too, (F₃ F₄)] your Houses. (F₂ F₃ F₄).

118 kinsman (Q₁)] Cozen (Q₂ F₃ F₄); Cozin (Q₃ Q₄ F₁ F₂); cousin (Q₅).

125 (stage direction)] om. Qq.

127 Alive in triumph, and] A liue in tryumph and (Q₁); He gan in triumph and (Q₂); He gon in triumph and (Q₃ Q₄); He gone in triumph [Triumph (F₄)], and (Q₅ F₃ F₄); He gon in triumph, and (F₁ F₂).

129 fire-ey'd] fier eyed (Q₁); fier end (Q₂); fier and (Q₃); fire and (Q₄ Q₅ F₁ F₂); fire, [Fire, (F₄)] and (F₃ F₄).

145 and others] *and all* (Qq Ff).

152 O Prince! O husband!] O Prince, O Cozen, husband, (Q₂); O Prince, O Cozin, Husband, (F₁); O prince!—O husband! (Capell).

171 agile] agill (Q₁ Q₄ Q₅); aged (Q₂ Q₃ F₁); able (F₂ F₃ F₄).

188 owe? (Q₅)] owe. (Q₂ Q₃ Q₄ Ff).

189 *Mon.*] *Capu.* (Q₂); *Cap.* (Q₃ Ff); *Moun.* (Q₄); *Mou.* (Q₅).

193 hate's (Knight)] hates (Q₁); hearts (Qq Ff); hates' (Capell).

197 I will (Q₁ Q₄ Q₅ F₂ F₃ F₄)] It will (Q₂ Q₃ F₁).

Scene 2, 6 runaway] runnawayes (Q₂ Q₃ Q₄); run-awayes (F₁ Q₅); run-awaies (F₂ F₃); run-aways (F₄); run-away (Blackstone conj.); runagate's (Becket conj.¹); rumourers' (Singer₂); run-abouts' (Keightley); rude day's (Dyce).

9 By (Q₄ Q₅ F₂ F₃ F₄)] And by (Q₂ Q₃ F₁).

15 grown (Rowe)] grow (Qq Ff).

21 he (Q₅)] I (Q₂ Q₃ Ff); hee (Q₄).

37 weraday (Q₂)] weladay (Q₃ Q₄ Q₅ F₃ F₄); welady (F₁ F₂).

47 death-darting (F₁ Q₂ Q₄ Q₅)] death arting (Q₃).

49 shut (Capell)] shot (Qq Ff).

49 make thee (Johnson conj.; Steevens 1778)] makes thee (Qq F₁); makes the (F₂ F₃ F₄).

51 of (Ff Q₅)] om. Q₂ Q₃ Q₄.

56 swounded (Q₁)] sounded (Q₂ Q₃ Q₄ F₁ F₂ F₃); swouned (Q₅); swooned (F₄).

66 dear-lov'd (Pope)] deare loude (Q₁); dearest (Qq Ff).

71 Qq F₁ F₄ give the whole line to Juliet; F₂ F₃ give 'O God!' to Juliet and 'Did . . . blood' to the Nurse.

72 It did . . . it did!] Given to the Nurse in Q₁ Q₅ F₂ F₃ F₄; continued to Juliet in Q₂ Q₃ Q₄ F₁.

73 O serpent . . . face] Given to Juliet in Q₁ Q₅ F₂ F₃ F₄; to the Nurse in Q₂ Q₃ Q₄ F₁.

76 Dove-feather'd raven (Theobald)] Rauenous douefeatherd rauē (Q₂); Rauenous douefeatherd Rauen (Q₃); Rauenous doue, feathred Rauen

¹ *Shakspeare's Himself Again*, 1815, p. 214. Becket prints 'runagate's,' but explains the word as a plural: 'the eyes of runagates, rebels, or love-apostates.'

(Q₄); Ravenous dove, feathred raven (Q₅); Rauenous Doue-feather'd Rauen (F₁); Ravenous Dove, feather'd Raven (F₂ F₃ F₄).

79 damned (Q₄ Q₅ F₂ F₃ F₄)] dimme (Q₂ Q₃); dimne (F₁).

135 maiden-widowed] Hyphen inserted by Rowe.

Scene 3, 1 (stage direction)] *Enter Frier* (Q₁). All the rest make Romeo enter here with the Friar.

3 (stage direction)] *Enter Romeo* (Q₁); om. Qq Ff.

15 Hence (Q₁)] Here (Qq Ff).

20 banishment (Hanmer)] banished (Qq Ff).

21 banishment (Q₁)] banished (Qq Ff).

39–44 Qq arrange thus: 39, 41, 43, 40, 41, 42, 44. Ff arrange thus: 39, 41, 43, 40, 44 (omitting l. 42).

52 Thou (Q₄ Q₅)] Then (Q₂ Q₃ F₁); om. F₂ F₃ F₄.

52 a little (Qq)] om. Ff. Q₁ reads: 'Thou fond mad man, heare me but speake a word.'

61 madmen] mad man (Q₂); mad men (Q₃ Q₄ Q₅); Mad men (F₁).

70 (stage direction)] *Enter Nurse, and knocke* (Q₂); *Enter Nurse, and knockes* (Q₃ F₁ F₂); *Enter Nurse and knocks* (F₃ F₄); *Nurse knocks [knockes* (Q₅)] (Q₄ Q₅).

73 *Knock* (F₂ F₃ F₄)] *They knocke* (Q₂ Q₃); *Knocke* (Q₄ Q₅ F₁).

75 *Knock* (F₃ F₄)] *Slud knock* (Q₂); *Slud knocke* (Q₃); *Knocke againe* (Q₄ Q₅); *Knocke* (F₁ F₂).

80 *Enter Nurse* (Rowe)] after l. 78 in Qq Ff.

82 Where is (Q₁)] Wheres (Q₂ F₁).

85, 86 O . . . predicament] Part of the Nurse's speech in Qq Ff. Corrected by Farmer.

91 *rises*] *He rises* (Q₁); om. Qq Ff.

92 Well (Malone)] Wel (Q₁); om. Qq Ff.

108 (stage direction)] *He offers to stab himselfe, and Nurse snatches the dagger away.* (Q₁); om. Qq Ff.

110 denote (Q₁ Q₄ Q₅ F₁)] deuote (Q₂ Q₃); do [doe (F₂)] note (F₂ F₃ F₄).

113 Or (Q₁)] And (Qq Ff).

117 lives (F₄)] lies *or* lyes (Qq F₁ F₂ F₃). Q₁ reads 'Lady too, that liues in thee?'

138 too (Q₁ F₂ F₃ F₄)] om. Qq. F₁.

141 light (Q₂ Q₃ Q₅ Ff)] lights (Q₁ Q₄).

143 misbehav'd and (Q₅)] misbehaude and (Q₁); mishaued and (Q₂ Q₃); misbehau'd and (Q₄); mishaped and (F₁); mis-shaped and a (F₂ F₃); mis-shapen and a (F₄).

144 pout'st upon] puts vp (Q₂ Q₃); powts vpon (Q₄); poutst upon (Q₅); puttest vp (F₁).

163 is (Q₁)] sir (Qq F₁ F₂ F₃); Sir (F₄).

164 *Exit*] *Exit Nurse* (Q₁ after l. 165); om. Qq Ff.

168 disguis'd (Q₄ Q₅ Ff)] disguise (Q₂); disguisd (Q₃).

Scene 4, 8 no time (Q₁)] no times (Qq Ff).

13 be (Q₃ Q₄ Q₅ Ff)] me (Q₂).

20 A . . . a (Qq F₁ F₂ F₃)] A . . . A (F₄); On . . . o' (Theobald); **O'** . . . o' (Capell).

23 We'll] Well, (Q₂); Weele (Q₃ Q₄ F₁); Wee'll (Q₅).

30 A] a (Qq Ff); o' (Capell).

34 very very late **(Q₁)**] very late (Qq); late (Ff).

Scene 5 (stage direction) aloft, at the window] *at the window* (Q₁); *aloft* (Qq Ff).

13 exhales (Q₁ Q₃ Q₄ Ff)] exhale (Q₂ Q₅).

31 chang'd (Rowe)] change (Qq Ff).

36 (stage direction) (Rowe₂)] *Enter Madame and Nurse* (Q₂); *Enter Madam and Nurse* (Ff).

42 *He goeth down.*] *He goeth downe.* (Q₁); om. Qq Ff.

43 my lord, my love, my friend] my Lord, my Loue, my Frend (Q₁); loue, Lord, ay husband, friend (Q₂); Loue, Lord, ay Husband, Friend (F₁); Love, Lord, ah Husband, Friend [friend (F₃)] (F₂ F₃ F₄).

53 our time (Q₃ Q₄ Q₅ Ff)] our times (Q₂); the time **(Q₁).**

54–57 Given to Romeo in Q₂ Q₃; to Juliet in Q₁ and the rest.

55 thee, . . . below] thee . . . below (Q₁); thee now, thou art so lowe (Q₂ Q₃ Q₄ F₁ F₂); thee now thou art so low (Q₅); thee now, thou art so low (F₃ F₄).

62 renowm'd (Q₄)] renowmd (Q₂ Q₃); renown'd (Q₅ Ff).

68 (stage direction)] after 'back' (l. 64) in Qq Ff; corrected by Capell.

83 him (Q₄ Q₅ F₂ F₃ F₄)] om. Q₂ Q₃ F₁.

95, 96 him—dead—Is (Theobald)] him. Dead Is (Qq Ff).

102 Tybalt] om. Qq F₁; *Tybalt* (F₂ F₃ F₄).

107 I (Q₄ Q₅ F₂ F₃ F₄)] om. Q₂ Q₃ F₁.

127 air] Ayre (Q₄); aire (Q₅); earth (Q₂ Q₃ F₁).

132 Thou counterfeit'st] Thou countefaits (Q₂); Thou counterfaits (Q₃ F₁); Thou counterfeits (Q₄ F₂); Thou counterfeitst (Q₅); Thy counterfeits (F₃); Thy Counterfeit's (F₄).

140 gives you (Q₅ F₂ F₃ F₄)] giue you (Q₂); giues you (Q₃ Q₄ F₁).

146 bridegroom] Bride (Q₂); Bridegroome (Q₃ Q₄ Q₅ F₁).

150 How . . . choplogic?] How, how, howhow, chopt lodgick, (Q₂); How now, how now, chopt lodgick, (Q₃ Q₄); How now? how now? chopt logick? (Q₅); How now? How now? Chopt Logicke? (F₁ F₂); How now? How now? Chopt Logick (F₃ F₄); Whats here, chop logicke. (Q₁). Corrected by Steevens.

152 And . . . you] om. Ff.

162 a (Qq Ff)] o' (Theobald).

173 Q₂ gives to the Nurse 'Father, ô Godigeden.' So Q₃. Q₄ Q₅ make the necessary correction. F₁ follows Q₃, as usual. The other Folios omit 'Father' but give the rest of the line to the Nurse. Q₁ is correct: '*Cap*: Oh goddegodden.'

177–179 Day . . . hath been (Pope)] Day, night, early, late, at home, abroad, | Alone, in company, waking or sleeping, | Still my care hath beene (Q₁); Day, night, houre, tide, time, worke, play, | Alone in companie, still my care hath bene (Q₂). The other Quartos and the Folios follow Q₂.

181 princely] Princely (Q₁); noble *or* Noble (Qq Ff).

182 train'd] trainde (Q₁); liand (Q₂); allied (Q₃ Q₄); alli'd (Q₅); Allied (Ff).

228 thou this (Q₁)] thou (Qq Ff).

236 *Exit* (Q₄ Q₅ F₂ F₃ F₄)] om. Q₂ Q₃ F₁; *She lookes after Nurse* (Q₁).

Act iv, Scene 1, 7 talk'd] talke (Q₂ Q₃ Q₄ F₁ F₂); talkt (Q₅); talk (F₃ F₄).

10 do (Q₂)] doth (Q₁ Q₃ Q₄ Q₅ F₁ F₂); should (F₃ F₄).

45 cure (Q₁ Q₅)] care (Q₂ Q₃ Q₄ Ff).

46 Ah (Q₁)] O (Qq Ff).

72 slay (Q₁ Q₄ Q₅ F₃ F₄)] stay (Q₂ Q₃ F₁); lay (F₂).

78 yonder (Q₁)] any (Qq Ff).

81 shut (Q₁)] hide (Qq Ff).

83 chapless (F₃ F₄)] chaples (Q₁); chapels (Q₂); chappels (Q₃ F₁); chaplesse (Q₄ Q₅); chapplesse (F₂).

85 shroud (Q₄ Q₅)] om. Q₂ Q₃; graue (F₁).

92 the (Q₂)] thy (Q₃ Q₄ Q₅ Ff).

94 distilled (Q₁)] distilling (Qq Ff).

100 To paly (Q₅)] Too many (Q₂ Q₃); Too paly (Q₄); To many (F₁); To mealy (F₂ F₃ F₄).

105 forty (Q₃ Q₅ Ff)] fortie (Q₁ Q₂ Q₄); fifty (Maginn conj.); thirty (Marsh conj.).

110 After l. 110 Q₂ inserts 'Be borne to buriall in thy kindreds graue.' Q₃ Q₄ Q₅ Ff also have this line. Hanmer omitted it.

115, 116 and he . . . waking (Q₃ Q₄ Q₅)] an he . . . walking (Q₂); om. Ff.

Scene 2, 9 (stage direction)] *Exit Seruingman.* (Q₁); om. Qq Ff.

26 becomed (Ff)] becomd (Q₂ Q₃); becommed (Q₄ Q₅).

45 him up (F₂ F₃ F₄)] vp him (Q₂); him vp (F₁).

Scene 3, 16 life (Qq); fire *or* Fire (Ff).

30 Supplied by Steevens from Q₁; line omitted in Qq Ff.

50 O . . . wake (Hanmer)] O . . . walke (Q₂ Q₃ F₁); Or . . . wake (Q₄ Q₅); Or . . . walke (F₂); Or . . . walk (F₃ F₄).

59 Romeo . . . thee] *Romeo* I come, this doe I drinke to thee (Q₁); *Romeo, Romeo, Romeo,* heeres drinke, I drinke to thee (Q₂—and so substantially Qq Ff with various punctuation).

59 (stage direction)] *She fals vpon her bed within the Curtaines* (Q₁); om. Qq Ff.

Scene 4, 6–8 Go . . . watching] Qq Ff give this to the Nurse. Singer and some others assign it to Lady Capulet, following a conjecture of Z. Jackson's (*Shakspeare's Genius Justified*, 1819, p. 424). Q_1 supports Qq Ff.

13 jealous hood (Q_5 F_2 F_3)] iealous hood (Q_2 Q_3 Q_4 F_1); jealous-hood (F_4).

13 (stage direction)] after 'there' (l. 14) in Qq Ff.

21 faith (Q_4 Q_5)] father (Q_2 Q_3); Father (F_1); Faith (F_2 F_3 F_4).

23 (stage direction)] after 'day' in Qq Ff.

28 *Exeunt* (Capell)] om. Qq Ff.

Scene 5, 1 Enter *Nurse* (Hanmer)] om. Qq Ff.

9 needs must (Q_2)] must needs (the rest).

15 weraday] wereaday (Q_2); weleaday (Q_3); weladay (Q_4 Q_5 F_1 F_2 F_3); wel-a-day (F_4).

16 (stage direction) (Q_1 F_4)] om. Qq; after 'here' (F_1 F_2 F_3).

32 *with Musicians* (Q_5)] *with the Musitians* (Q_4); om. Q_2 Q_3 Ff.

36 See, there (F_4)] there (Qq F_1); see there (F_2 F_3).

41 long (Q_3 Q_4 Q_5 Ff)] loue (Q_2).

51 behold (Q_3 Q_4 Q_5 Ff)] bedold (Q_2).

65 Confusion's cure] confusions care (Q_2); confusions, care (Q_3 Q_4 Q_5); confusions: Care (F_1 F_2 F_3); Confusions: Care (F_4); Confusion's Cure (Theobald).

81 In all (Q_1)] And in (Qq Ff).

82 fond (F_2 F_3 F_4)] some (Qq F_1).

95 (stage direction)] *Exeunt manet.* (Q_2); *Exeunt: manet.* (Q_3); *Exeunt manent Musici.* (Q_4); *Exeunt. Manent Musici.* (Q_5); *Exeunt* (Ff).

101 (stage direction)] *Exit omnes. Enter Will Kemp.* (Q_2); *Exeunt omnes. Enter Will Kempe.* (Q_3); *Exeunt omnes. Enter* Peter. (Q_4 Q_5); *Enter Peter* [Peter (F_4)] (Ff).

107 of woe (Q_4 Q_5)] om. Q_2 Q_3 Ff.

107 O . . . comfort me] om. Ff.

124 Then . . . wit] given to Peter in Q_4 Q_5; continued to the Musician in Q_2 Q_3 Ff.

128 grief] griefe (Q_1); griefes (Qq F_1 F_2); griefs (F_3 F_4).

129 And . . . oppress] om. Qq Ff; And dolefull dumps the minde oppresse (Q_1).

135 Pretty! (Pope)] Pretie, (Q_1); Prates, (Q_2); Pratee, (Q_4 Q_5); Pratest, (Q_3 Ff).

139 Pretty too! (Pope)] Prettie too: (Q_1); Prates to, (Q_2); Pratest to, (Q_3 F_1 F_2); Pratee to, (Q_4); Pratee too: (Q_5); Pratest too, (F_3 F_4).

Act v, Scene 1, 11, booted] *booted* (Q_1); om. Qq Ff.

15 How . . . Juliet?] How fares my *Juliet?* (Q_1); How doth my Lady *Iuliet* [*Juliet* (Q_5 F_3 F_4)]? (Qq Ff).

18 Capel's] *Capels* (Qq F₁ F₂ F₃); *Capulet's* (F₄); Capels' (Malone).

24 e'en (Collier)] in (Q₂); euen *or* even (the rest).

24 defy you (Pope)] denie you (Q₂ Q₃ Q₄ F₁); deny you (Q₅ F₂ F₃ F₄); defie my (Q₁).

33 (stage direction)] *Exit* after 'lord' (l. 32) (Q₂ Q₃ Q₄ Q₅); *Exit Man* after 'lord' (Ff).

38 'a] a (Q₂ Q₃ Q₄); he (Q₅ F₂ F₃ F₄); om. F₁.

57 (stage direction)] om. Qq.

70 starveth in (Q₅ F₂ F₃ F₄)] starueth in (Q₂ Q₃ Q₄ F₁); stareth in (Otway, *Caius Marius*); stare within (Pope).

76 pay (Q₁ Q₄ Q₅)] pray (Q₂ Q₃ Ff).

Scene 3, *with . . . torch*] om. Qq Ff. Q₁ has '*Enter Countie Paris and his Page with flowers and sweete water.*'

3 yond yew tree] this Ew-tree (Q₁); yond young (*or* yong) Trees (*or* trees) (Qq Ff).

21 (stage direction) *Balthasar* (Q₁); *Peter* (Q₂ Q₃ Ff); Balthazer *his man* (Q₄ Q₅).

21 (stage direction) with . . . iron] supplied from Q₁; om. Qq Ff.

40, 43 Given to Balthasar in Q₁ Q₄ Q₅; to Peter in Q₂ Q₃ Ff.

48 (stage direction)] om. Qq Ff; supplied in Q₁ before l. 45.

68 conjuration (Capell)] coniurations (Q₁); commiration (Q₂); commisseration (Q₃ F₁); commiseration (Q₄ Q₅ F₂ F₃); Commiseration (F₄).

70 *They fight* (Q₁)] om. Qq Ff.

71 *Page* (Q₄ Q₅)] om. Q₂ Q₃; *Pet.* (Ff); *Boy* (Q₁).

102 Shall I believe (Theobald)] I will beleeue, Shall I beleeue (Q₂ F₁).

107–120 Between l. 107 and 108 Q₂ inserts:

> Depart againe, come lye thou in my arme,
> Heer's to thy health, where ere thou tumblest in.
> O true Appothecarie!
> **Thy drugs are quicke. Thus with a kisse I die.**

Then it goes on with ll. 108–120. Q₃ Ff follow the same derangement. Corrected in Q₄ Q₅.

107 palace (Q₄ Q₅)] pallat (Q₂); pallace (Q₃); Pallace (F₁).

136 unthrifty] vnthriftie (Q₂); vnluckie (Q₃ Q₄ F₁); unluckie (F₂); unlucky (Q₅ F₃ F₄).

137 yew (Pope)] yong (Q₂); young (Q₃ Q₄ Q₅ Ff).

147 *Juliet rises*] *Iuliet rises* (Q₁ before l. 147); om. Qq Ff.

170 rest (Hazlitt)] rust (Qq Ff). Q₁ reads: 'Rest in my bosome.'

170 (stage direction)] *She stabs herselfe and falles* (Q₁); *Kils herselfe* (F₁); om. Qq.

189 (stage direction)] *Enter Capels* (Q₂ Q₃); *Enter* Capulet *and his Wife* (Q₄ Q₅ Ff).

190 that they so (Q₃ Q₄ Q₅ Ff)] that is so (Q₂).

191 The (Pope)] O the (Qq Ff).

194 our (Johnson and Heath conj.; Capell)] your (Qq Ff).

199 slaughter'd (F₃ F₄)] Slaughter (Q₂); Slaughterd (Q₃); slaughtred (Q₄ Q₅); Slaughter'd (F₁ F₂).

205 it (Q₂)] is (the rest). Q₁ has 'it is sheathed.'

209 more early (Q₁)] now earling (Q₂); now early (Q₃ Q₄ Q₅ Ff).

232 that (Q₄ Q₅)] thats (Q₂ Q₃); that's (Ff).

258 awaking (Q₃ Q₄ Q₅ F₁ F₃ F₄)] awakening (Q₂); a waking (F₂).

268 his (Q₁ Q₂)] the (the rest).

271 in this (Q₁)] to this (Qq Ff).

272 *Bal.* (Q₅)] *Balth.* (Q₂ Q₃ Q₄); *Boy* (Ff).

299 raise (Q₅ Ff)] raie (Q₂ Q₃); rayse (Q₄).

301 such (Q₁ Q₂)] that (Q₃ Q₄ Q₅ Ff).

310 *Exeunt omnes* (Ff)] om. Qq.

GLOSSARIAL INDEX

223

bones, ii, 4, 37

book (by th'), according to rule, i, 5, 112; (without), i, 2, 61

bosom, confidences, secret counsels, iii, 5, 242

bound, under bonds, i, 2, 1

bounty, generosity, ii, 2, 133

bout, a match, a turn, i, 5, 19

brain (bear a), to have a good mind, i, 3, 29

brave, noble, iii, 1, 121

break, to wound or bruise, i, 2, 53; i, 3, 38; to declare one's self insolvent, iii, 2, 57

breathe, to utter, ii, Prologue, 10

bring, to conduct, iii, 2, 129

broad, notorious, ii, 4, 91

broke, *p.p.*, broken, iii, 5, 40

broken, bruised, wounded, i, 2, 53

brotherhood, position as a friar, v, 2, 17

buckler, a small shield, i, 1, 1

burn, daylight, i, 4, 43

burthen, *n.*, burden, i, 4, 22

burthen, *v.*, to burden i, 4, 23

but, unless, ii, 2, 76

butt-shaft, an arrow for target practice, ii, 4, 17

by-and-by, immediately, ii, 2, 151; iii, 1, 175; iii, 3, 76; iii, 4, 35; v, 3, 284

By'r Lady, i, 5, 35

by th' book, according to rule, i, 5, 112

cage, a basket, ii, 3, 7

caitiff, *adj.*, miserable, v, 1, 52

can, may be able to do, ii, 6, 3

cancell'd, *p.p.*, made of no effect, iii, 3, 98

candle-holder, i, 4, 38

canker, the rose canker (caterpillar), ii, 3, 30

cank'red, eaten with rust, i, 1, 102; malignant, rancorous, i, 1, 102

cannot choose, cannot help, i, 3, 50; iii, 5, 78

care, eager desire, iii, 5, 23

careful, solicitous for one's welfare, iii, 5, 108

carry it away, to win the day, get the victory, iii, 1, 77

carry coals. *See* coals

carry no crotchets, iv, 5, 120

case, one's condition, state, iii, 3, 85; situation, iv, 5, 100; a mask, i, 4, 29

catch'd, *p.p.*, caught, iv, 5, 48

Catling, a small catgut lutestring, iv, 5, 132

cause (first and second), ii, 4, 26

centre, ii, 1, 2

challenge, to claim, iii, 5, 216

change, to exchange, iii, 5, 31

chapless, jawless, iv, 1, 83

charge, weighty matters, v, 2, 18

charnel house, iv, 1, 81

check'ring, variegating, ii, 3, 2

cheer, *n.*, viands, iv, 5, 87

cheer, *v.*, to revive, iii, 3, 25

cheerly, *interj.*, cheer up, enjoy yourselves, i, 5, 90

cheveril, a kind of kid leather, ii, 4, 87

chinks (the), plenty of coin, i, 5, 119

choler, anger, i, 1, 5; i, 5, 91

choose (cannot), cannot help, i, 3, 50; iii, 5, 78

choplogic, a subtle arguer, splitter of hairs, iii, 5, 150

churl, a niggard, v, 3, 163

circled orb, sphere, ii, 2, 110

circumstance, detailed information, ii, 5, 36; v, 3, 181

civil, *adj.*, of fellow citizens, Prologue, 4; decorous, sober, iii, 2, 10

Cleopatra, ii, 4, 43

clos'd, *p.p.*, shut up, confined, v, 2, 29

close, *adj.*, reserved, i, 1, 156

closely, in concealment, v, 3, 255

closet, a private room, iv, 2, 33

clout, a piece of cloth, ii, 4, 216

clown, a servant, i, 2 (*stage direction*)

clubs, a rallying cry, i, 1, 80

coals (carry), to submit tamely to insult, i, 1, 1

cock (the second), iv, 4, 3

cock-a-hoop (set), i, 5, 83

cockatrice, a basilisk, iii, 2, 47

cock'rel, a young cock, i, 3, 53

coil, disturbance, racket, fuss, ii, 5, 67

coldly, coolly, iii, 1, 55

collar (out of), i, 1, 6

combin'd, *p.p.*, brought into harmonious union, ii, 3, 60

come about, to come to pass, come true, i, 3, 45

come near ye (am I)? have I scored a point on you? i, 5, 22

comfort, to sustain, iii, 3, 56

comfortable, helpful, v, 3, 148

commend me to, give my respects or regards to, ii, 4, 182, 204, 223; iii, 3, 155; iii, 4, 9

commission, authority, iv, 1, 64

common, general, i, 1, 109

compare, *n.*, comparison, iii, 5, 240

compass, limits, iv, 1, 47

complain, to address pathetic words of love, ii, Prologue, 7

compliment, ceremony, conventional forms of speech, ii, 2, 89; *pl.*, ceremonious language and behaviour, ii, 4, 20

cónceal'd, iii, 3, 98

conceit, conception, idea, thoughts, iv, 3, 38; understanding, ii, 6, 30

conceive, to understand, ii, 4, 51

conduct, guidance, iii, 3, 131; a leader, a guide, iii, 1, 129; v, 3, 116

conduit, iii, 5, 130

cónfessor, ii, 6, 21; iii, 3, 49

confidence, private conversation, ii, 4, 134

confines, *pl.*, limits, bounds, iii, 1, 6

confound, to destroy, ii, 6, 13

confusion, calamity, disaster, iv, 5, 65

conjuration, adjuration, solemn bidding, v, 3, 68

consequence, a future event, i, 4, 107

consort, to associate, ii, 1, 31; iii, 1, 47; associate with, iii, 1, 135

content, pleasing quality, i, 3, 84

content thee, calm yourself, i, 5, 67

contráct, *n.*, ii, 2, 117

contráry, to oppose, i, 5, 87

convert, to change, i, 5, 94

convoy, means of conveyance, ii, 4, 202

cope, to deal, iv, 1, 75

Cophetua (King), ii, 1, 14

cordial, a reviving medicine, a restorative, v, 1, 85

corse, a corpse, iii, 2, 54, 128; iv, 5, 80, 89, 93; v, 2, 29

cot-quean, a man who busies himself with women's affairs, iv, 4, 6

counsel, secrets, secret thoughts, ii, 2, 53; a secret, secrecy, ii, 4, 208; private conversation, i, 3, 9

counsellor, a confidential adviser, i, 1, 154

count, way of reckoning time, iii, 5, 46

counterfeit, *n.*, ii, 4, 49

counterfeit, *v.*, to imitate, iii, 5, 132

countervail, to counterbalance, ii, 6, 4

County, Count (*a title*), i, 2 (*stage direction*); i, 3, 105; iii, 5, 219; iv, 1, 49; iv, 2, 23, 29, 45; v, 3, 174

court-cubbert, a court-cupboard, side-board, i, 5, 7

courtship, the life and condition of a courtier, iii, 3, 34

create, *p.p.*, created, i, 1, 184

cross, perverse, iv, 3, 5

cross, *v.*, to thwart, v, 3, 20

crotchets (carry no), iv, 5, 120

crow, a short crowbar, v, 2, 21

crowkeeper, a guard against crows, i, 4, 6

crush a cup, i, 2, 84

cry a match, to claim the victory, ii, 4, 72

cry you mercy, beg your pardon, iv, 5, 141

cunning, skilful, iv, 2, 2

curfew bell, iv, 4, 4

cursy, *n.*, a curtsy, i, 4, 72

cursy, *v.*, to curtsy, ii, 4, 58

curtains, iv, 3, 59

Cynthia, the moon, iii, 5, 20

dainty. *See* make dainty

damnation (ancient), damned old crone, iii, 5, 237

date, limit, term, v, 3, 229

dateless bargain, a sale for ever, v, 3, 115

day, daylight, iv, 1, 101

daylight (burn), i, 4, 43

dear (*emphasizing*), iii, 3, 28; momentous, v, 3, 32

dear account, heavy reckoning, i, 5, 120

dear hap, happy fortune, ii, 2, 191

dear import, vast importance, v, 2, 19

deceiv'd, *p.p.*, mistaken, v, 1, 29

decree, *n.*, a decision, iii, 5, 139

decree, *v.*, to decide, iii, 3, 146

deflower, to ravish, iv, 5, 37

defy, to reject, repudiate, v, 3, 68

deliver, to report, iii, 5, 139

demesnes, domains, ii, 1, 20; iii, 5, 182

deny, to refuse, i, 5, 21

depend, to impend, overhang, iii, 1, 124

descent, origin, source, v, 3, 218

desperate tender (a), iii, 4, 12

despised, *adj.*, despicable, iii, 2, 77

despite (in), to spite thee, v, 3, 48

détestàble, iv, 5, 56; v, 3, 45

devise, to imagine, iii, 1, 72

Dian's wit, i, 1, 216

Dido, ii, 4, 42

different, opposed, hostile, i, 5, 92

digress from, to depart from, abandon, iii, 3, 127

discover, to disclose, reveal, ii, 2, 106; iii, 1, 147

discovery, investigation, i, 1, 157

discreet, sane, sanely discriminating, i, 1, 200

dishclout, a dishcloth, iii, 5, 221

dislike, to displease, ii, 2, 61

dismal, ill-omened, iv, 3, 19

disposition, state of mind, i, 3, 65

dispute, to discuss, iii, 3, 63

distempered, disordered, ii, 3, 33

distemp'rature, trouble in one's mind, ii, 3, 40

distraught, distracted, iv, 3, 50

division, modulation, harmonious variation, iii, 5, 29

doctrine, instruction, i, 1, 245

dog's name, ii, 4, 219

doom, judgment, decision, sentence, iii, 3, 4, 8, 9

double, *adv.*, with duplicity, deceitfully, ii, 4, 179

doublet, a jacket, iii, 1, 33

doubt, *n.*, hesitation, iv, 1, 87

doubt, *v.*, to suspect, v, 3, 44

doves, Love's birds, ii, 5, 7

down, gone to bed, iv, 5, 12

dram, a drink, a draught, v, 1, 60

golden sleep, ii, 3, 38
good-den. *See* God-den
good heart, i, 1, 191
goodly, fine, ii, 4, 107
goodman boy, i, 5, 79
good morrow, good morning, i, 1, 167; ii, 3, 31, 34; ii, 4, 115
good my friend, v, 3, 124
gore-blood, clotted blood, iii, 2, 56
gossamer, light filament of spider's web, ii, 6, 18
gossip, a friendly dame, an old woman friend, ii, 1, 11; iii, 5, 172, 175
gown, a dressing gown, i, 1, 81
grace, *n.*, favour, ii, 3, 86; moral virtue, ii, 3, 28; virtue, efficacy, ii, 3, 15
gracious, charming and beauteous, ii, 2, 113
grandsir, grandsire, old gentleman, ii, 4, 32
grave (married to her), iii, 5, 141
grave, dignified, i, 1, 100
green, sallow, ii, 2, 8; (eye), light hazel, iii, 5, 222; (in earth), freshly laid in the grave, iv, 3, 43
green-sickness, *adj.*, chlorotic, iii, 5, 157
grievance, cause of sorrow, i, 1, 164
gypsy, ii, 4, 43
gyves, fetters, ii, 2, 181

hall (a), clear the floor, make room, i, 5, 28
hap, fortune, ii, 2, 191
haply, perchance, v, 3, 165
happy, fortunate, iii, 3, 137–140; opportune, fortunately discovered, v, 3, 169
harlotry, *n.*, a good-for-nothing, iv, 2, 14
have at thee (you), i, 1, 79; iv, 5, 124; v, 3, 70
haviour, behaviour, ii, 2, 99
hay, home thrust, iii, 4, 27
he, *n.*, man, v, 1. 67
head, source, origin, v, 3, 218
heart (good), i, 1, 191; *pl.*, hearts (my), good fellows, brave boys, i, 5, 88
heartless, cowardly, i, 1, 73
Heart's ease, a tune, iv, 5, 102–105
heaviness, sadness, grief, iii, 4, 11; iii, 5, 109
heavy, melancholy, sad, sorrowful, i, 1, 144; i, 4, 12; iv, 5, 18; gloomy, ii, 2, 158
heel (by my), iii, 1, 39
Helen, ii, 4, 43
help me after, to help me to follow thee, v, 3, 164
Hero, ii, 4, 43
hid, *p.p.*, hidden, iii, 2, 141
high-lone, alone without assistance, i, 3, 36
highmost, loftiest, ii, 5, 9

hilding, worthless creature, jade, ii, 4, 43; iii, 5, 169
him, himself, i, 5, 68
hind, a menial, i, 1, 73
his, its, i, 4, 108; ii, 6, 12; iv, 1, 97; iv, 5, 70; v, 3, 268
hoar, mouldy, ii, 4, 140
hold, *interj.*, iv, 1, 122; iv, 4, 1; v, 1, 59
holidam, halidom, i, 3, 43
holp, *p.p.*, helped, i, 2, 48
homely, plain, ii, 3, 55
honest, honourable, i, 5, 126; ii, 5, 56; iii, 2, 62; respectable, ii, 1, 28; trusty, ii, 5, 80
hood (a jealous), iv, 4, 13
hood, to cover with a hood (as a hawk), iii, 2, 14
hoodwink, to blindfold, i, 4, 4
hot, irritable, angry, ii, 5, 64
hour (*dissyllable*), ii, 5, 11; iii, 1, 200; v, 3, 253
house, a religious house, a monastery, v, 2, 9; (of the first), of the highest rank, ii, 4, 26
humorous, damp, ii, 1, 31
humour, moisture, current, iv, 1, 96; mood, feelings, i, 1, 136, 148; a whimsy, a fantastic notion, ii, 1, 7
hunt's-up, a morning call of the hunter, a morning song, iii, 5, 34
hurt, *n.*, a wound, iii, 1, 98
hurt, *p.p.*, wounded, iii, 1, 93, 95

I, ay, iii, 2, 45 ff.
idle, *adj.*, empty, silly, i, 4, 97
idle, *v.*, to float idly, ii, 6, 19
if that, if, ii, 2, 143
ill, an evil deed, a sin, iv, 5, 94
ill-beseeming, *adj.*, iii, 3, 113
ill-divining, forecasting evil, iii, 5, 54
impeach, to accuse, v, 3, 226
import (dear), vast importance, v, 2, 19
import, *v.*, to signify, v, 1, 28
importune, to question insistently, i, 1, 152
in (good time), i, 2, 45; (happy time), very opportunely, iii, 5, 112
inconstant toy, iv, 1, 119
inherit, to possess, have, i, 2, 30
iron wit, iv, 5, 125
it, its, i, 3, 52

Jack, a fellow, iii, 1, 12; a saucy fellow, ii, 4, 159; iv, 5, 148
jaunce, *n.*, a jolting, ii, 5, 26
jaunce, *v.*, to jolt, ii, 5, 53
jealous, suspicious, v, 3, 33
jealous hood, iv, 4, 13
joiner, one who makes furniture, etc., i, 4, 68

set up his rest (hath), has firmly resolved, is determined, iv, 5, 6

set up my everlasting rest, take up my abode forever, v, 3, 110

shall, who shall, iii, 5, 91

shield. *See* God shield

should, was (were) to, i, 2, 75; v, 3, 149

show, *n.*, appearance, iii, 2, 77

show, *v.*, to appear, look, i, 2, 103; i, 5, 50

shrift, confession, i, 1, 166; ii, 4, 192; ii, 5, 68; absolution, ii, 3, 56

shuts up, brings to a close, iv, 1, 101

sick, sickly, ii, 2, 8

siege, i, 1, 219

simples, medicinal plants, v, 1, 40

singleness, feebleness, tenuity, ii, 4, 70

single-sol'd, weak, thin, ii, 4, 70

singular, unique, ii, 4, 70

sirrah, i, 2, 34; i, 5, 31, 128; iv, 2, 2; iv, 4, 16; v, 3, 280

sir-reverence, i, 4, 42

skains-mates, cutthroat companions, ii, 4, 161

slack, to retard, check, iv, 1, 3

slip, a counterfeit coin, ii, 4, 51

slop, loose breeches, iv, 4, 48

slow, to retard, iv, 1, 16

slug-abed, iv, 5, 2

smatter, to babble, chatter, iii, 5, 172

so, provided that, ii, 2, 97; if, iii, 5, 18; (please you), if you please, i, 1, 163; iv, 3, 9

soft, *interj.*, i, 1, 202; ii, 2, 1; iii, 4, 18; iii, 5, 142

so ho, *interj.*, ii, 4, 136

solace, to take comfort, iv, 5, 47

solemnity, festival, celebration, festal rites, i, 5, 59, 65; iv, 5, 61

some minute (hour), a minute (an hour) or so, v, 3, 257, 268

something, *adv.*, somewhat, rather, ii, 4, 140

son, son-in-law, iii, 4, 16

soon at night, this (coming) night, ii, 5, 78

soon-speeding, *adj.*, quickly efficacious, v, 1, 60

sort out, to pick out, select, iii, 5, 110

sound, to plumb, iii, 2, 126

sounding, investigation, i, 1, 157

Soundpost, iv, 5, 139

sped, *p.p.*, done for, finished, iii, 1, 94

speed (be my), prosper me, v, 3, 121

spent, *p.p.*, used up, ii, 4, 140, 146

sphere (of a planet), ii, 2, 17

spinner, a spider, i, 4, 59

spite of (in), in defiance of, i, 1, 85. *Cf.* i, 5, 64

spleen, quarrelsome temper, irascibility, iii, 1, 162

splendour, brilliant beauty, i, 2, 105

spoke, *p.p.*, spoken, i, 4, 1, 7; ii, 2, 89; iv, 1, 28

spring, source, origin, v, 3, 218

stand, *n.*, standing, i, 5, 52

stand on, to insist on, ii, 3, 93; ii, 4, 36

star-cross'd, thwarted by unfavourable stars, ill-fated, Prologue, 6

startle, to spring up, rise with startling sound, v, 3, 194

starveth, v, 1, 70

state, one's condition, iii, 3, 166; iv, 3, 4; high rank, iii, 3, 34; stately array, i, 4, 70; ceremony, festival, iv, 3, 8

stay, to wait, i, 3, 105; iii, 1, 133; wait for, heed, i, 1, 219; wait patiently for, ii, 5, 36; linger, iii, 1, 141; stop, iv, 3, 58; detain, v, 3, 187; delay, v, 3, 251

stay dinner, to wait and dine, iv, 5, 149

stead, to benefit, ii, 3, 54

still, ever, always, i, 1, 178, 224; ii, 3, 27; iii, 3, 39; iii, 5, 130, 133, 179; v, 3, 106

still-waking, ever-wakeful, i, 1, 188

stint, to cease, stop, i, 3, 48, 57

stout, brave, valiant, iii, 1, 174, 178

straight, *adv.*, straightway, immediately, i, 3, 104; i, 4, 72, 73, 74; ii, 5, 73; iv, 4, 22; v, 1, 33, 79; v, 2, 21

strain, to force, ii, 3, 19; iv, 1, 47; do violence to, ii, 4, 55

strange, unfamiliar, iii, 2, 15; distant, offish, ii, 2, 101

stratagems, atrocities, iii, 5, 211

strucken, *p.p.*, struck, i, 1, 239

stumble (*ominous*), v, 3, 122

substance, reality, iii, 2, 77

sudden, immediate, iii, 5, 110, 137

sullen, dismal in sound, iv, 5, 88

sum, sum total, ii, 6, 34

supple government, iv, 1, 102

surcease, to cease, die away, iv, 1, 97

suspicion (of), suspected, v, 3, 222

swashing blow, a heavy downward stroke, i, 1, 69

sweet, *adj.*, perfumed, v, 3, 14; (my mother), dear, iii, 5, 200

sweet, *adv.*, sweetly, ii, 3, 32

sweeting, a sweet apple, ii, 4, 83

swits and spurs, ii, 4, 72

swound, to swoon, iii, 2, 56

sympathy (woful), agreement in sorrow, iii, 3, 85

tackled stair, a rope ladder, ii, 4, 200

take, to understand, comprehend, i, 4, 46; ii, 4, 131

take me with you, let me understand you, iii, 5, 142

take post, to hire post horses, v, 1, 21

take the wall, i, 1, 16

wax (a man of), i, 3, 76; (a form of), iii, 3, 126

wax, to grow, i, 5, 128

ways, *n. pl.*, roads, paths, iv, 1, 79

ways, *adv.*, (go thy), go along, ii, 5, 45

we (*the royal*), i, 1, 108; iii, 1, 192, 201; v, 3, 189, 194

weak, unmanly, unworthy of a gentleman, ii, 4, 181

weakest goes to the wall, i, 1, 17

weeds, clothes, v, 1, 39

well, in bliss, in heaven, iv, 5, 76; v, 1, 17

well-flower'd, ii, 4, 64

well-govern'd, well-conducted, well-behaved, i, 5, 70

well said, well done, i, 5, 88

wench, girl, lass, ii, 4, 4; ii, 5, 45; iii, 3, 143

weraday, *interj.*, welladay, iii, 2, 37; iv, 5, 15

what, whatever, ii, 6, 3

what, *interj. of impatient calling*, i, 3, 3, 4

what dost thou? what hast thou to do? iii, 5, 61

what (know), to know what's what, i, 5, 86

when that, when, iii, 3, 62

which, who, iii, 3, 123; iii, 5, 80; v, 3, 250

whiles, while, as long as, v, 3, 300

who, him who, i, 1, 137

whoreson, fellow, iv, 4, 20

wild-goose chase, ii, 4, 74

will, *n.*, desire, ii, 3, 28

will none, will not have it, iii, 5, 140

wink, to shut, be closed, iii, 2, 6

winking at, shutting my eyes to, v, 3, 294

wit, intellect, mind, iii, 3, 125, 130; iv, 5, 125; wisdom, common sense, i, 4, 49; iii, 5, 74; (Dian's), i, 1, 216

with, by, i, 1, 158, 195, 197, 226; ii, 2, 83; ii, 3, 40; ii, 4, 13 ff.; iii, 3, 134; by means of, v, 3, 166, 293

withal, with, i, 5, 117, 145; iii, 1, 81; therewith, thereby, i, 1, 119; also, at the same time, iii, 1, 159

without, outside of, iii, 3, 17

without-book, recited from memory, i, 4, 7. Cf. i, 2, 61

wits, intellect, iv, 1, 47; (five), five senses, i, 4, 47 (cf. ii, 4, 77)

woes, woful objects, v, 3, 179

womb, belly, v, 1, 65; v, 3, 45

word, a watchword, motto, i, 4, 40

world's, from this world, iii, 3, 20

worm, the rose caterpillar, i, 1, 158

worms' meat, food for worms, iii, 1, 112

worser, worse, ii, 3, 29; iii, 2, 108

worth, one's possessions, ii, 6, 32

worthy, noble, of high rank, iii, 5, 146

wot, know, iii, 2, 139

wretch, a term of affection, i, 3, 44

writ, *pret.*, wrote, v, 3, 246; *p.p.*, written, i, 2, 44, 45; v, 2, 4; written down, iv, 2, 1; v, 3, 82

wrong (do), to treat in an unfriendly way, i, 1, 203

wrought, *p.p.*, procured, iii, 5, 145

year, *pl.*, years, i, 3, 2

years (much in), advanced in age, iii, 5, 46

yet (*emphatic*), iii, 3, 57

yond, yonder, i, 5, 130; v, 3, 3

your (*indefinite*), i, 2, 52, 53

zounds, iii, 1, 52, 102

PRINTED IN THE UNITED STATES OF AMERICA